CBT: Science Into Practice

Series Editor

Nikolaos Kazantzis, Cognitive Behavior Therapy Research Unit,
Melbourne, VIC, Australia

This series addresses topics that reflect current thinking in the field of cognitive behavior therapy, the most widely accepted form of therapy across mental health disciplines. Despite the consensus that CBT is an effective treatment modality, much of the existing clinical literature focuses on single facets, such as specific disorders or populations. Mostly it does not take into account the latest evidence for transdiagnostic change mechanisms and processes. This series provides guidance on how the latest evidence can be translated into practice. Volumes focus on enhancing flexibility in both the selection and delivery of techniques tailored to individual clients. Each provides clinical insights enhanced by case studies and vignettes to ensure relevance for the practicing professional.

Laura A. Payne
Editor

Psychosocial Interventions for Chronic Pain in Women and Girls

Springer

Editor
Laura A. Payne
Department of Psychiatry, McLean Hospital
Belmont, MA, USA

ISSN 2946-5419 ISSN 2946-5427 (electronic)
CBT: Science Into Practice
ISBN 978-3-031-98875-2 ISBN 978-3-031-98876-9 (eBook)
https://doi.org/10.1007/978-3-031-98876-9

This Springer imprint is published by the registered company Springer Nature Switzerland AG
The registered company address is: Gewerbestrasse 11, 6330 Cham, Switzerland

To Andrew and Byron, my two biggest champions. And to Mom and Dad, for supporting me always.

Foreword

I am delighted that the book *Psychosocial Interventions for Chronic Pain in Women and Girls* is being published in the **CBT: Science into Practice** book series at a pivotal moment in the evolution of pain management. Chronic pain is a pervasive health challenge, and the need to improve outcomes for women and girls, who have often been underserved or overlooked in pain research and care, has never been more evident. Over the past several decades, the field has recognized that effective pain treatment must extend beyond the purely biomedical framework. A biopsychosocial approach, which addresses psychological and social dimensions alongside the physical, represents a critical innovation in meeting the needs of those who do not respond adequately to standard medical treatments.

Modern pain science is grounded in this holistic empiricism—evaluating not only new medical interventions but also the cognitive, emotional, and behavioral factors that influence each patient's pain experience. By embracing routine assessment of psychosocial variables, such as stress, coping styles, and social support in parallel with biological indicators, clinicians can tailor interventions in real time to individual needs. This integrated perspective offers a pathway to refine treatment dynamically, ensuring that therapy remains responsive to factors like mood fluctuations or life stressors that can exacerbate pain. In short, the biopsychosocial model isn't just a theoretical ideal; it is the foundation of personalized pain management, and it underpins the innovative strategies highlighted in this volume.

This volume, edited by Dr. Laura A. Payne featuring contributions from many of the leading experts in the field, provides a comprehensive guide to state-of-the-art Cognitive- Behavioral Therapies (CBTs) and broader psychosocial treatments for chronic pain in female populations. The book synthesizes a burgeoning body of research and clinical wisdom into a compelling and accessible resource; it is an essential guide for clinicians, researchers, and trainees committed to enhancing pain management through evidence-based, gender-informed care. Across its chapters, readers will find not only thorough reviews of theory and empirical evidence, but also practical insights and techniques that can be directly applied to improve the lives of women and girls living with pain.

In the opening chapter, Dr. Payne offers an insightful overview that frames the unique needs of women and girls with chronic pain. She illuminates the systemic disparities that have pervaded pain research and treatment, such as the historical underrepresentation of female patients in clinical studies and the tendency for women's pain reports to be minimized or dismissed in practice. This introductory chapter not only sets the stage by highlighting how hormonal factors, pain cognitions like catastrophizing, and societal roles uniquely affect women and girls, but also challenges outdated notions that chronic pain is ever purely biological. It artfully lays the groundwork for the innovative approaches that follow, underscoring that a holistic, gender-responsive lens is crucial for tangible relief and recovery.

The book's structure is effective. Part I—Interventions with Adults—comprises a series of chapters focusing on adult women, each tackling a different chronic pain condition or therapeutic approach. The diversity of interventions explored in this section is notable. Readers are introduced to Emotional Awareness and Expression Therapy (EAET) as a means to uncover and address the often-unspoken emotional conflicts that can manifest as physical pain. They will find integrative psychosocial strategies for managing musculoskeletal pain in women, combining cognitive-behavioral techniques with lifestyle and physical therapy considerations. Innovative applications of CBTs are showcased for conditions that have historically been under-recognized or stigmatized. For example, one chapter demonstrates how Pain Reprocessing Therapy, a cutting-edge approach rooted in neuroscience, can alleviate migraine headaches by retraining the brain's responses to pain signals. Another chapter provides an Acceptance and Commitment Therapy (ACT) intervention tailored for women with endometriosis and persistent pelvic pain, illustrating how acceptance, mindfulness, and values-based action can help patients transcend the life constraints imposed by chronic pain. The section encompasses conditions once rarely discussed in clinical literature: a dedicated chapter on persistent genital arousal disorder (PGAD) sheds light on a perplexing and distressing condition, offering a psychosocial framework to understand and manage symptoms that were long kept in the shadows. Throughout Part I, the chapters blend established therapies with emerging ones, and they include case vignettes and clinical guidelines that translate theory into practice. Clinicians will appreciate how these contributions balance scientific rigor with real-world application, offering actionable strategies for diverse scenarios, from tailoring mindfulness exercises for menstrual pain to implementing cognitive and behavioral techniques for bladder pain syndrome.

Part II—Interventions with Adolescents and Young Adults—turns the focus to younger females, underscoring the vital importance of developmental context in pain treatment. Adolescent girls and young women with chronic pain face a different set of challenges, including juggling school or work, social life, and family dynamics, all the while dealing with pain that can derail normal development. The chapters in this section recognize that treating a 15-year-old with chronic pain is not the same as treating a 50-year-old, and they offer guidance tailored to this reality. Traditional CBT techniques are adapted to treat vulvodynia, a debilitating genital pain condition, in both women and adolescent girls, highlighting how cognitive restructuring and gradual exposure can reduce pain and distress in this sensitive area. One chapter explores how CBTs can be translated into the digital realm to engage the "digital native" generation: it discusses the adaptation of therapy from the clinic room to online platforms, detailing how interactive apps and Internet-based programs can deliver CBTs effectively to adolescent and young adult females. Another chapter focuses on the treatment of juvenile fibromyalgia in girls, illustrating how classic CBT principles, like teaching pacing, cognitive reframing, and relaxation techniques, are adapted for a pediatric context. By presenting strategies that range from modern telehealth tools to age-appropriate therapeutic exercises, Part II ensures that the volume addresses the lifespan of female pain, from adolescence into adulthood.

One of the most compelling aspects of this book is the way it bridges cutting-edge scientific evidence with compassionate clinical practice. The contributors do not merely catalog interventions; they delve into why these approaches work, elucidating the psychosocial mechanisms of change that underlie successful pain treatment. Across chapters, readers will find discussions of key concepts such as pain catastrophizing, avoidance behavior, and the role of trauma and stress in exacerbating pain. Throughout the volume, there is also a recognition of the importance of the therapeutic relationship and patient empowerment in pain management. Whether it's a therapist working face-to-face with a woman with pelvic pain, or a digital program guiding a teenager through relaxation exercises, the human element shines through: the book consistently shows how empathy, validation of the patient's experience, and collaborative goal-setting amplify the effectiveness of psychosocial techniques.

Importantly, *Psychosocial Interventions for Chronic Pain in Women and Girls* does not shy away from the real-world challenges involved in translating these approaches into practice. The authors and editor give thoughtful consideration to potential barriers and how they might be overcome. The book addresses strategies for interdisciplinary collaboration, encouraging mental health professionals, physicians, and physical therapists to work in concert so that psychosocial care becomes a seamless part of pain treatment. Cultural considerations are also explored: readers are reminded that women and girls from diverse backgrounds may have different beliefs about pain and therapy and that interventions must be culturally sensitive and tailored to the individual's context. The honesty and pragmatism in addressing challenges enhance the book's utility: readers will not only be inspired by what can be done, but also guided in how to actually do it within the constraints of real clinical environments. This book challenges all of us, clinicians, researchers, and health-care leaders, to fully embrace a gender-informed, biopsychosocial approach to treating chronic pain.

The editor's expertise and dedication to advancing psychosocial pain research are evident throughout this volume. Dr. Laura A. Payne is a renowned clinical psychologist and a leading scholar in the study of chronic pain in women. As Director of the Clinical and Translational Pain Research Program at McLean Hospital and Assistant Professor of Psychology at Harvard Medical School, she brings a powerful combination of clinical acumen and research excellence. Dr. Payne's career has been distinguished by innovative contributions at the intersection of mental health and pain medicine. Early in her training, she co-authored the development of the Unified Protocol for Transdiagnostic Treatment of Emotional Disorders, underscoring her skill in creating broad-reaching psychological interventions. She has since applied that innovative mindset to the domain of pain, where she investigates how factors like hormonal cycles, stress, and emotion regulation impact pain outcomes in female patients. Her scholarly work and leadership in multidisciplinary research initiatives have solidified her reputation as a leading voice in this field. This background makes her ideally suited to edit a volume of this kind. With such distinguished expertise to draw on, Dr. Payne is eminently qualified to helm this book.

Readers will finish the book equipped with new knowledge and tools, but also with a sense of optimism and empowerment, ready to translate these pages into better care for their patients. In sum, *Psychosocial Interventions for Chronic Pain in Women and Girls* is a much-needed and invaluable contribution to the field. It arrives at a time when clinicians and researchers are keenly aware of the necessity for more inclusive and holistic pain management approaches. This volume will undoubtedly become a critical resource for practitioners and scholars who are committed to advancing gender-informed, evidence-based approaches to pain management. I wholeheartedly applaud Dr. Payne and all the contributing authors for their exceptional work in bringing this volume to life. Their collective efforts have charted a path forward that promises not only to enhance therapeutic outcomes but also to ensure that the millions of women and girls living with chronic pain are met with the understanding, respect, and effective care they deserve.
Melbourne, Australia

Cognitive Behavior Therapy Research Unit Nikolaos Kazantzis
Melbourne, VIC, Australia

Beck Institute for Cognitive Behavior Therapy
Philadelphia, PA, USA

Conflicts of Interest

Kazantzis disclosed his royalties from the Guilford Press (Therapeutic Relationship in Cognitive Behavior Therapy; Cognitive and Behavior Theories in Clinical Practice); Routledge (Using Homework Assignments in Cognitive Behavior Therapy); Springer Nature publishers (CBT: Science into Practice Book Series; Handbook of Homework Assignments in Psychotherapy: Research, Practice, & Prevention). He also disclosed editor stipend from the Association for Behavioral and Cognitive Therapies for his role as Editor-in-Chief for *Cognitive and Behavioral Practice* (Elsevier).

Praise for *Psychosocial Interventions for Chronic Pain in Women and Girls*

"Few conditions affect quality-of-life to a greater degree than unrelenting chronic pain, but most research to date on treating this difficult condition has focused on men. Now, one of the world experts on chronic pain in women, Dr. Laura Payne, has assembled a series of state-of-the-art treatment protocols for the 26% of women and girls who live with this debilitating problem in all of its manifestations. This book will be the go-to resource for every clinician treating chronic pain in women."

—David H. Barlow, *PhD, ABPP, Professor of Psychology and Psychiatry Emeritus, Founder, Center for Anxiety and Related Disorders (CARD), Boston University*

"Finally there is a book on pain dedicated to women and girls! This is long in coming, given that many chronic pain conditions are more prevalent in women than in men. What is also unique about this book is the inclusion of details about the various psychological interventions and also case examples of how these interventions are used with individuals. Both the types of pain unique to women as well as the variety of different psychological interventions are described in detail. This book is a "must" for any clinician who treats women or girls and for investigators who include women in their pain research. I highly recommend this valuable book."

—Lonnie Zeltzer, MD, Founder, President, Creative Healing for Youth in Pain, Emerita Distinguished Professor of Pediatrics, Anesthesiology, Psychiatry and Biobehavioral Sciences, David Geffen School of Medicine at UCLA

"Psychosocial Interventions for Chronic Pain in Women and Girls is an essential and timely contribution to the field. Dr. Payne and the contributors confront the persistent stigma surrounding women's pain with scientific rigor and compassion, offering evidence-based interventions that empower both providers and patients. This book is a vital resource for anyone committed to advancing equitable, effective pain care."

—Christine B. Sieberg, *PhD, EdM, MA, Staff Psychologist, Center for Health Outcomes & Interdisciplinary Research at Mass General Brigham & Associate Professor of Psychology in the Department of Psychiatry at Harvard Medical School*

"This timely volume addresses a critical gap in pain management literature by focusing on the unique experiences of women and girls with chronic pain. The authors provide evidence-based guidance that elegantly translates current research into practical tools for clinicians. At a time when we increasingly recognise the gendered dimensions of pain, this book is an essential resource for practitioners, which offers the specialised knowledge healthcare providers need to deliver more effective and tailored care for these individuals."

—Johan W.S. Vlaeyen, *PhD, Maastricht University, Netherlands, KU Leuven University, Belgium*

Contents

About the Editor

Laura A. Payne is a clinical psychologist at McLean Hospital and Assistant Professor of Psychology in the Department of Psychiatry at Harvard Medical School. She completed her undergraduate degree in psychology from the University of California, Los Angeles (UCLA), and subsequently her PhD from Boston University Center for Anxiety and Related Disorders. During her graduate work, she was an initial co-developer and co-author of the *Unified Protocol for Transdiagnostic Treatment of Emotional Disorders*—a transdiagnostic cognitive-behavioral treatment for emotional disorders—and her dissertation focused on evaluating two key components of the Unified Protocol and applying them to individuals with obsessive-compulsive disorder. During her postdoctoral fellowship at the UCLA Pediatric Pain Program, she extended these concepts to the treatment of pain, adapting the Unified Protocol to address both pain and emotions (anxiety/depression) in a sample of adolescents with chronic pain. Dr. Payne was awarded an NIH Postdoctoral National Research Service Award to understand the relationship of emotion regulation strategies to acute pain in children with chronic pain, and she was recognized for her work in 2010 with the UCLA Chancellor's Award for Postdoctoral Research. She then continued to explore central nervous system pain mechanisms in adolescent girls and young adult women with primary dysmenorrhea (PD; menstrual pain without an identified cause), through both a UCLA Bridge Award and then through an NIH Career Development Award. She also received a UCLA Children's Discovery and Innovation Institute Seed Grant to explore the feasibility and acceptability of a behavioral intervention for reducing pain catastrophizing in girls and young women with PD. Dr. Payne has since continued her research exploring centralized pain mechanisms involved in adolescents and adults with menstrual pain, including brain, behavior, psychological, and hormonal factors involved in the transition to chronic pain in this population. In 2019, she moved her lab to McLean Hospital/Harvard Medical School where she subsequently received additional NIH and Department of Defense grants to further her research. Clinically, Dr. Payne provides evidence-based psychological care to women with all types of chronic pain, with a particular focus on pelvic and genital pain.

Chapter 1
Introduction: Addressing the Unique Needs of Women and Girls with Chronic Pain

Laura A. Payne

Chronic pain is defined as pain lasting 3 months or longer, and current estimates suggest that 60 million people in the United States are experiencing chronic pain, making it one of the most common and costly public health issues (Zajacova et al., 2025). The field of pain has advanced tremendously in the past several decades. Deeper understandings of neurobiological, inflammatory, hormonal, behavioral, and psychological factors contributing to the experience of pain has allowed for the development and refinement of treatment approaches to directly target these mechanisms. This progress has also forced a reconciliation with the notion that the experience of chronic pain for all people is solely due to structural or tissue damage in the body, with the most effective treatment approaches focusing holistically on biological, psychological, and social factors (Gatchel et al., 2007). As a result, we have been able to more comprehensively treat pain and relieve suffering for many people, although effective treatments can still be difficult to access by the vast majority of people who suffer from chronic pain (Brennan et al., 2019).

Pain in Women and Girls

Despite these advances, research on pain in women and girls significantly lags behind pain research generally, even though women and girls experience chronic pain, including high-impact chronic pain, at higher rates than men (Mogil, 2020). This divergence between men and women appears to start in adolescence (Boerner

L. A. Payne (✉)
McLean Hospital, Belmont, MA, USA

Department of Psychiatry, Harvard Medical School, Boston, MA, USA
e-mail: LPayne@mclean.harvard.edu

L. A. Payne (ed.), *Psychosocial Interventions for Chronic Pain in Women and Girls*, CBT: Science Into Practice, https://doi.org/10.1007/978-3-031-98876-9_1

et al., 2024). For example, migraine, fibromyalgia, musculoskeletal pain, temporomandibular joint disorder (TMJ), and irritable bowel syndrome are all more common in women than men (Fillingim et al., 2009; Mogil, 2012). Additionally, there are a number of conditions that exist exclusively in women, including chronic pelvic pain (CPP), endometriosis (a condition where endometrial-like tissue grows outside of the uterus and can result in CPP and infertility), dysmenorrhea (menstrual pain), and vulvodynia (pain in and around the vulva), and estimates suggest that CPP affects up to 26% of women world-wide (Lamvu et al., 2021). Despite this high prevalence, gynecologic pain conditions are significantly underfunded when compared to male dominant diseases (Bergeron et al., 2020; Ellis et al., 2022; Kirk et al., 2024; Rice et al., 2020).

In 2014, the NIH required the inclusion of sex as a biological variable in all funded research (Clayton & Collins, 2014), with the goal of better understanding sex differences in risk for disease (Bale & Epperson, 2017). While this was a major advancement for research on female-specific mechanisms in disease and drug response, there is still tremendous room for improvement. Efforts to include female humans and animals in pain research (and at least document the sex of study participants) have been somewhat successful, although preclinical studies using rodents and other animals are still not fully reporting potential sex differences. For example, in a recent paper examining bias in pain research, Plumb et al. (2023) found "only 49% mouse and 30% rat articles in 2021 reported the use of both sexes" (p. 1777). This suggests we still have a long way to go in our efforts to both understand and report differences in pain research unique to females.

With regard to clinical care for pain, women and girls also experience bias in diagnosis and treatment. A recent review of published articles on pain found that women with chronic pain were more likely to be assigned a psychological "cause" of their pain as opposed to a somatic cause (Samulowitz et al., 2018). Women presenting to the emergency room for abdominal pain are less likely to receive any analgesia (including opiates) and, if they are prescribed analgesics, they wait longer for the analgesics compared to men (Chen et al., 2008).

Impact on Treatment

The systemic inequities in pain research (failure to document sex of research participants, disaggregate results by sex, and fund female-dominant or female-specific pain conditions) and clinical care (dismissal of women's symptoms, restriction of analgesia treatments) limits our ability to understand unique factors contributing to women's and girls' pain experience, which has a direct impact on tailoring and delivery of effective treatments. Consistent with the biopsychosocial model of pain, providers must consider biological vulnerabilities impacting women and girls, including hormonal factors (both within and across menstrual cycles and across reproductive life stages and transitions), differences in brain structure and function, and genetic variability and susceptibility to pain—all of which are important in providing care, albeit the relative importance of each of these components is likely to vary significantly across individuals (Bartley & Fillingim, 2013; Fillingim, 2017). Importantly, psychosocial variables including stress, family roles, relationship satisfaction, sexual desire and activity, daily activities, trauma, mental health (e.g., anxiety and depression), and many others, must also be recognized as important risk and protective factors when working with women and girls who experience pain (Edwards et al., 2016; Gebhardt et al., 2024).

Women and girls also experience unique psychosocial stressors related to their experiences of pain. For example, women with endometriosis-associated pain report lower levels of quality of life, decreased sexual activity and enjoyment, and higher levels of shame than women without endometriosis (Della Corte et al., 2020), while men with chronic pain are more likely to avoid talking about pain and experience frustration and grief (Samulowitz et al., 2018). Furthermore, the role that psychosocial variables play in women's pain appears to be different from men. For example, a recent study found that women with low psychosocial resources (defined as self-efficacy and instrumental and social support) were at greater risk for endorsing frequent pain 18 months later compared to men, with instrumental support being the most protective variable for women (Samulowitz et al., 2023).

Treatment approaches for women and girls with chronic pain have reflected these inequities and biases for hundreds of years, and even as recently as the 1960s, in the second edition of the Diagnostic and Statistical Manual of Mental Disorders (DSM-II; American Psychiatric Association, 1968), pain and chronic symptoms were categorized under the diagnosis of "hysterical neurosis" (Shetty et al., 2020), with treatments focusing primarily on hypnosis and psychoanalysis (North, 2015). Treatment for pain has unquestionably improved since then, but some pain conditions continue to go under-recognized. For example, dysmenorrhea (pain during menstruation) affects the majority of reproductive-age girls and women, with approximately 25% of girls and women experiencing severe pain each menstrual period and at least a portion go on to develop chronic pain (Gagnon et al., 2022). Yet, little is known about why so many girls and women experience this disabling condition. In their 2011 commentary "Don't Dismiss Dysmenorrhea," Berkley & McAllister highlight "this situation is appalling, considering the evidence that moderate-to-severe dysmenorrhea not only has a serious and chronic impact on quality of life, but also . . . is likely a 'harbinger of more pain to come later in life'" (p. 1940, Berkley & McAllister, 2011).

Where We Are Now

The last 20 years of pain treatment and research has revolutionized the field, with new psychosocial treatments, specifically cognitive-behavioral therapy (CBT) for pain, being developed, tested, and refined, and this has included a focus on some of the individualized needs of girls and women from a biopsychosocial perspective. Once hidden from public discourse, pelvic and genital pain conditions, including vulvodynia, persistent genital arousal disorder, and CPP, are now more widely and openly discussed, with specific treatments available for individuals with these conditions. Other conditions, such as fibromyalgia, musculoskeletal pain, and migraine, are better understood as the field of pain neuroscience has advanced considerably. Efforts to make effective treatments more accessible through digital technologies have also changed the delivery of care, making treatment more accessible to women and girls. These newer models have had a powerful positive effect on many women and girls living with chronic pain.

Of note, examination of sex differences in chronic pain has been an important area of research for decades, but our understanding of sex and gender has evolved. While "sex" is typically considered the biological characteristics and attributes that define males versus females, it is important to acknowledge that individuals may be born with sex characteristics that are not in alignment with their identified gender(s), which is defined as the social construction of identities typically associated with males and females (Schudson et al., 2019). For the purposes of this book, most chapters use the terms "women" and "girls" to refer to those who were assigned female sex at birth, although it is expected that some clients do not identify with the female gender despite possessing sex characteristics and organs associated with female sex. However, given that the individualized treatment approaches presented in this book acknowledge the unique experiences of each client as a part of the therapy, the treatment approaches described may still be applicable regardless of identified gender.

The importance of considering and treating all aspects of pain from the biopsychosocial model cannot be overstated. Outdated views that chronic pain results from purely biological *or* purely psychological causes continue to persist, but that is changing. When the field is able to fully embrace the biopsychosocial model, and consider how individual experiences, biology, stressors, and social relationships all impact pain experience, we will finally be able to provide the care to achieve tangible relief and full recovery for women and girls who are suffering with chronic pain.

References

American Psychiatric Association (Ed.). (1968). *Diagnostic and statistical manual of mental disorders* (2nd ed.). American Psychiatric Association.

Bale, T. L., & Epperson, C. N. (2017). Sex as a biological variable: Who, what, when, why, and how. *Neuropsychopharmacology, 42*(2), 386–396. https://doi.org/10.1038/npp.2016.215

Bartley, E. J., & Fillingim, R. B. (2013). Sex differences in pain: A brief review of clinical and experimental findings. *British Journal of Anaesthesia, 111*(1), 52–58. https://doi.org/10.1093/bja/aet127

Bergeron, S., Reed, B. D., Wesselmann, U., & Bohm-Starke, N. (2020). Vulvodynia. *Nature Reviews Disease Primers, 6*(1), 36. https://doi.org/10.1038/s41572-020-0164-2

Berkley, K. J., & McAllister, S. L. (2011). Don't dismiss dysmenorrhea! *Pain, 152*(9), 1940–1941. https://doi.org/10.1016/j.pain.2011.04.013

Boerner, K. E., Keogh, E., Inkster, A. M., Nahman-Averbuch, H., & Oberlander, T. F. (2024). A developmental framework for understanding the influence of sex and gender on health: Pediatric pain as an exemplar. *Neuroscience and Biobehavioral Reviews, 158*, 105546. https://doi.org/10.1016/j.neubiorev.2024.105546

Brennan, F., Lohman, D., & Gwyther, L. (2019). Access to pain management as a human right. *American Journal of Public Health, 109*(1), 61–65. https://doi.org/10.2105/ajph.2018.304743

Chen, E. H., Shofer, F. S., Dean, A. J., Hollander, J. E., Baxt, W. G., Robey, J. L., Sease, K. L., & Mills, A. M. (2008). Gender disparity in analgesic treatment of emergency department patients with acute abdominal pain. *Academic Emergency Medicine, 15*(5), 414–418. https://doi.org/10.1111/j.1553-2712.2008.00100.x

Clayton, J. A., & Collins, F. S. (2014). Policy: NIH to balance sex in cell and animal studies. *Nature, 509*(7500), 282–283. https://doi.org/10.1038/509282a

Della Corte, L., Di Filippo, C., Gabrielli, O., Reppuccia, S., La Rosa, V. L., Ragusa, R., Fichera, M., Commodari, E., Bifulco, G., & Giampaolino, P. (2020). The burden of endometriosis on women's lifespan: A narrative overview on quality of life and psychosocial wellbeing. *International Journal of Environmental Research and Public Health, 17*(13). https://doi.org/10.3390/ijerph17134683

Edwards, R. R., Dworkin, R. H., Sullivan, M. D., Turk, D. C., & Wasan, A. D. (2016). The role of psychosocial processes in the development and maintenance of chronic pain. *The Journal of Pain, 17*(9 Suppl), T70–T92. https://doi.org/10.1016/j.jpain.2016.01.001

Ellis, K., Munro, D., & Clarke, J. (2022). Endometriosis is undervalued: A call to action. *Frontiers in Global Women's Health, 3*, 902371. https://doi.org/10.3389/fgwh.2022.902371

Fillingim, R. B. (2017). Individual differences in pain: understanding the mosaic that makes pain personal. *Pain, 158*(Suppl 1), S11–S18. https://doi.org/10.1097/j.pain.0000000000000775

Fillingim, R. B., King, C. D., Ribeiro-Dasilva, M. C., Rahim-Williams, B., & Riley, J. L., 3rd. (2009). Sex, gender, and pain: A review of recent clinical and experimental findings. *The Journal of Pain, 10*(5), 447–485. https://doi.org/10.1016/j.jpain.2008.12.001

Gagnon, M. M., Moussaoui, D., Gordon, J. L., Alberts, N. M., & Grover, S. R. (2022). Dysmenorrhea across the lifespan: A biopsychosocial perspective to understanding the dysmenorrhea trajectory and association with comorbid pain experiences. *Pain, 163*(11), 2069–2075. https://doi.org/10.1097/j.pain.0000000000002649

Gatchel, R. J., Peng, Y. B., Peters, M. L., Fuchs, P. N., & Turk, D. C. (2007). The biopsychosocial approach to chronic pain: Scientific advances and future directions. *Psychological Bulletin, 133*(4), 581–624. https://doi.org/10.1037/0033-2909.133.4.581

Gebhardt, A. J., Andermo, S., & Arman, M. (2024). Relational vulnerability in motherhood-an existential perspective on pain and exhaustion among women. *Frontiers in Psychology, 15*, 1412385. https://doi.org/10.3389/fpsyg.2024.1412385

Kirk, U. B., Bank-Mikkelsen, A. S., Rytter, D., Hartwell, D., Marschall, H., Nyegaard, M., Seyer-Hansen, M., & Hansen, K. E. (2024). Understanding endometriosis underfunding and its detrimental impact on awareness and research. *npj Women's Health, 2*(1), 45. https://doi.org/10.1038/s44294-024-00048-6

Lamvu, G., Carrillo, J., Ouyang, C., & Rapkin, A. (2021). Chronic pelvic pain in women: A review. *JAMA, 325*(23), 2381–2391. https://doi.org/10.1001/jama.2021.2631

Mogil, J. S. (2012). Sex differences in pain and pain inhibition: Multiple explanations of a controversial phenomenon. *Nature Reviews. Neuroscience, 13*(12), 859–866. https://doi.org/10.1038/nrn3360

Mogil, J. S. (2020). Qualitative sex differences in pain processing: Emerging evidence of a biased literature. *Nature Reviews. Neuroscience, 21*(7), 353–365. https://doi.org/10.1038/s41583-020-0310-6

North, C. S. (2015). The classification of hysteria and related disorders: Historical and phenomenological considerations. *Behavioral Science, 5*(4), 496–517. https://www.mdpi.com/2076-328X/5/4/496

Plumb, A. N., Lesnak, J. B., Berardi, G., Hayashi, K., Janowski, A. J., Smith, A. F., Bailey, D., Kerkman, C., Kienenberger, Z., Martin, B., Patterson, E., Van Roekel, H., Vance, C. G. T., & Sluka, K. A. (2023). Standing on the shoulders of bias: Lack of transparency and reporting of critical rigor characteristics in pain research. *Pain, 164*(8), 1775–1782. https://doi.org/10.1097/j.pain.0000000000002874

Rice, L. W., Cedars, M. I., Sadovsky, Y., Siddiqui, N. Y., Teal, S. B., Wright, J. D., Zorbas, A., & Del Carmen, M. G. (2020). Increasing NIH funding for academic departments of obstetrics and gynecology: A call to action. *American Journal of Obstetrics and Gynecology, 223*(1), 79.e71–79.e78. https://doi.org/10.1016/j.ajog.2020.03.022

Samulowitz, A., Gremyr, I., Eriksson, E., & Hensing, G. (2018). "Brave Men" and "Emotional Women": A theory-guided literature review on gender bias in health care and gendered norms towards patients with chronic pain. *Pain Research & Management, 2018*, 6358624. https://doi.org/10.1155/2018/6358624

Samulowitz, A., Haukenes, I., Grimby-Ekman, A., Bergman, S., & Hensing, G. (2023). Psychosocial resources predict frequent pain differently for men and women: A prospective cohort study. *PLoS One, 18*(3), e0283222. https://doi.org/10.1371/journal.pone.0283222

Schudson, Z., Beischel, W., & Anders, S. (2019). Individual variation in gender/sex category definitions. *Psychology of Sexual Orientation and Gender Diversity, 6*. https://doi.org/10.1037/sgd0000346

Shetty, S. A., Chandini, S., Fernandes, S. L., & Safeekh, A. T. (2020). Hysteria: A historical perspective. *Archives of Medicine and Health Sciences, 8*(2), 312–315. https://doi.org/10.4103/amhs.amhs_220_20

Zajacova, A., Grol-Prokopczyk, H., & Nahin, R. L. (2025). Pain among US adults before, during, and after the COVID-19 pandemic: A repeated cross-sectional study using the 2019-2023 National Health Interview Survey. *medRxiv*, 2024.2010.2024.24316018. https://doi.org/10.1101/2024.10.24.24316018

Part I
Interventions with Adults

Chapter 2
Emotional Awareness and Expression Therapy for Chronic Pain

Shoshana Krohner, Maisa Ziadni, Howard Schubiner, and Mark A. Lumley

Introduction: Background

Chronic pain is one of the most pervasive and challenging conditions worldwide (Cohen et al., 2021), often persisting long after physical injuries have healed or in the absence of clear structural abnormalities or tissue damage. Most chronic pain conditions are more prevalent in women compared with men, including fibromyalgia, spinal pain, headache, abdominal pain, and temporomandibular disorder. This pattern of differences in men's and women's pain is apparent from adolescence onward (Keogh, 2022). Emerging research reveals that, for many individuals, chronic pain is not simply a physical phenomenon but the result of brain-based and psychological processes (Jepma et al., 2018; Meulders, 2020; Seymour, 2019; Tracey, 2010; Vlaeyen & Crombez, 2020). Emotional Awareness and Expression Therapy (EAET) is a relatively new, evidence-based treatment for chronic pain that views most chronic pain as reversible and targets the psychological roots of chronic pain (Lumley & Schubiner, 2019). This chapter explores the principles, mechanisms, empirical evidence, and clinical applications of EAET, highlighting how breaking cycles of fear and avoidance can lead to profound and lasting relief from chronic pain.

S. Krohner (✉)
Department of Psychiatry and Behavioral Sciences, Montefiore Medical Center/Albert Einstein College of Medicine, Bronx, NY, USA
e-mail: shoshana.krohner@einsteinmed.edu

M. Ziadni
Stanford University School of Medicine, Palo Alto, CA, USA

H. Schubiner
College of Human Medicine, Michigan State University, Pleasant Ridge, MI, USA

M. A. Lumley
Department of Psychology, Wayne State University, Detroit, MI, USA

L. A. Payne (ed.), *Psychosocial Interventions for Chronic Pain in Women and Girls*, CBT: Science Into Practice, https://doi.org/10.1007/978-3-031-98876-9_2

An important advance in understanding and treating chronic pain is the distinction between secondary and primary pain (Treede et al., 2019). Secondary pain arises from identifiable pathological processes in the body, whereas primary pain (also referred to as nociplastic, neuroplastic, or centralized pain) lacks a clear somatic driver and is largely caused by processes in the brain and spinal cord (Fitzcharles et al., 2021). Primary pain includes conditions such as fibromyalgia, irritable bowel syndrome, chronic pelvic pain, and many cases of non-specific musculoskeletal pain (Yunus, 2007). The neurophysiology of primary pain reveals that pain is not the result of physical injury or structural abnormalities but rather the result of learned neural circuits (Dale et al., 2018; McCarberg & Peppin, 2019; Woolf, 2011). In response to repeated stress or perceived danger, the brain can become hypersensitive, amplifying pain signals or "misfiring" to generate pain spontaneously, absent tissue damage or injury (Jepma et al., 2018; Meulders, 2020; Seymour, 2019; Vlaeyen & Crombez, 2020). The overlap of brain regions that process physical pain and emotions (Eisenberger & Leiberman, 2004; Kross et al., 2011), as well as elevated rates of psychosocial stress and trauma in patients with pain (Dalechek et al., 2024; You et al., 2019), especially women, suggest that learned emotional patterns can influence pain experience. Furthermore, processes like interoception and predictive coding demonstrate that the brain constructs pain based on expectations, not just stimuli (Baliki & Apkarian, 2015; Barrett & Simmons, 2015; Petzschner et al., 2017). As these neural circuits repeatedly fire, pain can become the brain's default response to physical or emotional stimuli that are perceived as dangerous, explaining why pain can persist without clear somatic drivers.

Consistent with this model, EAET views chronic primary pain as the result of a learned neural response that is perpetuated by an emotional fear-avoidance cycle. EAET is designed to leverage the brain's remarkable ability to change and reorganize itself, aiming to directly address the underlying causes of chronic primary pain to substantially reduce or even eliminate chronic pain. In EAET, individuals learn to reinterpret pain signals as non-threatening and build greater capacity to experience and process difficult emotions, ultimately breaking the emotional fear-avoidance cycle and eliminating chronic pain.

EAET has been developed through a series of clinical trials in multiple pain populations with varying intervention formats, including individual and group EAET, therapy duration ranging from 1 session to 9 sessions, and delivery modes including in-person, telehealth, and self-guided internet-based. These studies are reviewed in several publications (Maroti et al., 2025; Lumley et al., 2022; Lumley & Schubiner, 2019). EAET has been effective in treating a range of centralized and primary pain conditions that are common among women, such as fibromyalgia (Lumley et al., 2017), irritable bowel syndrome (Thakur et al., 2017), pelvic pain (Carty et al., 2019), non-specific musculoskeletal pain (Krohner et al., 2024), and medically unexplained symptoms (Maroti et al., 2022; Ziadni et al., 2018). Several studies of group EAET have demonstrated its superiority to cognitive behavioral therapy in reducing some pain-related outcomes, especially pain intensity (Lumley et al., 2017; Yarns et al., 2020, 2024a, 2024b).

Theoretical Foundations of EAET

In EAET, chronic primary pain is viewed as a reversible condition (Lumley & Schubiner, 2019). The EAET model is grounded in evidence showing that chronic primary pain is a brain-based, learned phenomenon—suggesting that it can be unlearned and changed. Acute pain is a natural and protective creation of the brain, designed to alert a person to potential harm and ensure safety. Pain, however, is not merely a response to physical injury; it is a complex experience shaped by both sensory and emotional factors (Raja et al., 2020). As such, recent classifications of pain categorize chronic pain by three major mechanisms: (1) nociceptive pain, caused by musculoskeletal or visceral tissue injury; (2) neuropathic pain, arising from nerve damage; and (3) nociplastic pain, arising from altered pain processing in the central nervous system in the absence of ongoing tissue or nerve damage (Treede et al., 2019).

Research indicates that nociplastic pain arises from changes in how the brain processes sensory information (Dale et al., 2018; McCarberg & Peppin, 2019; Woolf, 2011). This understanding of the brain's role in nociplastic pain is critical to the EAET model, which adopts a predictive processing model—an increasingly supported view of brain functioning that explains how the brain actively constructs perceptual experiences. Predictive processing explains that the brain is not merely passively receiving information, but rather actively predicts or infers experiences based upon inputs from the environment, the body, and prior experiences. These predictions are compared to incoming sensory signals, and any discrepancies or "prediction errors" will drive updates to perception and experience (Baliki & Apkarian, 2015; Barrett & Simmons, 2015; Büchel et al., 2014; Petzschner et al., 2017; Tracey, 2010). In chronic primary pain, the brain's prediction process appears to become overly focused on threat and danger, amplifying pain even when there is no injury present or peripheral nociception. This process can lead to a self-sustaining loop where the brain continues to anticipate pain, thus reinforcing the experience of threat and danger, which in turn reinforces the prediction of threat (Jepma et al., 2018; Meulders, 2020; Seymour, 2019; Vlaeyen & Crombez, 2020). The role of perceived threat in chronic pain is further supported by elevated rates of trauma and adversity in those with nociplastic pain relative to secondary/neuroceptive/neuropathic conditions (Dalechek et al., 2024; You et al., 2019).

Emotional and Interpersonal Contributions to Pain

Chronic or persistent pain is generated or amplified, at least in part, when the brain predicts "danger." EAET targets not only the fear of bodily damage—which is the evolutionarily adaptive reason for the experience of bodily pain—but also broader perceived threats to oneself—one's memories, actions, thoughts, or interpersonal interactions—that evoke uncomfortable emotions and are often avoided. In the EAET model, it is the fear-driven avoidance of these perceived threats that sustains the brain's pain-alarm mechanism (Lumley & Schubiner, 2019). Some aspects of this model are not new; many scholars and clinicians have noted the central role of "experiential avoidance," whether conceptualized as an avoidance coping strategy or a defense (e.g., Barlow et al., 2011; Hayes et al., 1996) that can act as a primary driver of psychological and behavioral pathology. EAET builds on these theories, proposing that the avoidance of emotionally-charged experiences plays a central role in chronic pain. From this vantage point, gender disparities in pain may be understood through the lens of differential experiences of emotional threats. Although men tend to be exposed to more life-threatening traumatic events overall, women are more frequently exposed to specific trauma types that pose a higher risk for long-lasting emotional impact—particularly those occurring at a younger age and interpersonal traumas involving betrayal or violation of trust and safety, which are often accompanied by shame, stigma, and secrecy (Olff et al., 2007; Olff, 2017). Women also tend to report stronger perceptions of threat and loss of control during traumatic experiences, show higher levels of peritraumatic dissociation, and exhibit more dysregulation in the stress response system compared to men. At the same time, gendered socialization shapes which emotions are accessible or permissible for women to openly express (Olff, 2017). For many women, cultural expectations may contribute to the suppression of agentic emotions such as anger and assertiveness in favor of more relational or affiliative modes of being (Fischer et al., 2004). Viewed through the lens of EAET, these factors may explain the higher prevalence of chronic pain in women (Keogh, 2022) and support the theory that an emotion-fear avoidance cycle drives chronic pain and that reclaiming disavowed emotional states may be central to recovery.

A key framework in EAET is the two-triangle model (Malan & Parker, 1995), drawn from psychodynamic theory and therapies. The Triangle of Conflict, with three poles—Defenses, Feelings/Affect, and Anxiety (i.e., symptoms)—describe how people defend against or avoid adaptive emotions—such as anger at injustice, sadness over loss, or love in seeking connection—due to punitive or traumatic life experiences and social constraints. The Triangle of Person maps how these internal conflicts play out in three types of relationships: persons connected to the patient from their past (like parents), their present, and the therapist. An example of the triangles as an interpretative mechanism is provided in the case presentation below. The defensive mechanisms that enable avoidance of one's adaptive feelings are common and usually were healthy or useful at one time or in certain contexts; however, when the use of defenses becomes excessive or rigid, one is deprived of the valuable insights and motivations that are generated by experiencing one's adaptive feelings. Moreover, chronic defensive blocking or avoidance of adaptive emotions will drive the emergence of symptoms, traditionally labeled as "anxiety," but which actually includes a range of affective and bodily states that are best thought of as inhibitory, thereby keeping the person stuck, trapped, withdrawn, hurting, etc. Importantly, one of these symptoms is the experience of bodily pain—the key focus in this book—although there are others, including anxiety, depression, fatigue, numbness, and shame.

EAET integrates multiple therapeutic approaches to facilitate emotional engagement and processing of avoided emotions. It draws from several short-term dynamic psychotherapies, notably intensive short-term dynamic psychotherapy (ISTDP), which targets relational conflicts between anger, guilt, and sadness/connection, relying on various techniques that encourage physiological activation in experiencing and expressing emotion. EAET has commonalities with the psychodynamic model of affect phobia, which desensitizes patients to feared emotions, Emotion-focused therapies, employing techniques like focusing and empty chair work, cognitive behavioral therapies, emphasizing exposure to feared stimuli and emotional processing, as well as expressive writing and rescripting therapy, using these techniques to process and resolve distressing experiences. How these therapies and techniques are used in EAET will be elaborated below.

Despite differing techniques, these approaches share a core principle: reversing emotional avoidance to reduce symptoms, especially pain. A distinguishing feature of EAET is its focus on core interpersonal and self-related needs, guiding the selection of emotional experiences to target. Drawing from developmental, social-cognitive, and personality research, EAET highlights two fundamental interpersonal needs: relatedness/communion/sociability and autonomy/agency/independence (e.g., Deci & Ryan, 2012; Helgeson, 1994). Humans need to trust, depend on, and be vulnerable with others, while at the same time, protecting themselves, setting boundaries, and confronting injustice. Emotions support the pursuit of these needs: connection is fostered by sadness, love, adaptive guilt, healthy fear, and gratitude, whereas autonomy is strengthened by adaptive anger (Lazarus, 1991). EAET also acknowledges a third fundamental need—self-integrity—encompassing self-care, self-competence, and self-esteem (Howell, 2017; Steele, 1988), which are underpinned by the emotions of pride and self-compassion. Another guiding principle for intervention in EAET is the distinction between adaptive (primary) emotions and secondary/defensive and inhibitory emotion states. Adaptive emotions—for example, anger in response to injustice, sadness after loss, self-compassion in response to shame—connect to real experiences and promote healing. In contrast, defenses or chronic avoidance foster secondary emotions like helplessness, numbness, or frustration, which perpetuate the threat-response cycle to adaptive emotions and sustain pain symptoms. As such, pain reduction in EAET is achieved by promoting the experience of adaptive emotions, reducing perceived threat/anxiety, and reducing secondary feelings.

Beyond in-session work with emotions, EAET aims to help individuals apply emotional insights to their real-life relationships. Patients are encouraged to express their emotional needs to people in their lives, when appropriate and potentially helpful, using skilled interpersonal communication. Changing interpersonal patterns can be difficult; however, doing so is considered crucial to reversing avoidance patterns, resolving conflicts, and ultimately reducing pain.

EAET Techniques and Application

Overview of the Process of EAET

EAET progresses through a series of four steps or stages, which build upon each other. These are: (1) educating the patient about the neuroscience and psychology of pain, (2) obtaining a psychosocial history including the disclosure of traumas and conflicts, (3) engaging in techniques of experiencing, expression, and resolution or emotional conflicts, and (4) encouraging adaptive communication of feelings and needs in actual relationships. Each of these steps or processes will be described in turn.

Step 1: Presentation of the Model Patients with chronic pain typically enter therapy with the belief that their pain stems from bodily damage; this view is consistent with the evolutionary value of acute pain. In EAET, they are introduced to an alternative model—chronic pain is a brain-based perception that is influenced by psychological and emotional processes. The therapist presents neuroscience findings and compelling stories to illustrate this model, such as the classic story of a construction worker who landed on a nail that pierced his boot but not his foot, yet he had tremendous pain. Patients learn about predictive processing, helping them understand that the brain integrates nociceptive signals with broader safety and threat perceptions, sometimes generating pain as a false alarm—an overlearned protective response rather than an indicator of bodily injury. In this step, the therapist explores the patient's pain history and symptoms as well as other stress-related conditions (e.g., migraines, bowel issues). Patients have usually received biomedical/bodily explanations for their symptoms, so skepticism is common. To address this, therapists conduct an "evidence-search," identifying signs of neuroplastic pain, such as migrating pain or pain that is triggered by stressful experiences. Provocative testing, where patients vividly imagine actions that routinely cause pain, often elicits painful sensations in session, providing additional evidence that the brain, rather than the body, is driving pain. Step 2 further explores brain-pain connections through emotional activation. If patient skepticism persists, patients are invited to remain open to testing these ideas as treatment progresses.

Step 2: Psychosocial History and Emotional Disclosure This step explores the patient's psychosocial history to identify links between emotionally difficult life experiences and chronic pain. The therapist guides the patient in reviewing past and ongoing challenges from birth to present, noting any connections between emotional stress and health problems, such as pain onset or exacerbation. Patients are often surprised to see patterns, such as headaches in childhood, linked to when they were bullied in school. This process can help patients see how unresolved emotional conflicts may contribute to somatic symptoms. The goal of this step is to open the patient to the possibility that life experiences—and how the person emotionally responded to those experiences—are important, and those difficult experiences and subsequent emotional processes are often the drivers of somatic symptoms, including pain.

Encouraging emotional disclosure is key in EAET, as many patients hesitate to share distressing or traumatic experiences. The therapist is attentive to the patient's anxiety levels throughout such disclosures and actively validates and empathizes with any challenges in revisiting difficult life experiences. This step is also an opportunity for additional assessment, with the therapist checking in with the patient's bodily sensations during their discussion of emotional conflicts, to note any changes in pain or tension and highlight the mind-body connection when apparent. This is often a powerful experience for patients to begin to recognize the influence of emotions and unresolved conflicts on their perception of physical sensations, and this process suggests treatment goals to target in Step 3. Reducing fear of these emotional experiences deactivates the brain's pain-alarm system, decreasing the pain.

Step 3: Experience, Express, and Resolve Emotions Related to Avoided Experience This core step of EAET focuses on emotional processing through "experience-express-resolve" (EER)—a primary EAET technique that aims to help patients unlearn their fear of emotional memories and experiences by activating, expressing, and resolving them safely in session. As noted earlier, we target three classes of emotions: agentic emotions, particularly anger; connecting emotions, particularly sadness/grief and tenderness/love; and positive-self emotions, particularly pride and self-compassion. EER begins by recalling an interpersonal conflict, vividly picturing it, and noticing bodily responses. Patients are encouraged to express their activated emotions without censor or inhibition, often through imagined conversation or action. The therapist's task is to supportively guide patients toward the fullest and authentic expression of their feared emotions by reducing their use of defenses and to regulate anxiety as needed. The overarching goal is to reduce anxiety/fear of adaptive emotions and to support the healthy integration of complex emotions in interpersonal relationships. Oftentimes, this work begins with patients experiencing and expressing their anger, as it is a commonly avoided/conflicted feeling, especially in close relationships. Once anger is adequately dealt with, patients often spontaneously shift toward connecting feelings (e.g., guilt, grief, compassion), and therapists support this transition by encouraging full experience and expression of these feelings. The EER process is revisited across a few sessions, often progressing from present-day to older conflicts or traumas. Over time and with repetition, this process fosters increased capacity to tolerate previously avoided emotions, which is typically accompanied by reductions in defense use and anxiety and pain symptoms. The increase in emotional awareness, empowerment, and self-expression from engaging in EER work also paves the way for the final step of EAET: changing real-life relationships.

Step 4: Encouraging Adaptive Communication of Needs and Feelings in Actual Relationships EAET emphasizes that while emotional work in therapy reduces pain, addressing emotional avoidance in real relationships strengthens and sustains these benefits. Many patients struggle with expressing either assertive or connecting emotions in their relationships, and learning to communicate their needs enhances long-term symptom relief. Interpersonal expression becomes less anxiety-provoking after in-session emotional processing, as patients gain clarity about their feelings and needs. Relationship goals may include "repair"—expressing both connection and assertiveness for closer and more honest relationships—or "realignment"—setting clearer boundaries, sometimes including ending harmful relationships. This step may directly follow EER during a session or be a planned focus of later sessions. This work is often supported by role-playing interactions and/or therapist modeling. Changed relationships can have a powerful effect on reducing fear and pain and other symptoms, helping the person become more fully functioning, integrated, and healthy.

EAET Case Study: Woman with Fibromyalgia

Case Background

The patient is a 54-year-old White woman for whom her Catholic faith is very central to her life. She was an only child and experienced significant childhood trauma, including physical and verbal abuse from her mother. She described that her father seemed to work a lot to avoid being home with her mother, and that though he was aware of the abuse, he did not intervene. She developed migraines at age 8, which caused frequent school absences and trips to the school nurse. When she was in her 30s, her mother apologized for her actions, and she states that she has since forgiven her; however, her father has never acknowledged his silence about the abuse, and the patient has never confronted him.

The patient reported a pattern in her 20s of dating men who were controlling or abusive toward her. At 29, she moved out of state and away from her family of origin. Around this time, she began experiencing low back stiffness and pain, without any precipitating injuries. Medical evaluations were unremarkable. The pain limited her physical activity, and she began avoiding strenuous activities or walking for long periods. She reported wanting a child but never conceiving. When she married in her early 30s, her husband was not open to having a child together. Her back pain worsened at this time, and she began experiencing pelvic pain, which made sex painful. Medical evaluations at this stage revealed mild disc degeneration at two lumbar levels. At 35, she was diagnosed with primary ovarian insufficiency and reported abandoning the dream of having a child one day. At age 45, her husband lost his job, which increased financial stress, and her father passed away suddenly. She began experiencing intense, burning pain in her lower back that often radiated into her legs. The pain was debilitating, leaving her unable to stand for more than a few minutes, climb stairs, drive, or manage household responsibilities. She reports intense fear of pain flares, resulting in spending much of her time in bed at home. Medical evaluations suggested nerve impingement as the cause of this burning pain; however, the foraminal narrowing and bulging disc were only on the right side, and she had pain down both of her legs. Her neurological exam was normal and, therefore, surgery was not recommended.

Three years later, at age 48, she developed upper back and neck pain and began intermittently experiencing pain in her arms and hands as well as her legs. She was diagnosed with fibromyalgia. Medical evaluations found evidence of degenerative disc disease and disc bulging at several levels. The cumulative effects of these physical limitations deeply impacted her quality of life, limiting her ability to engage in household responsibilities, go to church, or see friends. Though her marriage remained stable over the years, it lacked any physical intimacy for the last 5 years, which she reports is due to her husband's apparent disinterest. She reports that when she tries to address their intimacy with him, her husband becomes withdrawn or verbally explosive, to which she responds by further minimizing her needs or wishes. She reports that her pain worsens during times of conflict or stress at home.

Detailed evaluation of the pain characteristics during the intake process revealed that the pain is experienced throughout her middle and lower back, pelvic region, upper and lower extremities, and head. Consistent with a neuroplastic pain presentation, the location of the pain often shifts from upper to lower back during the course of the day, is often worse in the morning, and is exacerbated by the weather, light touch, and stressful situations. Additionally, pain intensity fluctuated during the intake process in accordance with the discussion of historical and current psychological stressors, worsening when the patient was recounting these experiences.

Case Formulation and Treatment Plan

The patient's chronic pain is primarily driven by learned neural circuits that amplify and sustain pain despite minimal ongoing nociceptive input. Her pain worsened during emotional distress—marital conflict, fertility challenges, financial struggles, and father's death—highlighting the brain's role in maintaining symptoms. Childhood trauma, including abuse and lack of parental protection, likely contributed to neural sensitization and hypervigilance, making her more susceptible to chronic pain. Adult relational stress, including challenging marital dynamics, reinforced these pathways by perpetuating helplessness and fear. Her history suggests a pattern of maintaining attachment and suppression of valid anger about past and present violations. Avoidance behaviors, such as bed rest and fear of movement, further strengthened maladaptive neural patterns. Her fear of pain sustains a fear-pain cycle, where focus on pain amplifies intensity. Medical findings, including disc degeneration and nerve impingement, are common in middle-aged people and rarely fully explain her symptoms. The pain's inconsistency and responsiveness to non-harmful stimuli further indicate a neuroplastic condition. From an EAET perspective, the patient's pain results from the brain's misinterpreting safe sensations and experiences as threats due to ingrained neural patterns and unresolved emotional conflicts.

Treatment Phases with Therapist-Client Dialogue

Beginning Phase (Step 1/Sessions 1–2): Building Rapport, Pain Education, Initial Intervention

**Note: This excerpt is from Session 1. The EAET model is new to the patient. The therapist provides pain neuroscience education, collects pain history, and evaluates for indicators of neuroplastic pain and/or amplified pain.*

Therapist: So, let's take a look at how you think about your pain. When you think about moving or doing an activity that has triggered pain in the past, what thoughts come to mind?

Patient: Oh, all kinds of thoughts…or I guess you know, worries. I get afraid that I'll do something that will put me in worse pain, and so I, well, I suppose that is why I stay on this bed so much. It's my safe place, you know, I'm most comfortable when I'm on it. I don't really move around much anymore. I don't exercise because I'm afraid that I will injure myself. I would say that my pain disorder has put my body at risk for the rest of my life.

Therapist: When you say that you believe your body is at risk for the rest of your life, that really clarifies to me that you feel a lot of fear and threat. I can understand why you would want to stay on the bed where it feels safe! And, if we were to go back to our model for chronic pain—remember how I said that pain is our brain's danger signal? So, the fear that you experience, about being in pain or the pain getting worse, that fear actually activates that danger signal in our brain and can trigger a pain response.

Patient: Oh! So, you're saying that because I'm so afraid of being in pain when I move around, that's what sets off the pain I feel? It's not because I'm moving around too much, or...uh, you know, overextending myself?

Therapist: Yes, well the thing is that pain is our brain's way of letting us know it perceives danger. So, if our brain perceives a threat, it fires down that neural circuit and creates pain to protect us. As amazing as our brains are at detecting danger, they can also make mistakes and perceive danger even when we are actually safe. Our brains have also evolved to detect emotional threats, and so chronic pain can also be triggered by emotional stressors. Let me pause here, and check in. What are your thoughts right now about this idea?

Patient: I'm not sure. I do notice that there's a lot of fear for me. And when I'm feeling more stressed about things going on in my life, that my pain is usually worse. I never thought about it this way, though, and I don't know if it all applies to my case exactly. But I'll just have to be open-minded, I guess.

Therapist: I appreciate your willingness to keep an open mind, and I also can really understand why you would be a bit skeptical at this point—we're just getting to know each other, and you've had all of your other providers reinforce that there are things wrong in your body that are causing your pain. I'd be surprised if you didn't have any doubts about what I'm telling you at this point! How about we just continue to explore this together and see if we can confirm one way or another. Does that sound okay?

Patient: Yes, that sounds fine to me. Like I said, I'm willing to try and see. I am open to anything at this point.

Beginning Phase (Step 2/Sessions 2–3): Psychosocial History and Emotional Disclosure

**Note: This is Session 2. The patient notes she is open to the EAET model, and noted that when she is stressed (e.g., a fight with her husband) or is fearful about being in pain, her pain tends to worsen. This session focuses on developing understanding of links between the patient's psychosocial history, especially stressful or emotionally-conflicted experiences, and her pain symptoms.*

Therapist: I'm wondering if we can spend a bit more time today exploring any potential connections between stress, emotions, and your pain symptoms. Let's start with things that may have been difficult or stressful in your childhood and work up to present day. Does that sound okay to you?

Patient: Okay, sure. So, my childhood was pretty hard actually because my mother, she was very angry a lot and she kind of took some of her anger out on me when I was little. I guess I did things to upset her, or that's just what she did to teach me right and wrong.

Therapist: How did she take her anger out on you? Was it verbal or physical?

Patient: It was both yes. She umm, she would just get very mad, and she would call me all sorts of names, and just be very mean. And a lot of the time she would wind up you know, being physical too, you know. Hitting me or using a belt. And I didn't really know why it would happen, because I really tried to be a good kid, you know. I tried to listen and do well in school, and I don't know.

Therapist: I'm wondering what it's like for you now to revisit this. What kinds of emotions are coming up for you right now?

Patient: (tearful) I suppose it makes me feel very sad, very hurt, and sad.

Therapist: Yes, it's heartbreaking that you went through that. Was there anyone there who protected you? Did your father ever step in?

Patient: My father? No, not really. I think maybe he was afraid to upset my mom, and so he didn't do anything to protect me. I don't remember him being around that much, he worked a lot—maybe to get away from my mom because she could be mean to him, too.

Therapist: As all of these memories are coming up for you now, can we take a look at how your body might be responding? What do you notice?

Patient: Well, oh, I feel a lot of tightness in my throat and chest. And I, I'm in a lot of pain right now, it's just shooting down into my legs really bad now.

Therapist: Okay, so that's good to notice that your pain seems to be responding to these emotional memories—is there maybe some discomfort or anxiety about discussing how your parents hurt you as a child?

Patient: It's very difficult (tearful), I don't really like to think about it. That they hurt me like that, it's terrible. And I've decided that I forgave my mom, because I didn't want to hold on to that hurt anymore.

Therapist: I can understand the wish to put it behind you, because this is so painful to look at. At the same time, because your body seems to respond when it comes up and there's a lot of emotions, I'm wondering if it could be helpful to you to, help you feel less pain and also move forward, to begin by taking a look at the feelings that are there toward your parents for this.

Patient: I don't know if I can. It just hurts too much.

Therapist: This is really painful for you to be with, but I also think it would help you heal and move forward. What if we took it very slowly, just a step at a time, and we can always step back if it feels like too much? I'll be there with you every step of the way.

Patient: Okay, I guess I can try that.

Middle Phase (Step 3/Sessions 4–6): Processing Unresolved Trauma and Conflicts

**Note: This is Session 5. The patient and therapist have a shared goal of targeting previously avoided affects related to her childhood trauma and current relational dynamics. The patient reports having some days with substantially reduced pain, which is new for her, and she recognizes that her pain is triggered by her fear of healthy emotions. Yet, because she continues to experience anxiety and avoidance, this session focuses on facilitating affect exposure to adaptive anger and grief in the context of her relationship with her father, who was silent during the abuse. The prior session targeted unresolved anger and grief about the abuse she suffered from her mother. During that session, pain flared when the patient revisited memories of the abuse and then subsided following the experience and expression of anger toward her mother, followed by self-compassion and grief for her childhood self.*

Patient: You know, some of the homework was really difficult for me. I just don't think these things are resolved yet. With my father especially, I still see my father is, he's like the nicest man you would ever know. It's difficult to think about him as someone doing something wrong to me. And I think that's probably why I've never addressed this before, because I don't want to see him as anything but always doing the right thing.

Therapist: It can be really uncomfortable to consider the negative impact your dad had when he didn't protect you from your mother.

Patient: Yes, it is. Oh wow. There it goes again. I'm feeling pain in my back already.

Therapist: Okay, so your brain starts to go into that kind of threat response when these feelings come up about your dad, and the pain signal turns on. Can we explore that a bit more? When you think about your dad's role, how he didn't protect you…what do you feel toward him, about that?

Patient: Anger. And I feel just alone. I felt very alone at that moment, and just like where was my protector? And…did he love me because he was allowing this abuse to happen? That is not what you do to somebody you love. But I also see him as afraid.

Therapist: Right, we can imagine that your dad may have had his own limitations that impacted how he handled it—his own set of challenges. But that had an impact on you. Can you notice how the emotions are felt in your body right now?

Patient: The same way we talked about the other day. You know, how this area (gesturing at her throat) just gets really tight. And it's in my throat, you know, I just feel the tears coming.

Therapist: Can you let those tears come out? Don't hold them back. These are important tears for yourself, for when you felt alone with no one there to protect you.

Patient: (crying). It's just that if a child I loved was being treated that way, I would immediately step up no matter the consequences, and I'd protect them. How could my own father not protect me?

Therapist: Is that anger coming back in now, then? Thinking about how you deserved a father who would protect you.

Patient: Yes, it is. I just feel like I want to scream and hit the wall or something.

Therapist: I'm wondering if it feels difficult to allow yourself to imagine your anger, wanting to hit, coming out like this toward your dad, because you see him as vulnerable too?

Patient: Oh no, I don't like that at all. You mean, hit my father?

Therapist: So, remember that we're talking about experiencing your feelings for your own healing. And that this is different than what you would do with those feelings in real life, with your dad. Right now, your brain is telling you these feelings are dangerous, and so the pain signal is turning all the way up. Can we see what it would be like to be open to your feelings, so that you don't have to be in pain?

Patient: Okay (tearful). I can try.

Therapist: Maybe we can start with something that's a bit more accessible, like how you would express this anger toward Dad with your words and tone of voice. Imagine he's sitting here with you, what would your anger want to say to him?

Patient: I'm just really mad at you, Dad. I was a child, and you didn't act like a decent father. I was hurt…and I'm in a lot of pain, Dad. (crying) Oof.

Therapist: Go on.

Patient: (shouts) You need to say I'm sorry, Dad! Say you're sorry for not standing up for me!

Therapist: Now, just noticing what that was like, just to get a little bit of that anger out right now.

Patient: Oh, that was really hard for me. But…I already feel my body feeling lighter, sitting straighter…and the pain is better. It's not all gone. But it's better.

Final Phase (Step 4/Session 7–8): Reinforcing Gains and Fostering Healthy Relational Change

**Note: This is Session 7 (of 8). The patient has tackled anger toward her husband and parents in prior sessions and has further developed her capacity to experience feelings of self-compassion, sadness, and longing for closeness/love. The patient reports she has had little to no pain for several weeks. However, her pain recurred following an argument with her husband and then resolved quickly following her practicing assertive communication. This session is focused on reinforcing her new, healthier pattern of recognizing and experiencing her emotions and engaging in healthy interpersonal communication, the benefits for her pain and broader psychological health, and beginning to discuss maintenance of these positive changes following termination.*

Patient: I said to him, "You know I'm finally feeling like myself again. All these years I lost, I didn't get to enjoy myself or my life, and I finally am getting back to me." And then you know what he said? He said, "You know I also haven't felt like myself in years." And you know, I really understood that. I mean, my disability really affected us both, and it's been hard on our relationship.

Therapist: What I think is so beautiful about that moment between the two of you is, that in a way, you seemed to come closer together because you opened up about the painful stuff with each other. And it seems like you may have learned that even though he gets angry a lot, that at least part of what he's feeling underneath is a lot of the sadness that you have also been feeling—a lot of shared sadness between you two.

Patient: Yes, that's exactly what it was. That was hard for me to hear, because I didn't want him to be sad because of me you know.

Therapist: I'm noticing how quickly you go to "it's because of me." As if you had been making a choice in all of this, as if you're to blame.

Patient: It's just constantly hearing all the time from him, you know "I wish you could do more work" and him complaining about all of the things he does for me. It's been cyclical this whole time, that I start apologizing because of the things he has to do, and I have felt like it's my fault.

Therapist: So, what are your thoughts about that now?

Patient: It's not. it's not my fault. Logically, I know that. I don't always feel like that, even though I know I should. I think I'll have to work on that.

Therapist: It's a work in progress with the guilty feeling, and that's okay. I'm curious what happened with the pain flare you had, after this conversation with him that was more productive for the two of you.

Patient: Yes, well the couple of days after the first conversation, you know the argument with him, I was feeling a lot more pain than I've felt in a while. And I tried to work through it, remind myself there is no danger, and to focus on you know, figuring out what I was feeling. And looking back, it was amazing because I could see exactly what happened. Because I had been feeling great for a few weeks, you know. And then all of a sudden, I have this extreme pain that I felt like I had to go back and get an oxycodone or something. It was just amazing how that switch just went on like that.

Therapist: Right! And you were trying to feel it, but your brain was trying to protect you from feeling it. And so there's that fear again, and your brain is saying, "Oh, no! This is scary, I would much rather feel physical discomfort than this emotional pain. So let me look for the easiest neural circuits and fire down that—your back.

Patient: Yeah, I mean, that's still amazing to me. And after I did that, you know. Before that second conversation, I tried to figure out what I was feeling and got the anger out—I imagined myself standing up straight, standing over him, and pointing my finger at him and you know, I spoke strongly to him—I won't let you yell at me, don't speak to me like that. And the pain got a little better after that. And then after we talked again, I was back to feeling really good again. It just went away.

Therapist: Good for you! You noticed the pain response, you figured out what you were feeling and why, and then you found a way to express that in a productive way. What a powerful lesson you taught your brain about how it can be safe with emotional experience. And you had what sounds like a real, intimate conversation with your husband that helped you both feel more understood.

Patient: I just can't believe all of this, you know. I was thinking back to all the things you taught me, and how much better I feel. My pain made me miss many things, and now I'm finally able to do those things. I really want to thank you.

Therapist: I'm so pleased for you, too. With all these gains you've made, what are you looking forward to?

Patient: Walking more. Building myself back up to a place where I feel strong again. Because now I don't have pain holding me back, but my muscles are so weak because I haven't really been using them for so long. And I've got to keep working on asserting myself in my marriage and some other relationships. I realize that I've blocked my feelings for so long.

Case Summary: Applying the Triangles of Conflict and Person

As noted earlier, EAET is guided by the two-triangle model, which is depicted below (Fig. 2.1). On the left is the Triangle of Conflict, with its poles of adaptive feelings (F), defenses (D), and anxiety and other symptoms (A); and on the right is the Triangle of Persons, with its poles of past persons (P), current persons (C) and therapist (T). Below is a table that describes the poles of each triangle as they apply to the case of the woman with fibromyalgia and as were manifest in the beginning, middle, and late phases of her therapy (Table 2.1).

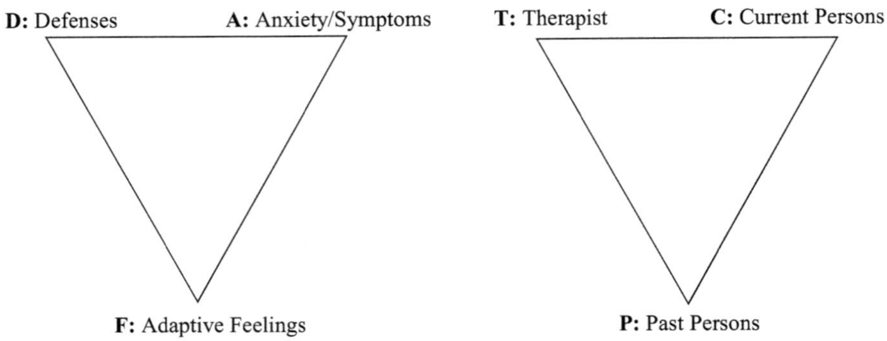

Fig. 2.1 Two-triangle model

Table 2.1 Example of two-triangle model

Triangle of conflict (Adaptive feeling/impulse—anxiety—defense)			
Triangle component	Treatment phase		
	Beginning	Middle	Late
Adaptive feelings	Anger toward parents is buried, as well as profound grief about the loss of a safe, nurturing childhood. Self-compassion and a desire for agency and emotional authenticity are masked by defenses	Anger, grief, and longing toward parents emerge and are experienced; healthy self-advocacy surfaces; emotional expression brings symptom relief	Anger, assertion, self-compassion, and shared sadness in relationships are expressed; sense of agency and emotional clarity increases; experiences a broad range of adaptive emotions, including empowerment, hope, and forgiveness
Anxiety/ pain symptoms	High anxiety about movement and pain; pain is chronic and persistent; pain flares with stress or fear	Anxiety increases during trauma processing; pain intensifies with emotional exposure (e.g., throat tightness, leg, and back pain); symptoms fluctuate based on unresolved affect	Pain re-emerges briefly during interpersonal conflict but resolves quickly after emotional processing and assertive expression; anxiety is more regulated and better understood as part of the emotional system
Defenses	Somatization, suppression, rationalization (e.g., premature forgiveness of mother)	Idealization of father, suppression of anger, intellectualization ("he was afraid") challenged; self-blame stemming from childhood attribution of responsibility for the abuse; ambivalence surfaces; begins to let go of avoidance and accept the complexity of feelings	Guilt and self-blame resurface but are addressed directly; greater capacity to experience and express feelings; use of assertiveness as a healthy alternative to emotional suppression or avoidance

(continued)

Table 2.1 (continued)

Triangle of conflict (Adaptive feeling/impulse—anxiety—defense)			
Triangle component	Treatment phase		
	Beginning	Middle	Late
Triangle of persons (Past relationships→current relationships→therapeutic relationship)			
Component	Treatment phase		
	Early	Middle	Late
Past persons	Central from the outset: Parents are addressed early, especially the mother's anger and abuse, and the father's emotional absence. These relationships are linked to the patient's chronic fear, somatic responses, and emotional avoidance	Deep focus on unresolved feelings toward both parents. The therapist helps the patient connect with rage toward the mother for the abuse, along with grief for her childhood. Relationship with father becomes nuanced—painful ambivalence, longing, and betrayal emerge	Continued work on integrating a fuller understanding of both parents. Patient engages with childhood from her present-day, resourced adult self, and is increasingly able to validate her emotional experience, assert her needs, and offer protection to herself in ways that were not possible during her childhood
Current persons	Husband noted early as a trigger for stress and pain. The relationship is emotionally charged but largely unexplored at first	The relationship with the husband is explored in more depth. Patient begins recognizing patterns of self-silencing, internalized guilt, and relational triggers for pain	Conflict with husband becomes a key arena for applying new skills: emotional awareness, assertiveness, and communication. Relationship improves, with increased intimacy and shared understanding
Therapist	The therapist is met with cautious openness. The patient shows compliance and deference early on, mirroring other relational patterns of self-silencing and fear of conflict. The therapist may be idealized or approached as an authority figure whose disapproval or judgment is feared	The patient begins to internalize a new relational template. She tests the relationship by expressing more vulnerable, conflicted, or intense emotions, and learns that doing so does not lead to punishment or rupture. This opens space for a corrective emotional experience, in which the patient no longer feels she must manage others' perceptions and responses to stay safe	The patient shifts toward empowered engagement. The therapist is now experienced as a collaborator—responsive other who supports the patient's autonomy, helps her make sense of her emotional world, and walks alongside rather than above her. This new dynamic allows the patient to begin trusting her own perceptions, validating her emotional experience, and taking an active role in her healing

Clinical Practice Guidelines and Considerations

Structuring EAET Sessions

Although a session-by-session manual has been developed for group-based clinical trials, EAET is most commonly viewed as a principle-guided therapy, not a rigid or scripted protocol, allowing for flexibility and tailoring in session-to-session targets. Although therapists may work with what the patient brings up, they should also actively guide them toward key treatment targets, particularly if avoidance or uncertainty arises. EAET therapists adopt an active and collaborative stance, supportively challenging patients to engage with uncomfortable but important emotional experiences while ensuring they feel supported.

Importantly, during EAET, patients are often encouraged to pause or delay engagement in biomedical interventions—such as medications, injections, physical therapy, or planned surgeries—to reduce reinforcement of medical explanations for pain and to clarify whether EAET is yielding benefits. As long as a clear disease-based cause of pain has been ruled out, pausing medical treatments during EAET does not usually pose a risk to the patient's health.

Common Challenges

Beyond the pain etiology considerations, psychological readiness must be assessed. EAET is an emotionally activating treatment, and as such, is not suitable for patients who have active suicidality or psychosis. Individuals with significant emotional fragility, such as severe dissociation, require a gradual, paced approach to prevent worsening of symptoms or re-traumatization. In such cases, the work would begin with more focus on monitoring anxiety and scaffolding regulation to build capacity for the titrated introduction of emotional exposures.

EAET involves patient discomfort and often therapist discomfort as well. As with any exposure-based or emotional-activation approach, therapists must develop the capacity to help patients experience temporary emotional distress. At the same time, therapists must balance attunement to the patient's anxiety, carefully regulating and titrating emotional intensity so that the sessions feel adequately challenging but never unsafe. EAET should provide a secure container for emotional exploration, where patients feel supported in confronting difficult emotions. Ensuring that the patient does not exceed their affect tolerance during emotional exposures involves close monitoring for signs of emotional flooding or excessive anxiety, and intervening as needed to help patients regulate anxiety.

Occasionally, pain, other somatic symptoms, and negative mood will initially worsen as patients begin processing avoided emotions. Therapists should normalize this response, explaining that discomfort arises from confronting previously avoided emotions and will decrease over time as they become more at ease with their feelings. Persistent symptom exacerbation, however, suggests the need for a more gradual approach, incorporating anxiety regulation techniques to mitigate excessive nervous system threat responses. Although most patients will exhibit mild defenses that resolve during EAET, some may have stronger defensive patterns that interfere with emotional processing. In EAET, therapists directly disrupt these defensive patterns, gently but firmly pointing them out in real-time and redirecting patients toward deeper emotional engagement. The therapeutic relationship can serve as a valuable tool for facilitating patient insight and personal change. In EAET, therapists encourage patients toward authentic expression of their emotions toward the therapist, and to practice assertive communication, where appropriate, with the therapist.

Concluding Thoughts

EAET is increasingly being considered a valid, evidence-based treatment option for neuroplastic pain conditions. A central strength of EAET lies in its flexibility—it can be adapted to various formats, settings, and contexts—making it more accessible to a wide range of patients. The approach encourages patients to confront and work through avoided emotional experiences, particularly those tied to trauma, unmet needs, and suppressed emotions. For many patients, including women, EAET promotes a renewed sense of one's emotional and relational capacities. It fosters safety in interpersonal experiences by encouraging healthy agency and self-protection alongside meaningful connection and care for others. The case presented in this chapter illustrates how chronic pain can become entangled with longstanding emotional conflicts and relational patterns in a woman with a history of early trauma and gendered experiences of emotional suppression. In such cases, targeting disavowed emotions like anger—often buried under layers of fear, shame, or the need to preserve relationships—becomes central to interrupting the brain's pain-alarm system. EAET offers a structured yet emotionally attuned pathway for accessing these core affective states and transforming them. As such, while the treatment has been demonstrably effective in reducing chronic pain among women, it often leads to deeper psychological and interpersonal shifts that extend beyond symptom relief.

Future research is needed to clarify the precise mechanisms of action of EAET and to identify other moderators of treatment response, as well as to identify the duration of sustained benefits of EAET. As chronic pain treatment continues to evolve, EAET stands out as a promising intervention that bridges advances in neuroscience with the enduring importance of emotional and relational healing in the treatment of chronic pain.

References

Baliki, M. N., & Apkarian, A. V. (2015). Nociception, pain, negative moods, and behavior selection. *Neuron, 87*(3), 474–491.

Barlow, D. H., Farchione, T. J., Fairholme, C. P., Ellard, K. K., Boisseau, C. L., Allen, L. B., & Ehrenreich-May, J. (2011). *Unified protocol for transdiagnostic treatment of emotional disorders: Therapist guide*. Oxford University Press.

Barrett, L. F., & Simmons, W. K. (2015). Interoceptive predictions in the brain. *Nature Reviews Neuroscience, 16*(7), 419–429.

Büchel, C., Geuter, S., Sprenger, C., & Eippert, F. (2014). Placebo analgesia: A predictive coding perspective. *Neuron, 81*(6), 1223–1239.

Carty, J. N., Ziadni, M. S., Holmes, H. J., Tomakowsky, J., Peters, K., Schubiner, H., & Lumley, M. A. (2019). The effects of a life-stress, emotional awareness and expression interview for women with chronic urogenital pain: A randomized controlled trial. *Pain Medicine, 20*, 1321–1329. https://doi.org/10.1093/pm/pny182

Cohen, S. P., Vase, L., & Hooten, W. M. (2021). Chronic pain: An update on burden, best practices, and new advances. *The Lancet, 397*(10289), 2082–2097.

Dale, J., Zhou, H., Zhang, Q., Martinez, E., Hu, S., Liu, K., et al. (2018). Scaling up cortical control inhibits pain. *Cell Reports, 23*(5), 1301–1313.

Dalechek, D. E., Caes, L., McIntosh, G., & Whittaker, A. C. (2024). Anxiety, history of childhood adversity, and experiencing chronic pain in adulthood: A systematic literature review and meta-analysis. *European Journal of Pain, 28*(6), 867–885.

Deci, E. L., & Ryan, R. M. (2012). Self-determination theory. *Handbook of Theories of Social Psychology, 1*(20), 416–436.

Eisenberger, N. I., & Lieberman, M. D. (2004). Why rejection hurts: A common neural alarm system for physical and social pain. *Trends in Cognitive Sciences, 8*(7), 294–300.

Fischer, A. H., Rodriguez Mosquera, P. M., Van Vianen, A. E., & Manstead, A. S. (2004). Gender and culture differences in emotion. *Emotion, 4*(1), 87.

Fitzcharles, M. A., Cohen, S. P., Clauw, D. J., Littlejohn, G., Usui, C., & Häuser, W. (2021). Nociplastic pain: Towards an understanding of prevalent pain conditions. *The Lancet, 397*(10289), 2098–2110.

Hayes, S. C., Wilson, K. G., Gifford, E. V., Follette, V. M., & Strosahl, K. (1996). Experiential avoidance and behavioral disorders: A functional dimensional approach to diagnosis and treatment. *Journal of Consulting and Clinical Psychology, 64*(6), 1152.

Helgeson, V. S. (1994). Relation of agency and communion to well-being: Evidence and potential explanations. *Psychological Bulletin, 116*(3), 412.

Howell, A. J. (2017). Self-affirmation theory and the science of well-being. *Journal of Happiness Studies, 18*, 293–311.

Jepma, M., Koban, L., van Doorn, J., Jones, M., & Wager, T. D. (2018). Behavioural and neural evidence for self-reinforcing expectancy effects on pain. *Nature Human Behaviour, 2*(11), 838–855.

McCarberg, B., & Peppin, J. (2019). Pain pathways and nervous system plasticity: Learning and memory in pain. *Pain Medicine, 20*(12), 2421–2437.

Keogh, E. (2022). Sex and gender differences in pain: Past, present, and future. *Pain, 163*(S1), S108–S116.

Krohner, S., Town, J., Cannoy, C. N., Schubiner, H., Rapport, L. J., Grekin, E., & Lumley, M. A. (2024). Emotion-focused psychodynamic interview for people with chronic musculoskeletal pain and childhood adversity: A randomized controlled trial. *The Journal of Pain, 25*, 39–52.

Kross, E., Berman, M. G., Mischel, W., Smith, E. E., & Wager, T. D. (2011). Social rejection shares somatosensory representations with physical pain. *Proceedings of the National Academy of Sciences, 108*(15), 6270–6275.

Lazarus, R. S. (1991). *Emotion and adaptation*. Oxford University Press.

Lumley, M. A., Schubiner, H., Lockhart, N. A., Kidwell, K. M., Harte, S., Clauw, D. J., & Williams, D. A. (2017). Emotional awareness and expression therapy, cognitive-behavioral therapy, and education for fibromyalgia: A cluster-randomized controlled trial. *PAIN, 158*, 2354–2363. https://www.ncbi.nlm.nih.gov/pmc/articles/PMC5680092/

Lumley, M. A., & Schubiner, H. (2019). Emotional awareness and expression therapy for chronic pain: Rationale, principles and techniques, evidence, and critical analysis. *Current Rheumatology Reports, 21*, 30. https://link.springer.com/article/10.1007/s11926-019-0829-6

Lumley, M. A., Yamin, J. B., Pester, B. D., Krohner, S., & Urbanik, C. P. (2022). Trauma matters: Psychological interventions for comorbid psychosocial trauma and chronic pain. *PAIN, 163*(4), 599–603. https://doi.org/10.1097/j.pain.0000000000002425

Malan, D., & Parker, L. (1995). *Individual psychotherapy and the science of psychodynamics*. CRC Press.

Maroti, D., Lumley, M. A., Schubiner, H., Lilliengren, P., Bileviciute-Ljungar, I., Ljótsson, B., & Johansson, R. (2022). Internet-based emotional awareness and expression therapy for somatic symptom disorder: A randomized, controlled trial. *Journal of Psychosomatic Research*, Article 111068. https://doi.org/10.1016/j.jpsychores.2022.111068

Maroti, D., Frisch, S., & Lumley, M. A. (2025). To feel is to heal—introduction to Emotional Awareness and Expression Therapy. *Schmerz*. https://doi.org/10.1007/s00482-025-00878-6

Meulders, A. (2020). Fear in the context of pain: Lessons learned from 100 years of fear conditioning research. *Behaviour Research and Therapy, 131*, 103635.

Olff, M., Langeland, W., Draijer, N., & Gersons, B. P. R. (2007). Gender differences in posttraumatic stress disorder. *Psychological Bulletin, 133*(2), 183–204.

Olff, M. (2017). Sex and gender differences in post-traumatic stress disorder: An update. *European Journal of Psychotraumatology, 8*(sup4). https://doi.org/10.1080/20008198.2017.1351204

Petzschner, F. H., Weber, L. A., Gard, T., & Stephan, K. E. (2017). Computational psychosomatics and computational psychiatry: Toward a joint framework for differential diagnosis. *Biological Psychiatry, 82*(6), 421–430.

Raja, S. N., Carr, D. B., Cohen, M., Finnerup, N. B., Flor, H., Gibson, S., et al. (2020). The revised International Association for the Study of Pain definition of pain: Concepts, challenges, and compromises. *Pain, 161*(9), 1976–1982.

Seymour, B. (2019). Pain: A precision signal for reinforcement learning and control. *Neuron, 101*(6), 1029–1041.

Steele, C. M. (1988). The psychology of self-affirmation: Sustaining the integrity of the self. In *Advances in experimental social psychology* (Vol. 21, pp. 261–302). Academic Press.

Thakur, E. R., Holmes, H. J., Lockhart, N. A., Carty, J. N., Ziadni, M. S., Doherty, H. K., Lackner, J. M., Schubiner, H., & Lumley, M. A. (2017). Emotional awareness and expression training improves irritable bowel syndrome: A randomized controlled trial. *Neurogastroenterology and Motility, 29*, e13143. https://doi.org/10.1111/nmo.13143

Tracey, I. (2010). Getting the pain you expect: Mechanisms of placebo, nocebo and reappraisal effects in humans. *Nature Medicine, 16*(11), 1277–1283.

Treede, R. D., Rief, W., Barke, A., Aziz, Q., Bennett, M. I., Benoliel, R., et al. (2019). Chronic pain as a symptom or a disease: The IASP classification of chronic pain for the International Classification of Diseases (ICD-11). *Pain, 160*(1), 19–27.

Vlaeyen, J. W., & Crombez, G. (2020). Behavioral conceptualization and treatment of chronic pain. *Annual Review of Clinical Psychology, 16*(1), 187–212.

Woolf, C. J. (2011). Central sensitization: Implications for the diagnosis and treatment of pain. *Pain, 152*(3), S2–S15.

Yarns, B. C., Lumley, M. A., Cassidy, J. T., Steers, W. N., Osato, S., Schubiner, H., & Sultzer, D. L. (2020). Emotional awareness and expression therapy achieves greater pain reduction than cognitive behavioral therapy in older adults with chronic musculoskeletal pain: A preliminary randomized comparison trial. *Pain Medicine, 21*, 2811–2822. https://doi.org/10.1093/pm/pnaa145

Yarns, B. C., Jackson, N. J., Alas, A., Melrose, R. J., Lumley, M. A., & Sultzer, D. L. (2024a). Emotional awareness and expression therapy or cognitive behavioral therapy for chronic pain in older veterans: A randomized clinical trial. *JAMA Network Open, 7*(6), e2417340. https://doi.org/10.1001/jamanetworkopen.2024.15842

Yarns, B. C., Molaie, A. M., Lumley, M. A., Zhu, T. A., Jazi, A. N., Ganz, D. A., & Melrose, R. J. (2024b). Video telehealth Emotional Awareness and Expression Therapy for older adults with chronic pain: A pilot study. *Clinical Gerontologist, 47*, 136–148. https://doi.org/10.1080/07317115.2022.2159909

You, D. S., Albu, S., Lisenbardt, H., & Meagher, M. W. (2019). Cumulative childhood adversity as a risk factor for common chronic pain conditions in young adults. *Pain Medicine, 20*(3), 486–494.

Yunus, M. B. (2007, June). Fibromyalgia and overlapping disorders: The unifying concept of central sensitivity syndromes. In *Seminars in arthritis and rheumatism* (Vol. 36, No. 6, pp. 339–356). WB Saunders.

Ziadni, M. S., Carty, J. N., Doherty, H. K., Porcerelli, J. H., Rapport, L. J., Schubiner, H., & Lumley, M. A. (2018). A life-stress, emotional awareness and expression interview for primary care patients with medically unexplained symptoms: A randomized controlled trial. *Health Psychology, 37*, 282–290. https://doi.org/10.1037/hea0000566

Chapter 3
Psychosocial Perspectives and Integrative Approaches in Managing Musculoskeletal Pain in Women

Monique Gilmore, Tiffany Parisi, Myrella Paschali, and Asimina Lazaridou

Introduction

Chronic musculoskeletal pain represents a significant public health concern due to its high prevalence, substantial healthcare costs, and profound impact on individual quality of life. Chronic musculoskeletal pain is the most common chronic pain condition, affecting approximately 30% of the population, and poses a major challenge for healthcare systems worldwide (El-Tallaway et al., 2021). As with many other chronic pain conditions, women are disproportionately affected. Women experience chronic musculoskeletal pain at higher rates, report greater pain intensity, and endure longer durations of pain compared to men (Ruau et al., 2012). The burden of chronic musculoskeletal pain not only affects the health system but also has pervasive effects on the daily lives of many women (Esteve et al., 2018; Hoffman et al., 2022; Lazaridou et al., 2020a, 2020b).

Individuals with chronic musculoskeletal pain experience persistent pain in musculoskeletal tissues, including skeletal muscles, bones, and joints. This ongoing pain compromises the ability to engage in daily movements without discomfort and can lead to regression in physical dexterity. Furthermore, musculoskeletal chronic pain is closely intertwined with psychological factors, particularly symptoms of

M. Gilmore (✉) · T. Parisi
Fielding Graduate University, Santa Barbara, CA, USA
e-mail: mgilmore@fielding.edu

M. Paschali
LVR-Klinik Düsseldorf, Department of Psychiatry and Psychotherapy, Heinrich Heine University, Düsseldorf, Germany

A. Lazaridou
Harvard Medical School, Boston, MA, USA

L. A. Payne (ed.), *Psychosocial Interventions for Chronic Pain in Women and Girls*, CBT: Science Into Practice, https://doi.org/10.1007/978-3-031-98876-9_3

depression and anxiety, which are reciprocally related to the experience of pain. Psychological interventions targeting both chronic pain and mental health symptoms are therefore critical for reducing the disproportionate burden experienced by women with musculoskeletal pain (Meints & Edwards, 2018).

Biopsychosocial Approach

The treatment of chronic pain through a biopsychosocial lens is supported by a robust body of research and is associated with improved patient outcomes (Gatchel et al., 2014). The biopsychosocial model of pain is an integrative framework that emphasizes the complex interplay between biological, psychological, and social factors in the experience and management of pain (Gatchel et al., 2014). This model is particularly relevant for understanding musculoskeletal pain in women, as women demonstrate greater pain prevalence than men and often experience more severe, frequent, and longer-lasting chronic pain conditions as a result of interacting biopsychosocial factors (Bingefors & Isacson, 2004).

Social Context

A biopsychosocial approach to chronic pain in women requires careful consideration of the social, biological, and psychological factors that influence diagnosis, treatment, and pain experience. Social context plays a critical role in shaping the clinical management of chronic pain. Women with chronic pain are more likely than men to make multiple visits to healthcare professionals before receiving an accurate diagnosis and treatment plan. They are also more likely to experience pain invalidation in healthcare settings and to attribute self-blame for their pain (Hoffman et al., 2022; Coady et al., 2024). Coady et al. (2024) found that greater experiences of pain invalidation were associated with higher levels of depressive symptomatology, with pain-related shame serving as a mediating variable in this relationship. Furthermore, experimental research has demonstrated that treatment and diagnosis can differ across cultural backgrounds. When controlling for all other symptoms, minority individuals were perceived as experiencing less pain compared to Caucasian individuals (Hirsh et al., 2010).

Biological Factors

Biological factors also significantly contribute to chronic pain in women, encompassing hormonal influences, genetic predispositions, neurobiological differences in pain processing, and immune system interactions. Hormonal fluctuations associated with menstruation, pregnancy, the postpartum period, and menopause, particularly involving estrogen and progesterone, affect pain perception and sensitivity, often complicating pain management efforts (Chen et al., 2020; Daneau et al., 2021; Fillingim et al., 2021). Changes in hormonal levels can heighten pain sensitivity and alter the course of chronic pain conditions (Bartley & Fillingim, 2013).

Genetic predispositions further contribute to chronic pain vulnerability, as women with certain genetic profiles may demonstrate heightened pain sensitivity and diminished endogenous pain inhibition, thereby increasing their susceptibility to chronic musculoskeletal pain (Zubieta et al., 2002). Central sensitization, defined as an increased responsiveness of neurons within the central nervous system, occurs more frequently in women and underlies conditions such as fibromyalgia and chronic pelvic pain (Clauw et al., 2019). This heightened neural response often leads to widespread pain that is disproportionate to the original injury or stimulus, posing significant challenges for traditional pain management strategies.

Neuroimaging studies have also identified sex differences in the structure and function of brain regions implicated in pain processing, including the anterior cingulate cortex, prefrontal cortex, and insula, which may contribute to the higher prevalence and severity of chronic pain among women (Mogil, 2020). In addition to neurological differences, women are more likely to develop autoimmune disorders such as lupus and multiple sclerosis, which are commonly associated with chronic musculoskeletal pain (Klein & Flanagan, 2016; Klyne et al., 2022). The interaction between the immune and nervous systems in these conditions can exacerbate pain and further complicate treatment efforts (Fairweather & Rose, 2004).

Psychological Factors

Psychological factors, particularly stress, also play a significant role in chronic pain. Chronic stress can alter pain processing by increasing pain sensitivity, known as hyperalgesia, and by prolonging recovery times (Stubbs et al., 2010). Dysregulation of the hypothalamic-pituitary-adrenal (HPA) axis, which governs stress responses, and abnormalities in cortisol levels have been implicated in the development and maintenance of chronic pain conditions (Fleshner et al., 2011).

In addition to stress, psychosocial factors significantly impact musculoskeletal pain (Lazaridou et al., 2020a, 2020b; Versluijs et al., 2023) and can detract from patients' quality of life, mental health, physical functioning, and physical outcomes (Holla et al., 2018; Martinez-Calderon et al., 2020; Lazaridou et al., 2020a, 2020b). Fatigue, sleep challenges, increased social isolation, pain catastrophizing, and depression are all correlated with chronic musculoskeletal pain (Evans et al., 2018; Franqueiro et al., 2023; Landmark et al., 2024; Martinez-Calderon et al., 2020). Chronic musculoskeletal pain can also result in a reduction of socio-emotional status, compromise employment opportunities (El Tallaway et al., 2021), and increase the risk of substance abuse. Moreover, higher pain intensity in individuals with chronic pain is associated with an increased risk of suicidal ideation, suicide attempts, and morbidity (Chen et al., 2023).

Treating Cognitions Associated with Chronic Pain

Cognitive behavioral therapy (CBT) is one of the most widely recognized and effective approaches for treating pain (Lazaridou et al., 2017, 2020a, 2020b) and specifically targets the reduction of pain catastrophizing (Gilliam et al., 2021; Lazaridou et al., 2017; Lee et al., 2023). Pain catastrophizing is a maladaptive cognitive distortion, characterized by patterns of negative automatic thoughts that distort objective reality, and has been shown to increase pain intensity, disability, emotional distress, and the overall pain experience (Landmark et al., 2024; Severeijns et al., 2001; Markfelder & Pauli, 2020). Pain catastrophizing is considered to underlie fear avoidance, a behavioral response that can lead to maladaptive coping strategies such as the avoidance of occupational therapy, physical exercise, and social connection. More intensive depressive symptoms and activity intolerance have been associated with higher levels of catastrophic thinking (Versluijs et al., 2023).

Women are often more receptive to adopting adaptive coping strategies and protective factors that CBT promotes, including cognitive reinterpretation of pain (Bartley & Fillingim, 2013). CBT interventions that specifically target pain catastrophizing aim to help individuals recognize catastrophic thoughts as they arise and to question these automatic thoughts, allowing for increased objectivity and more adaptive pain responses. This is done in combination with behavioral techniques designed to reduce fear-avoidance behaviors. Mindfulness-based interventions, such as cognitive reinterpretation of pain and nonjudgmental attending to pain cues, are also generally viewed more favorably by women than by men (Bartley & Fillingim, 2013). These interventions have been shown to improve depression symptoms and enhance quality of life, which can have a lasting impact (Hilton et al., 2017; Lazaridou et al., 2020a, 2020b).

Nonjudgmental awareness of pain can reduce pain-related emotional distress and foster greater acceptance of the pain experience, leading to a reduced pain burden and improved overall quality of life (Pester et al., 2023; Petrucci et al., 2021). Integrating CBT with mindfulness approaches offers a comprehensive strategy to address both cognitive distortions and emotional distress associated with chronic pain. Studies that integrate these frameworks demonstrate significant improvements in pain management and overall outcomes (Lee et al., 2024; Pester et al., 2023). Such interventions enable patients to develop more adaptive responses to pain, thereby reducing its impact on daily functioning (Garland et al., 2019a, 2019b; Pardos-Gascón et al., 2021).

Mindfulness Training for Primary Care (MTPC) has demonstrated significant benefits in enhancing emotional regulation and self-regulatory behaviors among patients with depression and chronic pain (Gawande et al., 2019; Schuman-Olivier et al., 2024). Following MTPC, increased activation has been observed in the insula, a brain region integral to interoception and emotional regulation, among individuals with severe depression (Datko et al., 2022). MTPC enhances interoceptive awareness, or the ability to perceive and trust internal bodily sensations. This heightened awareness has been shown to partially mediate the relationship between MTPC participation and improvements in health behaviors, including facilitating the initiation of action plans in individuals with depression and chronic pain.

Mindfulness-Oriented Recovery Enhancement (MORE) combines CBT interventions with mindfulness practices in an eight-session group therapy format to treat opioid addiction and chronic musculoskeletal pain (Garland, 2024). Participants in MORE first learn mindfulness meditation techniques to build meta-awareness and strengthen cognitive control, which helps manage automatic habits and reduces emotional biases in interpreting pain and cravings (Garland, 2024). They are then trained in reappraisal techniques, which involve reframing stressful experiences to mitigate negative emotions and reconsider the harmful outcomes of substance use. Mindfulness practices in this context also enhance individuals' ability to savor positive experiences, thereby promoting greater reward sensitivity, increased positive emotions, and a deeper sense of life meaning (Garland, 2016).

Neurobiological-Based Approaches

Although several emerging neurobiological therapeutic approaches to pain have demonstrated promise, Emotional Awareness and Expression Therapy (EAET) and Pain Reprocessing Therapy (PRT) have shown particularly strong results and are the focus of increasing clinical attention. Preliminary findings suggest that EAET substantially reduces pain (Lumley et al., 2012; Lumley & Schubiner, 2019; Yarns et al., 2020) by increasing clients' awareness of how stress and emotions interact with their pain experience, enhancing their understanding of how traumatic experiences contributed to the suppression of emotional expression, and guiding them in applying their increased emotional awareness to significant relationships in their lives.

Unlike many therapeutic approaches that do not directly address past trauma, EAET is distinguished by its focus on the traumatic experiences that have fostered patterns of emotional repression. Landmark et al. (2024) found that psychological distress related to lifetime stressors emerged as the most robust predictor variable of chronic pain. Wippert et al. (2017) found that when comparing various predictor variables for individuals with musculoskeletal pain, adverse critical life events considered to be life-changing were the strongest predictor of future pain on experience and disability compared to other predictor variables. Early life adversity, which includes different sources of adverse childhood experiences (ACEs), correlates with multiple chronic pain conditions, including musculoskeletal pain (Groenewald et al., 2020; Kaleycheva et al., 2021). This has raised questions about ACEs creating a vulnerability that is predictive of pain and depression (Antoniou et al., 2023a, 2023b). Trauma exposure may lead to dysregulation of the HPA axis and autonomic nervous system, resulting in altered pain processing and increased vulnerability to conditions such as fibromyalgia, myofascial pain syndrome, and other musculoskeletal disorders (Afari et al., 2014).

PRT has also demonstrated significant efficacy, with a randomized clinical trial showing substantial reductions in chronic back pain that were maintained at a 1-year follow-up (Ashar et al., 2022). Further supporting these findings, a subsequent study examining the role of mind-brain attributions in chronic pain recovery found that PRT significantly increased patients' attribution of their pain to psychological and neurological factors (Ashar et al., 2023). Patients who underwent PRT reported attributing their pain reduction to several key factors: cognitive reappraisal of pain, decreased catastrophizing, recognition of the impact of stress on pain, and enhanced social connections, including supportive interactions with both peers and therapists. Collectively, these elements appear to foster a more adaptive and resilient response to pain (Ashar et al., 2023). By reframing pain as a non-threatening experience and emphasizing the development of supportive therapeutic relationships, PRT may facilitate significant, enduring pain relief for individuals experiencing chronic pain conditions.

Addressing Behaviors Associated with Chronic Pain

Increasing Social Support

Behavioral activation is utilized as an intervention within cognitive behavioral therapy to promote greater social connectedness and enhance social interactions. Integrating group therapy directly into the treatment of individuals with chronic pain and fostering a supportive environment can significantly improve pain management outcomes (Driscoll et al., 2021; Pester et al., 2022). Psychosocial interventions that enhance social support and address interpersonal dynamics have been shown to improve pain outcomes (Boggero et al., 2024; Weiß et al., 2024). Social support serves as a buffer against the adverse effects of pain by providing emotional support, practical assistance, and validation of the pain experience (Franqueiro et al., 2023; Musich et al., 2022; Sturgeon et al., 2024). A study found that women who participated in group-based psychosocial interventions reported significant reductions in pain intensity as well as improved mental health outcomes. Increasing social support is correlated with reduced pain intensity, decreased pain-related disability, lower levels of loneliness, and improved physical and mental health status (Franqueiro et al., 2023), along with reduced symptoms of depression (Holla et al., 2018).

Accessibility is an important factor to consider when providing psychological treatment to women with chronic pain. Women often spend more time engaging in caretaking behaviors and household activities compared to men, which can reduce the time available for engaging in adaptive coping strategies. Encouragingly, evidence suggests that individuals with chronic health conditions may benefit from web-based psychological interventions that address depression, anxiety, and distress, according to a meta-analysis of 70 studies (Rini et al., 2021). Facilitator-directed web-based interventions were found to be more efficacious in reducing symptoms of depression than interventions lacking a facilitator. Most of the interventions reviewed were grounded in cognitive behavioral therapy principles (Rini et al., 2021).

Increasing Sleep

Obtaining sufficient sleep is imperative for maintaining physical and mental health. A reduced night of sleep leads to a rapid decline in cognitive functioning, emotional regulation, and immune system effectiveness (Gage & Baars, 2018). Women report higher rates of insomnia (Zeng et al., 2020) and often experience elevated levels of worry, intrusive thoughts, and rumination during the night (Sidani et al., 2019). Sleep deprivation lowers the pain threshold, thereby increasing the intensity of pain. Additionally, poor sleep quality is correlated with increased mental health challenges and a heightened risk for suicide (Cheatle et al., 2016; Cheatle, 2024). Other identified suicide risk factors include opioid prescribing patterns and opioid tapering processes (Mackey et al., 2020). Landmark et al. (2024) found that significant sleep disturbances were associated with increased pain intensity, fatigue, and emotional distress.

Cognitive therapy, mindfulness-based stress reduction (MBSR; Niazi & Niazi, 2011), and behavioral therapy can be utilized independently or in combination to improve sleep quality in individuals with chronic pain (Burns et al., 2022). These interventions not only enhance sleep but also contribute to improved physical functioning and mood. Activity scheduling designed to establish consistent routines and promote better sleep hygiene may be an important therapeutic component, alongside medical interventions aimed at increasing sleep quality and reducing hyperarousal caused by sleep deprivation. Addressing sleep difficulties is critical for mitigating the exacerbation of pain symptoms and improving overall quality of life.

Summary

Research underscores the necessity of adopting a comprehensive approach to pain management that addresses the biopsychosocial aspects of chronic pain. Integrating CBT, mindfulness-based interventions, physical therapy, and medication management, while enhancing collaboration among healthcare providers, is essential for improving patient outcomes and alleviating chronic pain (Clauw et al., 2019). Holistic methods combining CBT, mindfulness, and psychosocial interventions have been shown not only to decrease pain intensity but also to substantially enhance daily functioning and overall quality of life for women experiencing chronic pain (Clauw et al., 2019). These integrative strategies address the multifaceted nature of musculoskeletal pain by targeting its psychological, emotional, and social dimensions (Day et al., 2020; Serrat et al., 2021). A patient-centered, individualized approach remains crucial, particularly for women whose experiences of pain are highly variable and influenced by unique psychological backgrounds (Barret et al., 2021).

Implementation Considerations

In clinical applications, CBT interventions for chronic pain typically begin with psychoeducation regarding the impact of cognitive processes on the pain experience. Patients are introduced to the identification of automatic thoughts, particularly those reflecting catastrophizing patterns such as magnification and helplessness. Structured exercises, including thought records, are employed to facilitate the recognition of these patterns across various contexts. Following identification, cognitive restructuring techniques are utilized to encourage patients to examine the evidence supporting and refuting catastrophic cognitions and to generate more adaptive alternative thoughts. Behavioral experiments are often incorporated to help patients test these new cognitions in pain-provoking situations, reinforcing cognitive flexibility and perceived control.

Mindfulness-based strategies are introduced through structured practices such as body scans, mindful breathing, and nonjudgmental observation of pain sensations. Patients are guided to notice physical sensations without assigning evaluative judgments, thereby disrupting the habitual cognitive-affective amplification of pain. Home practice assignments and the integration of brief mindfulness exercises into daily routines support the generalization of skills beyond clinical settings. These interventions aim to foster cognitive flexibility, emotional regulation, and a more adaptive relationship with chronic pain.

Recommendations

Although current evidence supports the integration of CBT and mindfulness-based interventions into pain management, ongoing research is necessary for refining these approaches for enhanced efficacy and broader clinical application. One critical area for refinement involves the development of treatment strategies that cater to the individualized needs and unique pain profiles of women suffering from musculoskeletal pain (Clauw et al., 2019). Understanding the specific mechanisms through which CBT and mindfulness exert their therapeutic effects is pivotal for improving clinical outcomes. Future research should continue to investigate how these interventions influence pain perception, emotional regulation, and overall quality of life.

As the field continues to evolve, it will be important to focus on tailoring interventions to the diverse psychological and physiological experiences of patients. Research must explore the long-term effectiveness of integrated interventions, including the use of booster sessions and the inclusion of control groups in clinical trials to assess the sustained impact of these therapies (Day et al., 2020; Serrat et al., 2021). Adopting a holistic, patient-centered approach that emphasizes individualized treatment planning will be essential for advancing effective pain management strategies for women with chronic musculoskeletal pain (Barret et al., 2021).

References

Afari, N., Ahumada, S. M., Wright, L. J., Mostoufi, S., Golnari, G., Reis, V., & Cuneo, J. G. (2014). Psychological trauma and functional somatic syndromes: A systematic review and meta-analysis. *Psychosomatic Medicine, 76*(1), 2–11. https://doi.org/10.1097/PSY.0000000000000010

Antoniou, P., Darragh, M., & Eccleston, C. (2023a). Psychological interventions for chronic pain: Evidence and recommendations. *British Journal of Pain, 17*(1), 23–32. https://doi.org/10.1177/20494637221100012

Antoniou, G., Lambourg, E., Steele, J. D., & Colvin, L. A. (2023b). The effect of adverse childhood experiences on chronic pain and major depression in adulthood: A systematic review and meta-analysis. *British Journal of Anaesthesia, 130*(6), 729–746. https://doi.org/10.1016/j.bja.2023.03.008

Ashar, Y. K., Lumley, M. A., Perlis, R. H., Liston, C., Gunning, F. M., & Wager, T. D. (2023). Reattribution to mind-brain processes and recovery from chronic back pain. *JAMA Network Open, 6*(9), e2333846. https://doi.org/10.1001/jamanetworkopen.2023.33846

Ashar, Y., Perlis, R., Liston, C., Gunning, F., & Wager, T. (2022). Effects of pain reprocessing therapy on attributed causes of chronic back pain. *The Journal of Pain, 23*(Suppl 5), 27–28. https://doi.org/10.1016/j.jpain.2022.03.108

Barrett, D., Brintz, C. E., Zaski, A. M., & Edlund, M. J. (2021). Dialectical pain management: Feasibility of a hybrid third-wave cognitive behavioral therapy approach for adults receiving opioids for chronic pain. *Pain Medicine, 22*(5), 1080–1094. https://doi.org/10.1093/pm/pnaa361

Bartley, E. J., & Fillingim, R. B. (2013). Sex differences in pain: A brief review of clinical and experimental findings. *British Journal of Anaesthesia, 111*(1), 52–58. https://doi.org/10.1093/bja/aet127

Bingefors, K., & Isacson, D. (2004). Epidemiology, co-morbidity, and impact on health-related quality of life of self-reported headache and musculoskeletal pain—a gender perspective. *European Journal of Pain, 8*(5), 435–450. https://doi.org/10.1016/j.ejpain.2004.01.005

Boggero, I. A., Sangalli, L., Brasch, L., & King, C. D. (2024). Social health in young women with chronic pain. *Pain Reports, 9*(2), e1146. https://doi.org/10.1097/PR9.0000000000001146

Burns, J. W., Jensen, M. P., Thorn, B., Lillis, T. A., Carmody, J., Newman, A. K., & Keefe, F. (2022). Cognitive therapy, mindfulness-based stress reduction, and behavior therapy for the treatment of chronic pain: Randomized controlled trial. *Pain, 163*(2), 376–389. https://doi.org/10.1097/j.pain.0000000000002357

Cheatle, M. D., Foster, S., Pinkett, A., Lesneski, M., Qu, D., & Dhingra, L. (2016). Assessing and managing sleep disturbance in patients with chronic pain. *Anesthesiology Clinics, 34*(2), 379–393. https://doi.org/10.1016/j.anclin.2016.01.007

Cheatle, M. D. (2024). Pain, substance use disorder and suicide: On the edge. *Current Addiction Reports*. https://doi.org/10.1007/s40429-024-00585-9

Chen, Y., Navratilova, E., Dodick, D. W., & Porreca, F. (2020). An emerging role for prolactin in female-selective pain. *Trends in Neurosciences, 43*(8), 635–648. https://doi.org/10.1016/j.tins.2020.06.003

Chen, C., Pettersson, E., Summit, A. G., Boersma, K., Chang, Z., Kuja-Halkola, R., Lichtenstein, P., & Quinn, P. D. (2023). Chronic pain conditions and risk of suicidal behavior: A 10-year longitudinal co-twin control study. *BMC Medicine, 21*, 9. https://doi.org/10.1186/s12916-022-02703-8

Clauw, D. J., Essex, M. N., Pitman, V., & Jones, K. D. (2019). Reframing chronic pain as a disease, not a symptom: Rationale and implications for pain management. *Postgraduate Medicine, 131*(3), 185–198. https://doi.org/10.1080/00325481.2019.1574403

Coady, A., Godard, R., & Holtzman, S. (2024). Understanding the link between pain invalidation and depressive symptoms: The role of shame and social support in people with chronic pain. *Journal of Health Psychology, 29*(1), 52–64.

Daneau, C., Houle, M., Pasquier, M., Ruchat, S. M., & Descarreaux, M. (2021). Association between pregnancy-related hormones and lumbopelvic pain characteristics in pregnant women: A scoping review. *Journal of Manipulative and Physiological Therapeutics, 44*(7), 573–583. https://doi.org/10.1016/j.jmpt.2021.10.001

Datko, M., Lutz, J., Gawande, R., Comeau, A., To, M. N., Desel, T., Gan, J., Desbordes, G., Napadow, V., & Schuman-Olivier, Z. (2022). Increased insula response to interoceptive attention following mindfulness training is associated with increased body trusting among patients with depression. *Psychiatry Research: Neuroimaging, 327*, 111559. https://doi.org/10.1016/j.pscychresns.2022.111559

Day, M. A., Ehde, D. M., Burns, J., Ward, L. C., Friedly, J. L., Thorn, B. E., Ciol, M. A., Mendoza, E., Chan, J. F., Battalio, S., Borckardt, J., & Jensen, M. P. (2020). A randomized trial to examine the mechanisms of cognitive, behavioral and mindfulness-based psychosocial treatments for chronic pain: Study protocol. *Contemporary Clinical Trials, 93*, 106000. https://doi.org/10.1016/j.cct.2020.106000

Driscoll, M. A., Edwards, R. R., Becker, W. C., Kaptchuk, T. J., & Kerns, R. D. (2021). Psychological interventions for the treatment of chronic pain in adults. *Psychological Science in the Public Interest, 22*(2), 52–95. https://doi.org/10.1177/15291006211008157

El-Tallawy, S. N., Nalamasu, R., Salem, G. I., LeQuang, J. A. K., Pergolizzi, J. V., & Christo, P. J. (2021). Management of musculoskeletal pain: An update with emphasis on chronic musculoskeletal pain. *Pain and Therapy, 10*, 181–209. https://doi.org/10.1007/s40122-021-00235-2

Esteve, R., López-Martínez, A. E., Peters, M. L., Serrano-Ibáñez, E. R., Ruiz-Párraga, G. T., & Ramírez-Maestre, C. (2018). Optimism, positive and negative affect, and goal adjustment strategies: Their relationship to activity patterns in patients with chronic musculoskeletal pain. *Pain Research & Management, 2018*, 6291719. https://doi.org/10.1155/2018/6291719

Evans, E. A., Herman, P. M., Washington, D. L., Lorenz, K. A., Yuan, A., Upchurch, D. M., Marshall, N., Hamilton, A. B., & Taylor, S. L. (2018). Gender differences in use of complementary and integrative health by U.S. military veterans with chronic musculoskeletal pain. *Women's Health Issues, 28*(5), 379–386. https://doi.org/10.1016/j.whi.2018.07.003040367

Fairweather, D., & Rose, N. R. (2004). Women and autoimmune diseases. *Emerging Infectious Diseases, 10*(11), 2005–2011. https://doi.org/10.3201/eid1011.040367

Fillingim, R. B., King, C. D., Ribeiro-Dasilva, M. C., Rahim-Williams, B., & Riley, J. L. (2021). Sex, gender, and pain: A review of recent clinical and experimental findings. *The Journal of Pain, 10*(5), 447–485. https://doi.org/10.1016/j.jpain.2008.12.001

Fleshner, M., Maier, S. F., Lyons, D. M., & Raskind, M. A. (2011). The neurobiology of the stress-resistant brain. *Stress, 14*(5), 498–502. https://doi.org/10.3109/10253890.2011.596865

Franqueiro, A. R., Yoon, J., Crago, M. A., Curiel, M., & Wilson, J. M. (2023). The interconnection between social support and emotional distress among individuals with chronic pain: A narrative review. *Psychology Research and Behavior Management, 16*, 4389–4399. https://doi.org/10.2147/PRBM.S410606

Gage, N. M., & Baars, B. J. (2018). *Fundamentals of cognitive neuroscience: A beginner's guide* (2nd ed.). Academic Press.

Garland, E. L. (2024). Mindfulness-oriented recovery enhancement: Implementing an evidence-based intervention for chronic pain, opioid use, and opioid addiction in clinical settings. *British Journal of Clinical Pharmacology, 90*(12), 3028–3035.

Garland, E. L. (2016). Restructuring reward processing with Mindfulness-Oriented Recovery Enhancement: Novel therapeutic mechanisms to remediate hedonic dysregulation in addiction, stress, and pain. *Annals of the New York Academy of Sciences, 1373*(1), 25–37.

Garland, E. L., Hanley, A. W., Riquino, M. R., Reese, S. E., Baker, A. K., Salas, K., Yack, B. P., Bedford, C. E., Bryan, M. A., Atchley, R., Nakamura, Y., Froeliger, B., & Howard, M. O. (2019a). Mindfulness-Oriented Recovery Enhancement reduces opioid misuse risk via analgesic and positive psychological mechanisms: A randomized controlled trial. *Journal of Consulting and Clinical Psychology, 87*(10), 927–940. https://doi.org/10.1037/ccp0000390

Garland, E. L., Reese, S. E., Bedford, C. E., & Baker, A. K. (2019b). Adverse childhood experiences predict autonomic indices of emotion dysregulation and negative emotional cue-elicited craving among female opioid-treated chronic pain patients. *Development and Psychopathology, 31*(3), 1101–1110. https://doi.org/10.1017/S0954579419000622

Gatchel, R. J., McGeary, D. D., McGeary, C. A., & Lippe, B. (2014). Interdisciplinary chronic pain management: Past, present, and future. *American Psychologist, 69*(2), 119–130. https://doi.org/10.1037/a0035514

Gawande, R., To, M. N., Pine, E., Griswold, T., Creedon, T. B., Brunel, A., Lozada, A., Loucks, E. B., & Schuman-Olivier, Z. (2019). Mindfulness training enhances self-regulation and facilitates health behavior change for primary care patients: A randomized controlled trial. *Journal of General Internal Medicine, 34*(2), 293–302. https://doi.org/10.1007/s11606-018-4739-5

Gilliam, W. P., Schumann, M. E., Cunningham, J. L., Evans, M. M., Luedtke, C. A., Morrison, E. J., & Vowles, K. E. (2021). Pain catastrophizing as a treatment process variable in cognitive behavioural therapy for adults with chronic pain. *European Journal of Pain, 25*(2), 339–347. https://doi.org/10.1002/ejp.1671

Groenewald, C. B., Murray, C. B., & Palermo, T. M. (2020). Adverse childhood experiences and chronic pain among children and adolescents in the United States. *Pain Reports, 5*(5), e839. https://doi.org/10.1097/PR9.0000000000000839

Hilton, L., Hempel, S., Ewing, B. A., Apaydin, E., Xenakis, L., Newberry, S., et al. (2017). Mindfulness meditation for chronic pain: Systematic review and meta-analysis. *Annals of Behavioral Medicine, 51*(2), 199–213. https://doi.org/10.1007/s12160-016-9844-2

Hirsh, A. T., Jensen, M. P., & Robinson, M. E. (2010). Evaluation of nurses' self-insight into their pain assessment and treatment decisions. *The Journal of Pain, 11*(5), 454–461. https://doi.org/10.1016/j.jpain.2009.09.004

Hoffmann, D. E., Fillingim, R. B., & Veasley, C. (2022). The woman who cried pain: Do sex-based disparities still exist in the experience and treatment of pain? *The Journal of Law, Medicine & Ethics, 50*(3), 519–541. https://doi.org/10.1017/jme.2022.91

Holla, J. F. M., van Beers-Tas, M. H., van de Stadt, L. A., Landewé, R., Twisk, J. W. R., Dekker, J., & van Schaardenburg, D. (2018). Depressive mood and low social support are not associated with arthritis development in patients with seropositive arthralgia, although they predict increased musculoskeletal symptoms. *RMD Open, 4*(1), e000653. https://doi.org/10.1136/rmdopen-2018-000653

Kaleycheva, N., Cullen, A. E., Evans, R., Harris, T., Nicholson, T., & Chalder, T. (2021). The role of lifetime stressors in adult fibromyalgia: Systematic review and meta-analysis of case-control studies. *Psychological Medicine, 51*(2), 177–193. https://doi.org/10.1017/S0033291720004547

Klyne, D. M., Barbe, M. F., & Hodges, P. W. (2022). Relationship between systemic inflammation and recovery over 12 months after an acute episode of low back pain. *The Spine Journal, 22*(2), 214–225. https://doi.org/10.1016/j.spinee.2021.09.006

Klein, S. L., & Flanagan, K. L. (2016). Sex differences in immune responses. *Nature Reviews Immunology, 16*(10), 626–638. https://doi.org/10.1038/nri.2016.90

Landmark, L., Sunde, H. F., Fors, E. A., Kennair, L. E. O., Sayadian, A., Backelin, C., & Reme, S. E. (2024). Associations between pain intensity, psychosocial factors, and pain-related disability in 4285 patients with chronic pain. *Scientific Reports, 14*(1), 13477. https://doi.org/10.1038/s41598-024-64059-8

Lazaridou, A., Franceschelli, O., Buliteanu, A., Cornelius, M., Edwards, R. R., & Jamison, R. N. (2017). Influence of catastrophizing on pain intensity, disability, side effects, and opioid misuse among pain patients in primary care. *Journal of Applied Biobehavioral Research, 22*(1), e12081. https://doi.org/10.1111/jabr.12081

Lazaridou, A., Paschali, M., & Edwards, R. R. (2020a). Future directions in psychological therapies for pain management. *Pain Medicine, 21*(11), 2624–2626. https://doi.org/10.1093/pm/pnaa335

Lazaridou, A., Paschali, M., Schreiber, K., Galenkamp, L., Berry, M., Paschalis, T., Napadow, V., & Edwards, R. R. (2020b). The association between daily physical exercise and pain among women with fibromyalgia: The moderating role of pain catastrophizing. *Pain Reports, 5*(4), e832. https://doi.org/10.1097/PR9.0000000000000832

Lee, J., Lazaridou, A., Paschali, M., Loggia, M. L., Berry, M. P., Ellingsen, D. M., Isenburg, K., Anzolin, A., Grahl, A., Wasan, A. D., Napadow, V., & Edwards, R. R. (2024). A randomized controlled neuroimaging trial of cognitive behavioral therapy for fibromyalgia pain. *Arthritis & Rheumatology, 76*(1), 130–140. https://doi.org/10.1002/art.42672

Lee, J., Lazaridou, A., Paschali, M., Loggia, M., Ellingsen, D. M., Anzolin, A., et al. (2023). Cognitive behavioral therapy relieves fibromyalgia pain and modulates pain catastrophizing specific brain circuitry. *The Journal of Pain, 24*(4), 60. https://doi.org/10.1016/j.jpain.2023.02.179

Lumley, M. A., & Schubiner, H. (2019). Emotional awareness and expression therapy for chronic pain: Rationale, principles and techniques, evidence, and critical review. *Current Rheumatology Reports, 21*(1), 1–8. https://doi.org/10.1007/s11926-019-0829-6

Lumley, M. A., Sklar, E. R., & Carty, J. N. (2012). Emotional disclosure interventions for chronic pain: From the laboratory to the clinic. *Translational Behavioral Medicine, 2*(1), 73–81. https://doi.org/10.1007/s13142-011-0085-4

Mackey, K., Anderson, J., Bourne, D., Chen, E., & Peterson, K. (2020). Benefits and harms of long-term opioid dose reduction or discontinuation in patients with chronic pain: A rapid review. *Journal of General Internal Medicine, 35*(Suppl 3), 935–944. https://doi.org/10.1007/s11606-020-06253-8

Markfelder, T., & Pauli, P. (2020). Fear of pain and pain intensity: Meta-analysis and systematic review. *Psychological Bulletin, 146*(5), 411–450. https://doi.org/10.1037/bul0000228

Martinez-Calderon, J., Flores-Cortes, M., Morales-Asencio, J., & Luque-Suarez, A. (2020). Which psychological factors are involved in the onset and/or persistence of musculoskeletal pain? An umbrella review of systematic reviews and meta-analyses of prospective cohort studies. *The Clinical Journal of Pain, 36*(8), 626–637. https://doi.org/10.1097/AJP.0000000000000838

Meints, S. M., & Edwards, R. R. (2018). Evaluating psychosocial contributions to chronic pain outcomes. *Progress in Neuro-Psychopharmacology and Biological Psychiatry, 87*, 168–182. https://doi.org/10.1016/j.pnpbp.2018.01.017

Mogil, J. S. (2020). The translatability of pain across species. *Philosophical Transactions of the Royal Society B: Biological Sciences, 375*(1799), 20190324. https://doi.org/10.1098/rstb.2019.0286

Musich, S., Wang, S. S., Schaeffer, J. A., Kraemer, S., Wicker, E., & Yeh, C. S. (2022). The association of resilience, social connections, and internal locus of control with pain outcomes among older adults. *Geriatric Nursing, 48*, 43–50. https://doi.org/10.1016/j.gerinurse.2022.08.011

Niazi, A. K., & Niazi, S. K. (2011). Mindfulness-based stress reduction: A non-pharmacological approach for chronic illnesses. *North American Journal of Medical Sciences, 3*(1), 20–23. https://doi.org/10.4297/najms.2011.320

Pardos-Gascón, E. M., Narambuena, L., Leal-Costa, C., & Van-der Hofstadt-Román, C. J. (2021). Differential efficacy between cognitive-behavioral therapy and mindfulness-based therapies for chronic pain: Systematic review. *International Journal of Clinical and Health Psychology, 21*(1), 100197. https://doi.org/10.1016/j.ijchp.2020.08.001

Pester, B. D., Tankha, H., Caño, A., Tong, S., Grekin, E., Bruinsma, J., Gootee, J., & Lumley, M. A. (2022). Facing pain together: A randomized controlled trial of the effects of Facebook support groups on adults with chronic pain. *The Journal of Pain, 23*(12), 2121–2134. https://doi.org/10.1016/j.jpain.2022.07.013

Pester, B. D., Wilson, J. M., Yoon, J., Lazaridou, A., Schreiber, K. L., Cornelius, M., et al. (2023). Brief mindfulness-based cognitive behavioral therapy is associated with faster recovery in patients undergoing total knee arthroplasty: A pilot clinical trial. *Pain Medicine, 24*(6), 576–585. https://doi.org/10.1093/pm/pnac183

Petrucci, G., Papalia, G. F., Russo, F., Vadalà, G., Piredda, M., De Marinis, M. G., Papalia, R., & Denaro, V. (2021). Psychological approaches for the integrative care of chronic low back pain: A systematic review and metanalysis. *International Journal of Environmental Research and Public Health, 19*(1), 60. https://doi.org/10.3390/ijerph19010060

Ruau, D., Liu, L. Y., Clark, J. D., Angst, M. S., & Butte, A. J. (2012). Sex differences in reported pain across 11,000 patients captured in electronic medical records. *The Journal of Pain, 13*(3), 228–234. https://doi.org/10.1016/j.jpain.2011.11.002

Rini, C., Katz, A. W. K., Nwadugbo, A., Porter, L. S., Somers, T. J., & Keefe, F. J. (2021). Changes in identification of possible pain coping strategies by people with osteoarthritis who complete web-based pain coping skills training. *International Journal of Behavioral Medicine, 28*(4), 488–498. https://doi.org/10.1007/s12529-020-09938-w

Schuman-Olivier, Z., Gawande, R., Creedon, T. B., Comeau, A., Griswold, T., Smith, L. B., To, M. N., Wilson, C. L., Loucks, E. B., & Le Cook, B. (2024). Change starts with the body: Interoceptive appreciation mediates the effect of mindfulness training on behavior change – An effect moderated by depression severity. *Psychiatry Research, 342*, 116230. https://doi.org/10.1016/j.psychres.2024.116230

Serrat, M., Sanabria-Mazo, J. P., Almirall, M., Musté, M., Feliu-Soler, A., Méndez-Ulrich, J. L., et al. (2021). Effectiveness of a multicomponent treatment based on pain neuroscience education, therapeutic exercise, cognitive behavioral therapy, and mindfulness in patients with fibromyalgia (FIBROWALK study): A randomized controlled trial. *Physical Therapy, 101*(12), pzab200. https://doi.org/10.1093/ptj/pzab200

Severeijns, R., Vlaeyen, J. W., van den Hout, M. A., & Weber, W. E. (2001). Pain catastrophizing predicts pain intensity, disability, and psychological distress independent of the level of physical impairment. *The Clinical Journal of Pain, 17*(2), 165–172. https://doi.org/10.1097/00002508-200106000-00009

Sidani, S., Guruge, S., Fox, M., & Collins, L. (2019). Gender differences in perpetuating factors, experience and management of chronic insomnia. *Journal of Gender Studies, 28*, 402–413. https://doi.org/10.1080/09589236.2018.1491394

Stubbs, D., Krebs, E., Bair, M., Damush, T., Wu, J., Sutherland, J., & Kroenke, K. (2010). Sex differences in pain and pain-related disability among primary care patients with chronic musculoskeletal pain. *Pain Medicine, 11*(2), 232–239. https://doi.org/10.1111/j.1526-4637.2009.00760.x

Sturgeon, J. A., Zubieta, C., Kaplan, C. M., Pierce, J., Arewasikporn, A., Slepian, P. M., Hassett, A. L., & Trost, Z. (2024). Broadening the scope of resilience in chronic pain: Methods, social context, and development. *Current Rheumatology Reports, 26*(4), 112–123. https://doi.org/10.1007/s11926-024-01133-0

Versluijs, Y., Bandell, D., Kortlever, J., & Ring, D. (2023). The influence of symptoms of anger on pain intensity and activity intolerance. *Journal of Clinical Psychology in Medical Settings, 30*(2), 453–459. https://doi.org/10.1007/s10880-022-09894-5

Weiß, M., Gründahl, M., Jachnik, A., Lampe, E. C., Malik, I., Rittner, H. L., Sommer, C., & Hein, G. (2024). The effect of everyday-life social contact on pain. *Journal of Medical Internet Research, 26*, e53830. https://doi.org/10.2196/53830

Wippert, P. M., Fliesser, M., & Krause, M. (2017). Risk and protective factors in the clinical rehabilitation of chronic back pain. *Journal of Pain Research, 10*, 1569–1579. https://doi.org/10.2147/JPR.S134976

Yarns, B. C., Lumley, M. A., Cassidy, J. T., Steers, W. N., Osato, S., Schubiner, H., & Sultzer, D. L. (2020). Emotional awareness and expression therapy achieves greater pain reduction than cognitive behavioral therapy in older adults with chronic musculoskeletal pain: A preliminary randomized comparison trial. *Pain Medicine, 21*(11), 2811–2822. https://doi.org/10.1093/pm/pnaa145

Zeng, L. N., Zong, Q. Q., Yang, Y., Zhang, L., Xiang, Y. F., Ng, C. H., et al. (2020). Gender difference in the prevalence of insomnia: A meta-analysis of observational studies. *Frontiers in Psychiatry, 11*, 577429. https://doi.org/10.3389/fpsyt.2020.577429

Zubieta, J. K., Smith, Y. R., Bueller, J. A., Xu, Y., Kilbourn, M. R., Jewett, D. M., et al. (2002). μ-Opioid receptor-mediated antinociceptive responses differ in men and women. *Journal of Neuroscience, 22*(12), 5100–5107. https://doi.org/10.1523/JNEUROSCI.22-12-05100.2002

Chapter 4
Pain Reprocessing Therapy for Migraine Headaches in Women: Achieving Symptom Eradication and Recovery

Vanessa Blackstone

Migraine headaches are a highly prevalent and debilitating experience, disproportionately affecting women, yet research suggests that they are frequently misunderstood and inadequately treated. An estimated 18% of women worldwide experience migraine, compared to only 6% of men (Lipton et al., 2007; Vetvik & MacGregor, 2017). Despite the higher prevalence of migraine among women, studies indicate that they are more likely to encounter delayed diagnoses, symptom dismissal, and limited access to comprehensive treatment. These disparities have been attributed, in part, to implicit gender bias in clinical decision-making and longstanding misconceptions about women's pain reporting (Hoffmann & Tarzian, 2001; Samulowitz et al., 2018; Hamberg, 2008).

Historically, women's pain—especially migraine—has been over-pathologized, frequently attributed to stress, hormones, or emotional instability, rather than acknowledged as a legitimate physiological condition. This tendency reflects longstanding gender biases in medicine and sociocultural narratives about women's pain, where symptoms are more likely to be psychologized, dismissed, or misattributed—contributing to diagnostic delays and inadequate care (Bendelow, 2000; Hoffmann & Tarzian, 2001; Samulowitz et al., 2018; Martin, 1987).

Women experiencing migraine frequently encounter misdiagnosis, a lack of symptom validation, and treatment plans that fail to address the underlying mechanisms sustaining their pain (Unruh, 1996). Pharmacological interventions remain the standard approach, yet they often provide only partial relief for many women with migraine, leaving residual symptoms and disability (Buse et al., 2012; Lipton et al., 2001). Expanding treatment options means shifting the focus from controlling symptoms to retraining the brain's response to pain—an approach that prioritizes

V. Blackstone (✉)
Pain Psychology Center, Los Angeles, CA, USA
e-mail: vanessa@painpsychologycenter.com

L. A. Payne (ed.), *Psychosocial Interventions for Chronic Pain in Women and Girls*, CBT: Science Into Practice, https://doi.org/10.1007/978-3-031-98876-9_4

adaptability, self-trust, and nervous system safety rather than structural- or tissue-based assumptions about the nature of migraine.

Objectives of This Chapter

This chapter explores how Pain Reprocessing Therapy (PRT) can be applied to migraine pain in women, integrating:

- A review of existing literature on migraine prevalence, psychological contributions, and treatment limitations.
- A detailed case study, illustrating the use of PRT in a real-world clinical setting.
- Practical guidance for clinicians, including strategies for integrating PRT into migraine treatment plans.

By providing an evidence-based, clinician-focused perspective, this chapter aims to expand treatment options for women experiencing migraine pain, empowering both patients and providers with a brain-based approach to pain recovery.

The Challenges of Conventional Migraine Treatment

Limitations of Pharmacological Treatment

Standard biomedical treatment for migraine relies heavily on pharmacological interventions, including triptans, beta-blockers, and antidepressants. Yet studies indicate that women experiencing migraine often report lower satisfaction with treatment and greater difficulty in achieving sustained relief (Buse et al., 2012; Lipton et al., 2007). In addition to inconsistent efficacy, these medications are frequently associated with side effects, dependency concerns, and contraindications, leading many women to seek alternative options (Bigal & Lipton, 2008).

A key consequence of long-term reliance on acute medications is medication-overuse headache (MOH), characterized by a paradoxical increase in headache frequency due to the excessive use of symptom-abortive medications. MOH affects up to 1–2% of the general population and disproportionately impacts women, who are prescribed migraine medications at higher rates (Bigal & Lipton, 2008; Kristoffersen & Lundqvist, 2014). This phenomenon highlights the risks of a purely reactive model that prioritizes short-term suppression over long-term recovery.

While psychological and behavioral interventions are increasingly recognized as important components of migraine care, they are still not consistently integrated into standard treatment models. This underuse reflects a continued reliance on a biomedical framework that emphasizes structural and chemical explanations for pain while overlooking the complex neurobiological and psychological contributors to symptom persistence.

Ultimately, the limitations of pharmacological treatment—including side effects, risk of MOH, and the underutilization of effective integrative therapies—underscore the need for treatment models that address the nervous system's role in chronic pain. Such approaches offer a pathway beyond symptom management, supporting long-term recovery through cognitive reframing, nervous system retraining, and emotional processing.

The Intersection of Gender, Race, and Treatment Disparities

Women—particularly women of color—are more likely to have their pain dismissed, misdiagnosed, or inadequately treated due to implicit biases in healthcare (Hoffman et al., 2016). Studies indicate that Black and Hispanic women receive migraine prescriptions at significantly lower rates than white patients, despite similar symptom severity (Trawalter et al., 2012). These disparities reflect long-standing biases in medical treatment, where Black women's pain is often underestimated compared to that of white patients (Mathur et al., 2014).

Historically, migraine pain in women has been pathologized—frequently attributed to stress, emotional instability, or psychosomatic causes—rather than recognized as a legitimate and treatable condition. This perspective has led to delayed diagnoses, insufficient treatment, and emotional distress, which can reinforce symptom persistence and avoidance behaviors. Such gender biases in medical treatment are well-documented, with studies indicating that women's pain is often underestimated and misattributed to psychological factors, leading to disparities in care (Hoffmann & Tarzian, 2001; Samulowitz et al., 2018).

Taken together, these treatment disparities further underscore the need for multifaceted approaches like PRT, which validate patient experiences while addressing both the neurobiological and psychological factors involved in chronic pain.

Psychological Interventions Currently Used for Migraine Headaches

Given the biopsychosocial nature of migraine pain, several psychological interventions have been introduced as adjunct treatments for migraine. These include:

- Cognitive-Behavioral Therapy (CBT), which helps patients identify maladaptive thought patterns that contribute to pain sensitivity.
- Mindfulness-based interventions, which reduce stress and promote pain acceptance, lowering overall migraine burden.

- Acceptance and Commitment Therapy (ACT), which encourages patients to develop psychological flexibility, helping them manage pain without excessive fear or avoidance.

While these approaches have demonstrated effectiveness in stress management and emotional regulation, they do not directly target the neural mechanisms that sustain chronic pain (Schubiner & Betzold, 2021). Many traditional psychological treatments focus on helping individuals cope with pain rather than shifting the brain's interpretation of pain signals, leaving a crucial gap in migraine treatment.

Pain Reprocessing Therapy as an Alternative Approach

Pain Reprocessing Therapy (PRT) is a psychological intervention grounded in neuroscience, designed to retrain the brain's interpretation of pain signals, helping patients unlearn chronic pain as a conditioned response (Ashar et al., 2022). Rather than focusing on pain suppression, PRT helps individuals recognize pain as a non-dangerous misfiring of neural pathways, rather than an indication of structural damage.

In the context of migraine pain, PRT targets symptom preoccupation, fear, and avoidance, which contribute to symptom persistence and hypersensitivity. Many women experiencing chronic migraine develop anticipatory anxiety, constantly monitoring their bodies for signs of an impending attack. This hypervigilance reinforces pain sensitivity and maladaptive pain pathways, creating a cycle of stress and symptom exacerbation (Sullivan et al., 2001). By guiding patients to reframe their perception of pain, reinforce safety, and re-engage with life, PRT offers a promising avenue for long-term migraine recovery.

Chronic pain has traditionally been explained through a biomedical model, where symptoms are attributed to structural abnormalities or physiological dysfunction. However, advances in neuroscience and psychology suggest that pain is not always an accurate reflection of tissue damage. Instead, chronic pain can persist as a result of maladaptive neural pathways that reinforce and sustain symptoms even in the absence of an ongoing physical injury (Moseley & Butler, 2015; Schubiner & Betzold, 2021). PRT is an emerging, evidence-based intervention designed to target these maladaptive pathways by helping individuals retrain their brain's response to pain signals (Ashar et al., 2022).

Theoretical Foundations of Pain Reprocessing Therapy

The Role of the Brain in Pain Perception

Pain is not solely determined by nociceptive input from the body; rather, it is shaped by central processing mechanisms within the brain (Melzack & Wall, 1965). While acute pain serves a critical biological function—signaling potential harm and prompting protective responses—chronic pain is fundamentally different. When pain persists beyond expected healing periods, the nervous system undergoes sensitization, producing pain signals even in the absence of ongoing injury or threat (Apkarian et al., 2009; Woolf, 2011). This process, known as central sensitization, results in heightened pain sensitivity, prolonged episodes, and increased emotional distress surrounding bodily sensations (Latremoliere & Woolf, 2009).

The Role of Psychological Factors in Chronic Pain

The persistence of chronic migraine extends beyond a physiological phenomenon; it is reinforced by psychological and emotional factors that contribute to symptom amplification. Many women experiencing chronic migraine develop fear-based associations (i.e., conditioning), hypervigilance, and avoidance behaviors that inadvertently maintain their pain cycles. These maladaptive responses keep the nervous system in a heightened state of alertness, reinforcing central sensitization and making pain feel more severe and inescapable.

Fear, Hypervigilance, and Avoidance as Pain Reinforcers

Fear plays a central role in maintaining chronic pain, and women experiencing migraine often experience heightened anticipatory anxiety. Many find themselves constantly scanning their bodies for early warning signs of an attack, reinforcing a cycle of hypervigilance and symptom preoccupation. This hypervigilance increases pain sensitivity and stress, leading to greater migraine frequency (Sullivan et al., 2001). Avoidance behaviors—such as restricting physical activity, social engagements, or work responsibilities—can reinforce the brain's learned association between certain activities and pain. However, avoidance is not just about staying away from triggers; it also includes any attempt to stop, ignore, fix, or push through pain. This can look like canceling plans out of fear of worsening symptoms, rigidly tracking triggers, constantly researching new treatments, or trying to "push through" discomfort without acknowledging it.

These patterns condition the brain to interpret normal sensations as threats, heightening pain sensitivity over time (Vlaeyen & Linton, 2000). The more a person avoids or fights pain, the more the brain perceives it as dangerous, reinforcing the pain cycle. PRT works to disrupt this pattern by helping individuals engage with discomfort in a way that signals safety rather than fear, retraining the brain's response, and reducing its perception of threat.

Emotional Suppression and Its Role in Symptom Amplification

Emotional suppression, particularly the avoidance of anger, sadness, or fear, has been linked to increased pain sensitivity and prolonged pain episodes (Lumley et al., 2011). Many women experiencing migraine unconsciously suppress difficult emotions, leading to increased autonomic arousal and muscle tension, which can act as a migraine trigger. Research suggests that unprocessed emotional distress contributes to the activation of the same neural circuits involved in chronic pain, further reinforcing symptom persistence (Schubiner & Betzold, 2021). The pressure to pretend everything is okay or to push through stress and frustration without acknowledgment can further amplify this response. Ignoring what feels dysregulating does not resolve it; instead, it keeps the nervous system in a prolonged state of activation, making symptoms more persistent. Integrating emotional processing into migraine treatment is essential for disrupting these patterns.

How Chronic Pain Becomes Learned Pain

Chronic pain is not merely a persistent symptom but a reinforced neural pattern that the brain learns over time. When pain occurs repeatedly, the nervous system begins to misinterpret normal or mild bodily sensations as threats, increasing pain sensitivity (Schubiner & Betzold, 2021). This process, known as symptom amplification, occurs when the brain mistakenly perceives non-threatening stimuli as dangerous, strengthening pain pathways and prolonging symptoms (Ashar et al., 2022).

Several key mechanisms contribute to this learned pain response:

- Fear and Avoidance: Anticipatory anxiety about pain leads women experiencing migraine to avoid activities they believe will trigger discomfort. This avoidance reinforces the brain's association between movement and pain, increasing disability (Vlaeyen & Linton, 2000).
- Hypervigilance and Catastrophizing: Persistent focus on pain keeps the nervous system in a heightened state of alertness, making sensations feel more intense and reinforcing pain pathways (Sullivan et al., 2001).

- Emotional and Psychological Stress: Anxiety, unresolved trauma, and emotional suppression activate the same neural circuits involved in chronic pain, further amplifying symptoms (Ploghaus et al., 2001).

Pain is not just experienced—it is learned. Through repetition, the nervous system strengthens pain pathways, increasing sensitivity over time. This process aligns with the pain learning and unlearning framework outlined in *The Pain Reprocessing Therapy Workbook* (Blackstone & Sinaiko, 2024), which emphasizes how recognizing these patterns can help break the pain-fear cycle. However, just as pain can be learned, it can also be "unlearned" by leveraging the brain's neuroplasticity—the focus of PRT.

Neuroplasticity and Its Role in Chronic Pain

Although chronic pain can become an ingrained neural pattern, the brain remains capable of change through neuroplasticity—the process by which neural pathways are reshaped based on experience (Doidge, 2015). PRT leverages neuroplasticity to disrupt maladaptive pain pathways and reinforce new, non-threatening associations with bodily sensations (Ashar et al., 2022).

A critical component of this process is cognitive reframing, in which individuals reinterpret pain as a misfiring of the brain's protective system rather than evidence of injury (Schubiner & Betzold, 2021). A technique known as *somatic tracking*, developed at the Pain Psychology Center and later described in *The Way Out* by Alan Gordon (2021), was tested in a randomized clinical trial and demonstrated promising outcomes for individuals with chronic pain (Ashar et al., 2022). This practice helps individuals observe pain with curiosity rather than fear, reducing the brain's learned association between sensation and danger. Gradual exposure to movement encourages individuals to reintroduce activities they have previously avoided due to pain, effectively challenging the brain's expectation of harm (Vlaeyen & Linton, 2012). Additionally, PRT integrates emotional awareness strategies, helping individuals process emotions they may have suppressed due to the belief that their symptoms are purely physical.

Engaging in these practices helps individuals signal safety to their nervous system, reducing autonomic arousal and disrupting the conditioned pain response. Neuroplasticity makes it possible not only to decrease pain sensitivity but also to restore a sense of trust in the body's ability to move, function, and heal.

Core Principles of PRT

PRT is grounded in several core principles that support individuals in reprocessing pain as a neural phenomenon:

1. Reconceptualizing Pain as a False Alarm: Patients are educated to understand that chronic pain, while real, is often a result of the brain's misinterpretation of safe bodily signals as dangerous. This shift in perspective helps reduce fear and anxiety associated with pain (Pain Psychology Center, n.d.).
2. Attending to Pain with Non-Reactivity: Individuals are guided to observe their pain sensations with curiosity and non-reactivity, helping to diminish the brain's threat response. This practice aims to retrain the brain to interpret these signals accurately, i.e., not harmful (Pain Psychology Center, n.d.).
3. Addressing Underlying Emotional Threats: PRT involves exploring and processing emotional experiences that may contribute to the persistence of pain, such as stress, trauma, or repressed emotions. By resolving these emotional factors, the neural pathways maintaining the pain response can be altered (Pain Psychology Center, n.d.).

By focusing on these principles, PRT aims to help individuals unlearn maladaptive pain responses, thereby reducing or eliminating chronic pain symptoms.

Evidence-Based for PRT

A growing body of research supports the effectiveness of PRT in treating chronic pain conditions, including migraine headaches. A randomized controlled trial by Ashar et al. (2022) demonstrated significant pain reductions in individuals with chronic back pain, with 66% of participants becoming pain-free or nearly pain-free after treatment. Additionally, Schubiner and Betzold (2021) documented multiple case studies demonstrating that PRT techniques reduce pain-related distress and successfully rewire the brain's response to pain signals. Findings from Vlaeyen and Linton (2012) suggest that targeting fear-avoidance behaviors can support re-engagement in meaningful activities without exacerbating symptoms, breaking the cycle of pain-related anxiety and maladaptive protective responses.

While research remains preliminary in some areas, PRT has shown promise across a range of chronic pain conditions, most notably chronic back pain (Ashar et al., 2022). While formal research on its application to fibromyalgia is still emerging, PRT targets central sensitization and fear-based pain pathways—mechanisms that are also characteristic of fibromyalgia—suggesting it may hold promise for future exploration. In the context of migraine, research remains preliminary; however, initial case studies suggest that PRT can help women experiencing migraine reduce pain perception, regain function, and improve overall well-being by altering maladaptive neural pathways.

Understanding how PRT can be applied specifically to migraine requires further exploration of the psychological mechanisms that reinforce chronic pain. Because migraine often involves heightened neural sensitization, emotional distress, and maladaptive pain pathways, PRT presents an important opportunity to interrupt learned pain responses and promote long-term symptom relief.

Because PRT directly addresses the psychological and neuroplastic contributors to chronic pain, it presents a promising intervention for migraine treatment. The following section will examine PRT's clinical application in greater detail, demonstrating how individuals can reprocess pain and achieve symptom relief.

Clinical Application of PRT for Migraine

PRT provides a structured, brain-based approach to migraine treatment, helping women experiencing migraine interrupt the fear-based pain cycle that reinforces chronic symptoms. Chronic migraine is not merely a physical condition; it often represents a learned neural pattern shaped by fear, avoidance, and symptom preoccupation (Ashar et al., 2022). By shifting the brain's interpretation of pain from a threat response to a neutral signal, PRT works to reduce symptom amplification, reframe pain-related fear, and restore confidence in the body's resilience.

Pain persisting beyond expected healing periods is often sustained by neural pathways rather than ongoing tissue damage (Schubiner & Betzold, 2021). While migraine has traditionally been framed as purely neurological or vascular in origin, recent research suggests that fear, expectation, and learned pain responses play a significant role in symptom persistence (Seng et al., 2017). Many women experiencing chronic migraine develop hypervigilance to bodily sensations, preemptively scanning for signs of an impending attack. This heightened awareness reinforces pain perception and contributes to symptom amplification, where minor discomfort is interpreted as the onset of a full migraine episode. Additionally, avoidance behaviors, such as limiting activities or controlling environmental stimuli, further entrench the belief that a migraine is unmanageable and unpredictable, increasing distress and reducing confidence in the body's ability to cope.

PRT directly addresses these patterns by reducing the brain's fear response to symptoms, disengaging women experiencing migraine from excessive symptom monitoring, and reframing pathologizing narratives that reinforce helplessness. Through structured therapeutic interventions, individuals can learn to relate to pain differently, decreasing its intensity and frequency while restoring a sense of control over their lives.

Core Therapeutic Strategies

Somatic Tracking: Cultivating a New Relationship with Symptoms

Somatic tracking is a core PRT technique that fosters a non-reactive awareness of bodily sensations rather than an automatic fear response. Women experiencing chronic migraine often struggle with this practice because their symptoms are unpredictable, distressing, and sometimes debilitating. Unlike exposure therapy, which emphasizes tolerance and endurance, somatic tracking focuses on fostering safety through mindful attention. Instead of trying to push through or ignore discomfort, a client is encouraged to observe their symptoms with curiosity and openness, allowing their nervous system to respond with less alarm.

This approach is particularly useful for women experiencing migraine who have developed catastrophic interpretations of their pain. For example, a woman experiencing migraine who associates mild head pressure with an inevitable migraine attack may enter a cycle of anticipatory fear, increasing tension, and worsening symptoms. By guiding a client to track how their sensations shift over time rather than reacting with panic, the therapist helps disrupt this automatic cycle.

Client:	*"I don't understand how paying attention to my migraine will make it better. Focusing on it makes it worse."*
Therapist:	*"That makes sense. You've probably spent a lot of time trying to avoid or control pain, so this feels counterintuitive."*
Client:	*"Yeah, it feels like I'm just making it worse."*
Therapist:	*"That's understandable. What if instead of focusing on the pain itself, we just got curious about how it moves or changes?"*
Client:	*"I guess it feels like a dull pressure."*
Therapist:	*"And does it stay exactly the same, or does it shift, even slightly?"*
Client:	*"It's pulsing a bit."*
Therapist:	*"That's important. That means the pain isn't fixed—it changes. And if pain can change, the brain can learn to change its response to it."*

By guiding women experiencing migraine to adopt a more neutral—or even curious—stance in relation to their symptoms, somatic tracking gradually reduces the fear response. This shift decreases the brain's amplification of pain signals, creating the conditions necessary for recovery.

Exposure-Based Desensitization: Reducing Fear and Avoidance

Many women experiencing migraine structure their lives around preventing, minimizing, or escaping potential triggers, often due to years of navigating dismissive medical encounters and limited treatment options. While avoidance is a natural response to pain, it reinforces the belief that migraine is unpredictable and uncontrollable, leading to a cycle where fear-based restrictions become increasingly rigid, limiting daily activities and contributing to heightened stress and anxiety (Vlaeyen & Linton, 2000).

PRT addresses these avoidance patterns by helping a client gradually reintroduce feared activities in a controlled and manageable way. Unlike traditional exposure therapy, which often follows a hierarchical desensitization model, PRT encourages a more flexible, exploratory approach that prioritizes curiosity over endurance. The goal is not to force exposure to potential triggers but to help a woman experiencing migraine re-engage with life in ways that reduce their fear response. By approaching feared activities with openness rather than resistance, women experiencing migraine develop greater confidence in their ability to tolerate discomfort. Over time, this reduces the perceived threat of pain triggers and decreases symptom-related anxiety, restoring trust in their ability to navigate daily life with greater ease and confidence.

Cognitive Restructuring: Shifting Pain Narratives

Language plays a critical role in shaping the brain's response to pain. Women experiencing migraine, in particular, are often conditioned to internalize self-limiting narratives—whether due to medical invalidation, gendered pain biases, or societal messaging—reinforcing helplessness and symptom persistence (Sullivan et al., 2001). These beliefs are often formed over years of experiencing pain and receiving messages from medical professionals, family members, or personal experiences that frame migraine as an inescapable part of life.

You may have noticed throughout this chapter the intentional use of the singular term "migraine" rather than "migraines," as well as phrases like "a woman experiencing migraine" instead of "a woman with migraines." This shift in language reflects an important cognitive restructuring principle: reframing pain as an experience rather than an identity. Linguistic reframing in migraine care suggests that using the singular use of "migraine" can reduce over-identification with pain, reinforcing the idea that migraine is not a defining or unchangeable aspect of a person's life but rather a temporary state that can shift and be influenced (Yoga for Migraine, 2022). This perspective aligns with cognitive restructuring principles in PRT, where clinicians guide clients toward language that fosters adaptability, self-efficacy, and a sense of control over their response to pain. Blackstone and Sinaiko (2024) highlight that subtle shifts in language—such as referring to pain as a temporary experience rather than an unchangeable condition—can reduce fear and increase a sense of control over symptoms.

A woman experiencing migraine who frequently says, *"My migraines control my life"* might work toward adopting a more flexible perspective, such as, *"I am learning how to navigate this migraine differently."* Similarly, someone who believes, *"If I feel symptoms, my day is ruined,"* might shift toward thinking, *"Pain doesn't have to dictate my entire experience."* Though these adjustments may appear subtle, they can significantly influence how the brain processes pain signals, reducing reactivity and increasing a sense of agency. When language reinforces rigid, identity-based beliefs about pain, it strengthens fear and avoidance responses, further sensitizing the nervous system. By shifting how a person talks about migraine, they can begin to see it as a temporary state—something the brain can learn to interpret differently, rather than something they are powerless against.

Addressing Patient Skepticism

Skepticism is common among women experiencing migraine beginning PRT, particularly those who have seen multiple specialists, tried various treatments, and been told that their pain is purely neurological. Many fear that psychological approaches imply their pain is not real, which can create resistance to engaging in the process.

A central principle of PRT is meeting a client where they are, normalizing their skepticism, and inviting them to explore the concepts without demanding immediate belief. Clinicians can foster engagement by using real-life examples, highlighting moments when a woman's pain has already shifted, and reinforcing that the brain is capable of change.

Client: *"I don't buy into this whole 'pain reprocessing' idea. My migraines are real."*

Therapist: *I hear you. The pain you feel is very real, and nothing here is suggesting otherwise. What we're exploring is how the brain processes that pain—and how we can shift its response to it."*

By validating concerns while gently introducing new perspectives, therapists can help women experiencing migraine engage in PRT without feeling dismissed or pressured.

Bringing It All Together: A Multi-faceted Approach

PRT aims to help women experiencing migraine by addressing their preoccupation with symptoms, reinforcing safety, fostering autonomy through intentional routine changes, and guiding them through fear-based avoidance patterns. By integrating somatic tracking, exposure-based desensitization, and cognitive restructuring, a client gradually rewires their relationship with pain and regains control over their lives.

Chronic migraine extends beyond the experience of episodic pain; they often involve heightened pain sensitivity, emotional distress, and functional disruption, all of which can significantly impair daily life.

Case Study: A Woman's Journey Through PRT for Migraine

This case study presents the treatment course of "Emily," a 44-year-old woman, undergoing PRT for chronic migraine at the Pain Psychology Center in Los Angeles, CA. The purpose of this case study is to illustrate how PRT helps women experiencing migraine shift their relationship with pain, address fear-based patterns, and reclaim control over their lives. The client's name and some identifying details have been changed to protect her privacy.

Client Background and Presenting Concerns

Emily, a working professional and mother of two, had been experiencing chronic migraine for over a decade. Initially episodic, her migraine became consistent and unchanging, occurring several times per week with little variation in intensity or presentation. She described her migraines as unchanging—never improving, never shifting. This reinforced her belief that her condition was permanent, making her increasingly anxious about her ability to function.

Her migraine presented as a dull, throbbing pain that made it difficult to walk without carefully controlling each step. Noise sensitivity was particularly debilitating, as even moderate sounds could amplify her baseline 6/10 head pain to an unbearable 9/10, often triggering vertigo, nausea, and vomiting. She also experienced light sensitivity and difficulty tolerating quick movements, making it nearly impossible to be in a car, watch a screen, send emails, or even observe her kids playing. These symptoms left her feeling trapped in cycles of avoidance, struggling to eat, sit in one place for long periods, and often feeling like she had no option but to lie down in a dark, quiet room with the blinds drawn.

Emily described a constant, undercurrent of anticipatory anxiety, explaining that she was always "just getting through the task at hand" to avoid her symptoms worsening. She had tried nearly every available treatment, including neurology consultations, physical therapy, acupuncture, dietary modifications, and CBT. After years of medical visits and trial-and-error treatments with little relief, she felt exhausted and frustrated, deeply skeptical that PRT would be any different. She worried that this would be another waste of time and money. Despite her skepticism, Emily acknowledged that her current approach—rigidly managing symptoms and avoiding anything that might "set off" a migraine—was not working, and she was willing to try something different.

Understanding the Nervous System's Role: More Than Just Symptom Resolution

While Emily sought PRT specifically for migraine relief, the work extended beyond symptom reduction alone. In addition to nervous system regulation and pain reprocessing, sessions explored the deeper patterns that contributed to her chronic state of high alert. Emily grew up with a highly critical and emotionally invalidating parent, often being told she was "too emotional" or "too sensitive," which led her to feel ashamed of her emotions. Over time, she learned to suppress her feelings, push through discomfort, and anticipate criticism before it even came.

This pattern of emotional invalidation mirrored her experience with medical treatment, where she felt dismissed and told she was overreacting about her symptoms. The repeated experience of invalidation—both in childhood and in her medical care—reinforced her chronic state of vigilance, keeping her nervous system in a persistent state of high alert. The work together focused on both PRT-based techniques to address pain reprocessing, symptom preoccupation, and avoidance patterns, as well as somatic and narrative reframing work to help Emily understand why her nervous system defaulted to chronic vigilance and how to work with it rather than against it.

Early Treatment: Identifying Fear-Based Patterns and Pain Preoccupation

During the initial sessions, Emily described waking up each morning, immediately scanning her body to determine if it would be a "good" or "bad" migraine day. This preoccupation with symptoms kept her nervous system on high alert, reinforcing pain sensitivity and hypervigilance.

Emily: *"I wake up every morning scanning my body, wondering if today will be another bad day. And it always is."*
Therapist: *"That sounds exhausting. It makes sense that you're always on alert—your brain is trying to protect you from more pain."*
Emily: *"Yeah, I don't even think about it. It just happens."*
Therapist: *"Of course. It's become automatic. What if we tried pausing before checking, just to see how it feels? Not to change anything, just to notice."*
Emily: *"That sounds difficult, but I see how much time I spend bracing for migraine."*

By gradually reducing symptom-monitoring behaviors, Emily began to disrupt the automatic cycle of hypervigilance reinforcing her persistent migraine.

Application of PRT Techniques

One of Emily's greatest challenges in early treatment was learning to engage with pain differently. She was initially skeptical of somatic tracking, explaining that focusing on her symptoms made them feel worse.

Emily: *"I tried somatic tracking when I started getting a migraine. At first, it just made me more aware of the pain, and I panicked."*
Therapist: *"I can see why that would feel overwhelming. It's understandable to be hesitant when something feels like it's making things worse."*
Emily: *"Yeah, I wasn't sure if I was doing it right or if I should stop."*

Therapist: *"That makes sense. Instead of focusing on the pain itself, what if we just notice how it shifts—does it stay exactly the same or does it change, even slightly?"*

Emily: *"The pain wasn't just sitting there—it pulsed and moved a little. I never noticed that before."*

Through this small but critical shift in perspective, Emily begin to see pain as something that could change, rather than as an unavoidable, unmovable force in her life.

Emily had also developed avoidance behaviors, structuring her daily life around preventing a migraine. She avoided certain lighting, exercise, and even social engagements, fearing that any deviation from her controlled environment would trigger symptoms.

Emily: *"I avoid watching movies at night because I'm afraid the screen will make my migraine worse."*

Therapist: *"That's completely understandable. You've had enough experiences where that's happened, so of course it feels safer to avoid it."*

Emily: *"Yeah, I don't even think about it anymore—I just don't do it."*

Therapist: *"That makes sense. Avoidance can feel protective, but it can also reinforce the fear. What if we started small—just watching for two minutes, not to test yourself, but just to see how your brain responds?"*

Rather than forcing exposure, Emily engaged in small, manageable experiments to test her nervous system's adaptability. Over time, she realized that avoidance was reinforcing her anxiety more than preventing an actual migraine.

Outcome and Symptom Reduction

Over the course of 6 months of weekly sessions, Emily experienced a dramatic shift in her relationship with pain. Though the frequency of migraine decreased, the most profound change was in how she responded to discomfort. By the end of treatment, Emily considered herself symptom-free, with only occasional moments of "feeling uneasy." However, unlike before, these moments no longer created fear.

Emily: *"I used to panic when I felt anything that even remotely reminded me of a migraine. Now, I feel uneasy sometimes, but I know exactly what to do. And it is usually a sign of a need to slow down and take care of myself. I don't spiral anymore."*

She now maintains regular care for mental health support and continues to practice self-regulation techniques when needed. Though she occasionally experiences discomfort, she no longer views it as a threat or as a part of a rigid migraine pattern, reinforcing her new ability to respond with confidence rather than fear.

Final Reflection

Emily's journey through PRT illustrates how shifting away from fear-based symptom monitoring, challenging rigid pain beliefs, and retraining the brain's response to discomfort can lead to lasting relief. By the end of treatment, she no longer defined her life around migraine but instead saw herself as someone who had successfully reclaimed her well-being.

Practical Guidance for Clinicians

PRT offers a structured but adaptable framework for treating chronic migraine by shifting women experiencing migraine away from fear-based responses and avoidance behaviors. Given that migraine is often reinforced by heightened sensitivity to internal sensations, symptom monitoring, and rigid control strategies, clinicians must tailor their approach to each woman's needs while maintaining a clear emphasis on safety, cognitive shifts, and behavioral re-engagement. The case study presented in the previous section illustrates how this approach can unfold in real-world practice. While every client's journey is unique, the following treatment arc offers clinicians a flexible guide for applying PRT principles to migraine, informed by the authors' clinical experience and *The Pain Reprocessing Therapy Workbook* (Blackstone & Sinaiko, 2024). This section provides clinicians with structured guidelines for implementing PRT effectively in migraine treatment.

Assessing Readiness for PRT

Before initiating PRT interventions, clinicians are encouraged to assess a woman's current mindset, symptom-related fear, and preexisting beliefs about their experience with migraine. Many women experiencing migraine have been told that migraine is purely neurological or beyond their control, leading to skepticism about psychological interventions. Rather than attempting to dismantle these beliefs outright, clinicians should first seek to understand and validate their experiences, recognizing that skepticism is often rooted in years of frustration, failed treatments, and feeling dismissed by medical providers. Approaching these conversations with curiosity and care can foster the trust needed to begin therapeutic work.

A crucial first step is to gently explore the client's perspective with patience and curiosity:

- How does this client currently conceptualize their migraine?
- What treatments have they tried, and what are their expectations for recovery?
- Do they engage in symptom monitoring, avoidance behaviors, or rigid attempts at control?

- What emotional associations do they have with their symptoms—fear, frustration, or resignation?

For clients with high levels of skepticism or distress, the initial focus should be on validating their experiences and meeting them with empathy, rather than immediately challenging their beliefs. This same patience and understanding models the approach PRT invites them to take toward themselves. Once trust is built, discussions about nervous system adaptability and cognitive reframing can begin, laying the foundation for somatic tracking and exposure-based interventions in a way that feels safe rather than forced.

Once readiness is established, treatment can be gently structured across 8–12 sessions, paced according to the woman's nervous system capacity, emotional needs, and readiness. While PRT lends itself to a sequential flow—beginning with safety and education and gradually building toward exposure and reengagement—it is not a fixed protocol. Both clients and clinicians benefit from approaching this work with a "loose grip"—creating space for nonlinear movement and trusting that each step in the process offers an opportunity for rewiring. In her interview on *The Steady Coach* (Arthur, 2023), the author reflects on this approach, saying, "Sometimes we don't need a breakthrough—we need five gentle steps that don't scare our nervous system."

Table 4.1 offers one example of a flexible clinical arc for delivering PRT-informed migraine care—structured enough to support clinicians, but flexible enough to adapt to each client's pacing, symptoms, and readiness. While the example highlights an eight-session framework, this is not a one-size-fits-all model. Some clients may move more slowly, revisit sessions, or spend several sessions on the same theme. Clinical judgment, safety, and responsiveness should always guide the process.

PRT is not a rigid or purist approach. The goal is not symptom resolution in eight sessions, but a lasting shift in how clients relate to their pain, emotions, and sense of safety. For some clients, healing may begin with subtle internal shifts. For others, it may involve periods of plateau, flare-up, or life stress that require returning to earlier concepts. Clinicians are encouraged to trust their instincts and pace, offering clients repeated exposure to core PRT principles without rushing toward resolution.

Educating Women Experiencing Migraine on the Brain's Role in Pain Processing

A foundational aspect of PRT is helping women experiencing migraine understand that pain is a learned nervous system response that can change. This concept must be introduced in a way that validates their experience and opens space for new perspectives.

Rather than presenting pain neuroscience in a purely academic way, clinicians should integrate real-world examples tailored to the client's experiences. For example:

Table 4.1 Flexible PRT treatment arc for chronic migraine

Session	Guiding theme	Focus and clinical aim
1.	Establish safety and understanding	Begin by exploring how the client understands their migraine and what they have been told about it. Focus on validating their experience and gently introducing the concept that safety—not control—can foster meaningful change
2.	Introduce the brain's role in pain	Offer accessible psychoeducation about the nervous system's learned pain responses. Begin shifting the conversation from structural explanations to the possibility of neuroplastic change
3.	Identify openings for change	Support the client in noticing natural moments in symptoms (e.g., through distraction, laughter, connection). Use these observations to introduce reframing and nurture a sense of possibility
4.	Begin gentle observation	Introduce somatic tracking through safe or neutral sensations. Support the client in observing discomfort with curiosity rather than urgency or avoidance
5.	Explore emotional contributors	Invite the client to reflect on emotional patterns—such as pressure, frustration, or unresolved grief—that may influence their pain. Normalize these connections without overpathologizing
6.	Support meaningful re-engagement	Guide the client in gradually returning to previously avoided activities. Emphasize self-trust, pacing, and nervous system safety over symptom control
7.	Navigate fluctuations with stability	Frame flare-ups or extinction bursts as part of the healing process. Reinforce nervous system adaptability and strengthen emotional regulation strategies
8.	Integrate and sustain progress	Focus on integrating key practices such as tracking, emotional reflection, and safety-based thinking. Prepare the client to navigate future challenges with confidence and flexibility

Note. This table presents a flexible treatment arc for implementing Pain Reprocessing Therapy (PRT) in chronic migraine care. Clinicians should adapt session content based on individual readiness, symptom history, and pacing needs

- Instead of stating, *"Your migraine is neuroplastic and reversible,"*
  → Frame it as, *"Your nervous system has learned to respond a certain way, and it also has the ability to unlearn that response."*
- Instead of suggesting, *"Your pain is caused by fear,"*
  → Introduce it as, *"Pain and fear activate similar pathways in the brain, and the more we send safety messages, the less your nervous system needs to protect you with pain."*

Offering personalized examples of symptom shifts —such as headaches that lessen with distraction—reinforces the brain's capacity for change.

For clients who experience menstrual migraine or symptom flare-ups tied to hormonal changes, clinicians can validate these patterns while reinforcing the brain's ongoing capacity for change. Hormonal shifts may increase sensitivity in the nervous system, but they do not make recovery impossible. In fact, the anticipation of pain around one's cycle often triggers a protective response—such as increased fear, vigilance, or helplessness—which contributes to symptom amplification. Over time, this can lead clients to believe their pain is inevitable or untreatable during certain phases. PRT invites a different relationship: one that acknowledges biological influence without assuming loss of agency. Clinicians may encourage clients to notice how their pain and their distress about pain change across their cycle, reinforcing that the nervous system is not just reacting to hormones—it is responding to how safe or unsafe the experience feels. Supporting clients in tracking their internal state through the lens of safety—rather than control—can gradually reduce fear-driven amplification.

Guiding Women Experiencing Migraine Through Somatic Tracking

Somatic tracking is a critical PRT technique, but must be introduced carefully, especially for women experiencing intense migraine symptoms. Many report that focusing on symptoms increases distress and reinforces the belief that a migraine is unmanageable. To prevent this, clinicians should structure somatic tracking in a way that minimizes fear responses and encourages curiosity rather than resistance.

One essential component of this practice is recognizing not only the physical sensation of migraine but also the distress or resistance surrounding it. Many individuals experience anticipatory fear when they notice early migraine sensations, reinforcing pain sensitivity. These early signs—such as a slight throbbing, neck tightness, or vision changes—often trigger anxiety and dread, which can escalate the experience into a full-blown migraine. Instead of trying to suppress, control, or push away these sensations, somatic tracking invites individuals to observe both the physical discomfort and their emotional reaction to it.

For example, rather than simply noticing that a sensation is unpleasant, a client might explore:

- "How much distress am I feeling about this right now?"
- "Am I resisting this sensation, or am I allowing myself to be curious about it?"

This approach shifts the focus from trying to eliminate discomfort to understanding it in a way that signals safety to the nervous system. Additionally, for headache and migraine-specific tracking, Blackstone and Sinaiko (2024) suggest modifications such as:

- Practicing somatic tracking even when migraine symptoms are not present, as many individuals have ongoing sensations in the head or neck that can be explored before they escalate.
- Breathing into the belly rather than directly into the head or neck sensations, as shallow breathing in response to head pain can unintentionally activate the sympathetic nervous system.

- Observing the early signs of migraine without fear, recognizing that these sensations do not have to progress into pain.

By integrating these strategies, clinicians can help individuals reduce fear-based responses to migraine sensations and retrain their nervous system's interpretation of pain. Rather than focusing solely on symptom intensity, clients begin to notice physical and emotional shifts, building a sense of agency and reducing pain-related anxiety.

As clients become more skilled at observing their sensations with curiosity, it may also be helpful to introduce the idea that pain intensity and distress about pain are two disctinct experiences. In *The Pain Reprocessing Therapy Workbook* (Blackstone & Sinaiko, 2024), this distinction is explored through simple reflection: "How much pain am I in?" vs. "How much distress am I feeling about this right now?" For many women experiencing migraine, these questions can reveal that while physical pain may be present, the emotional response to it—fear, dread, urgency—may fluctuate more than the sensation itself. Helping clients track both their pain and their response to it builds nervous system awareness and reinforces the idea that how we relate to pain matters as much as the pain itself.

Reducing Avoidance and Reintroducing Feared Activities

Many women experiencing chronic migraine have developed avoidance behaviors, structuring their lives around preventing potential symptoms. While this response is understandable, it reinforces the belief that a migraine is uncontrollable. Clinicians should guide women in gradual, intentional engagement with activities they have been avoiding.

- Start with low-stakes experiments (e.g., watching a screen for 2 min instead of avoiding screens entirely).
- Focus on building confidence rather than endurance (e.g., *"This is not about proving anything, just gathering information about how your body responds."*).
- Encourage curiosity rather than hypervigilance (e.g., *"Let's notice how this feels without trying to predict or control the outcome."*).

By reframing these moments as opportunities for nervous system retraining rather than encounters with inevitable triggers, women experiencing migraine can gradually rebuild their confidence and flexibility.

Addressing Extinction Bursts and Nonlinear Progress

Healing from chronic migraine is a nonlinear process, and individuals may experience extinction bursts—temporary increases in symptoms as the brain unlearns old pain patterns and forms new, adaptive pathways (e.g., when the brain resists change by briefly amplifying discomfort before forming new patterns). These fluctuations are not setbacks but evidence that the brain is actively recalibrating, an essential step in breaking the cycle of learned pain (Schubiner & Betzold, 2021).

A common misconception is that recovery follows a straight, upward trajectory. However, healing is rarely linear, as illustrated in Fig. 4.1 (Blackstone & Sinaiko, 2024). While individuals often expect steady progress, true recovery involves periods of symptom fluctuation, moments of increased discomfort, and periods of stability before lasting improvements take hold. Figure 4.1 visually represents the difference between perceived and actual recovery, reinforcing the need to normalize temporary symptom increases as a natural part of the healing process.

Clinicians can support their clients by:

- Normalizing these symptom fluctuations, reminding them that temporary increases in pain do not mean they are regressing, but rather indicate that the brain is actively recalibrating.
- Revisiting past moments of progress to reinforce how far they have come, helping them trust in the process.
- Encouraging self-compassion rather than self-judgment, reinforcing that extinction bursts are signs that the nervous system is adapting, not failing.

Responding to these fluctuations with curiosity instead of fear is a key marker of long-term progress in PRT. When individuals recognize extinction bursts as part of the learning process rather than setbacks, they build confidence in their ability to navigate recovery without reinforcing fear-based pain pathways (Ashar et al., 2022). Clinicians may invite clients to reflect on moments of self-trust, flexibility, or emotional grounding remains available even in the presence of symptoms. This tool can be adapted from an exercise in *The Pain Reprocessing Therapy Workbook* (Blackstone & Sinaiko, 2024) that encourages clients to notice subtle internal shifts— reinforcing the idea that progress is measured not just in symptom absence but in how clients relate to the discomfort. Table 4.2 offers a client reflection tool that supports this approach by helping clients notice change beyond symptom intensity.

At times, clients may feel that progress has stalled, or that the tools are no longer working as they once did. When this happens, it is often not a sign of regression, but a reflection of deeper emotional demands, nervous system overload, or life circumstances that make regulation harder to access. Rather than introducing new strategies, clinicians can guide clients back to earlier practices—validating their efforts and helping them reconnect to moments of emotional resilience, curiosity, or small behavioral shifts. Returning to these tools with less pressure and more compassion

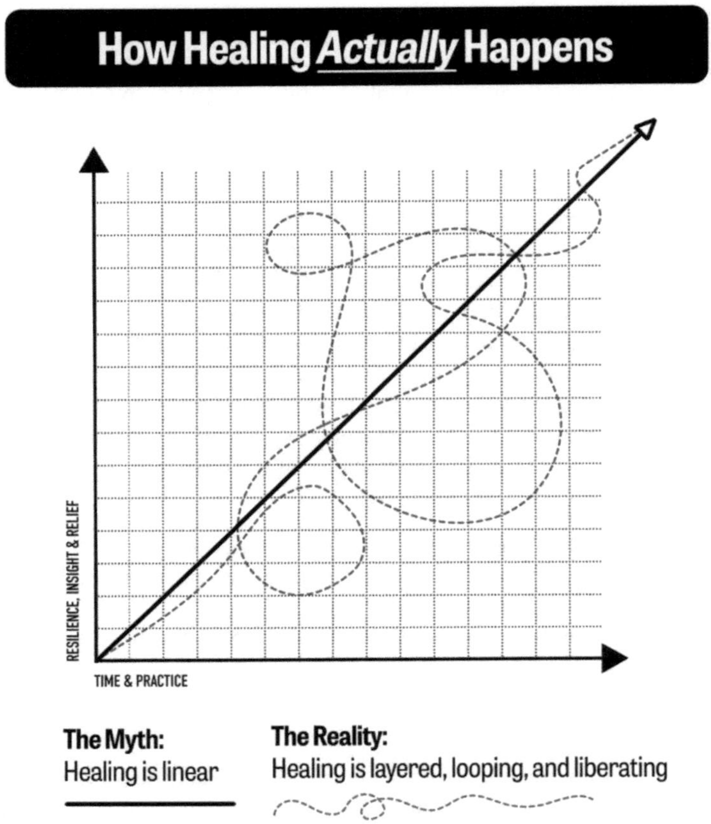

Fig. 4.1 How healing actually happens. Adapted from The Pain Reprocessing Therapy Workbook (Blackstone & Sinaiko, 2024)

Table 4.2 Client reflection tool—noticing change beyond symptom intensity

Use the following prompts to reflect on your experience with migraine outside of symptom severity. These can be explored independently or discussed with your therapist or coach
1. In the past few days, have there been moments where I felt **safe**, even if pain was present?
2. Have I responded to my symptoms with more **curiosity** or **compassion** than I might have in the past?
3. Did I return to an activity, place, or interaction I had been avoiding? What helped me feel ready?
4. Was there a time I could **pause**, breathe, or sit with discomfort without needing to fix it?
5. Even if the pain didn't change, did I feel any **emotional flexibility**, **reduced urgency**, or **greater self-trust**?

Note. These prompts are not intended to measure success, but rather to track how the nervous system is learning to relate differently to symptoms. Often, the most meaningful changes are internal —and quiet

reinforces that healing is rooted not in intensity or novelty, but in familiarity, flexibility, and relationship. Often, the nervous system does not need something new—it simply needs what has already been learned to be revisited with greater gentleness.

Conclusion

The case presented earlier in this chapter exemplifies how PRT can help clients shift from fear-based symptom control to resilience and adaptive flexibility—even in long-standing migraine cases. PRT offers an evidence-based approach to treating chronic migraine by shifting the brain's perception of pain from a threat to a neutral signal. Unlike traditional treatments that focus on symptom suppression, PRT targets the fear, avoidance, and symptom preoccupation that reinforce pain persistence. Through cognitive reframing, somatic tracking, and gradual exposure, individuals can retrain their nervous system, reduce pain-related anxiety, and restore a sense of control.

This chapter has outlined the theoretical foundations and clinical applications of PRT, demonstrating how chronic migraine is influenced by learned neural patterns rather than being purely biological. The presented case study illustrates how interrupting cycles of avoidance and hypervigilance fosters resilience and builds confidence in recovery. Clinicians are encouraged to introduce psychoeducation on neuroplasticity with curiosity rather than force, ensuring that somatic tracking and exposure are approached with flexibility to promote safety and tolerance.

PRT is not about eliminating all symptoms, but about changing how individuals relate to pain—reducing fear and restoring agency. Because healing is nonlinear, clinicians should emphasize that temporary symptom increases, or extinction bursts, are a normal part of nervous system retraining. Reinforcing safety, adaptability, and cognitive flexibility helps individuals reclaim their lives without being dictated by pain anticipation.

Further research should examine PRT's neurophysiological impact in migraine populations, supporting its integration into multidisciplinary pain care. As chronic pain treatment advances, PRT provides an evidence-based framework that fosters adaptability, empowerment, and long-term recovery.

References

Apkarian, A. V., Baliki, M. N., & Geha, P. Y. (2009). Towards a theory of chronic pain. *Progress in Neurobiology, 87*(2), 81–97. https://doi.org/10.1016/j.pneurobio.2008.09.018

Arthur, Y. (2023, October 3). *How PRT & tracking can help you recover from dizziness: Part 2 of interview w/Vanessa Blackstone* [Video]. The Steady Coach. YouTube. https://www.youtube.com/watch?v=PSmgkZZvh-I

Ashar, Y. K., Gordon, A., Schubiner, H., Uipi, C., Knight, K., Anderson, Z., et al. (2022). Effect of Pain Reprocessing Therapy vs Placebo and Usual Care for Patients With Chronic Back Pain: A Randomized Clinical Trial. *JAMA Psychiatry, 79*(1), 1–9. https://doi.org/10.1001/jamapsychiatry.2021.2669

Bendelow, G. (2000). *Pain and gender*. Prentice Hall.

Bigal, M. E., & Lipton, R. B. (2008). Overuse of acute migraine medications and migraine chronification. *Current Pain and Headache Reports, 13*(4), 301–307. https://doi.org/10.1007/s11916-009-0048-3

Blackstone, V., & Sinaiko, O. (2024). *The pain reprocessing therapy workbook: Using the brain's neuroplasticity to break the cycle of chronic pain*. New Harbinger Publications.

Buse, D. C., Manack, A. N., Fanning, K. M., Serrano, D., Reed, M. L., Turkel, C. C., & Lipton, R. B. (2012). Chronic migraine prevalence, disability, and sociodemographic factors: Results from the American Migraine Prevalence and Prevention Study. *Headache, 52*(10), 1456–1470. https://doi.org/10.1111/j.1526-4610.2012.02223.x

Doidge, N. (2015). *The brains' way of healing: Remarkable discoveries and recoveries from the frontiers of neuroplasticity*. Penguin Life.

Gordon, A. (2021). *The way out: A revolutionary, scientifically proven approach to healing chronic pain*. Avery.

Hamberg, K. (2008). Gender bias in medicine. *Women's Health, 4*(3), 237–243. https://doi.org/10.2217/17455057.4.3.237

Hoffmann, D. E., & Tarzian, A. J. (2001). The girl who cried pain: A bias against women in the treatment of pain. *The Journal of Law, Medicine & Ethics, 29*(1), 13–27. https://doi.org/10.1111/j.1748-720X.2001.tb00037.x

Hoffman, K. M., Trawalter, S., Axt, J. R., & Oliver, M. N. (2016). Racial bias in pain assessment and treatment recommendations, and false beliefs about biological differences between blacks and whites. *Proceedings of the National Academy of Sciences, 113*(16), 4296–4301.

Kristoffersen, E. S., & Lundqvist, C. (2014). Medication-overuse headache: A review. *Journal of Pain Research, 7*, 367–378. https://doi.org/10.2147/JPR.S46071

Latremoliere, A., & Woolf, C. J. (2009). Central sensitization: A generator of pain hypersensitivity by central neural plasticity. *The Journal of Pain, 10*(9), 895–926. https://doi.org/10.1016/j.jpain.2009.06.012

Lipton, R. B., Stewart, W. F., Diamond, S., Diamond, M. L., & Reed, M. (2001). Prevalence and burden of migraine in the United States: Data from the American Migraine Study II. *Headache, 41*(7), 646–657. https://doi.org/10.1046/j.1526-4610.2001.041007646.x

Lipton, R. B., Stewart, W. F., Diamond, S., Diamond, M. L., & Reed, M. (2007). Migraine prevalence, disease burden, and the need for preventive therapy. *Neurology, 68*(5), 343–349. https://doi.org/10.1212/01.wnl.0000252808.97649.21

Lumley, M. A., Cohen, J. L., Borszcz, G. S., Cano, A., Radcliffe, A. M., Porter, L. S., ... & Keefe, F. J. (2011). Pain and emotion: A biopsychosocial review of recent research. *Journal of Clinical Psychology, 67*(9), 942–968. https://doi.org/10.1002/jclp.20816

Martin, E. (1987). *The woman in the body: A cultural analysis of reproduction*. Beacon Press.

Mathur, V. A., Richeson, J. A., Paice, J. A., Muzyka, M., & Chiao, J. Y. (2014). Racial bias in pain perception and response: Experimental examination of automatic and deliberate processes. *The Journal of Pain, 15*(5), 476–484. https://doi.org/10.1016/j.jpain.2014.01.488

Melzack, R., & Wall, P. D. (1965). Pain mechanisms: A new theory, *150*(3699), 971–979. https://doi.org/10.1126/science.150.3699.971

Moseley, G. L., & Butler, D. S. (2015). Fifteen years of explaining pain: The past, present, and future. *The Journal of Pain, 16*(9), 807–813. https://doi.org/10.1016/j.jpain.2015.05.005

Pain Psychology Center. (n.d.). *How it works*. Retrieved October 10, 2024, from https://painpsychologycenter.com/how-it-works

Ploghaus, A., Narain, C., Beckmann, C. F., Clare, S., Bantick, S., Wise, R., Matthews, P. M., Rawlins, J. N., & Tracey, I. (2001). Exacerbation of pain by anxiety is associated with activity in a hippocampal network. *The Journal of Neuroscience: The Official Journal of the Society for Neuroscience, 21*(24), 9896–9903. https://doi.org/10.1523/JNEUROSCI.21-24-09896.2001

Samulowitz, A., Gremyr, I., Eriksson, E., & Hensing, G. (2018). "Brave men" and "emotional women": A theory-guided literature review on gender bias in health care. *Pain Research and Management, 2018*, Article ID 6358624. https://doi.org/10.1155/2018/6358624
Seng, E. K., Buse, D. C., Klepper, J. E., Mayson, S. J., Grinberg, A. S., Grosberg, B. M., Pavlovic, J. M., Robbins, M. S., Vollbracht, S. E., & Lipton, R. B. (2017). Psychological factors associated with chronic migraine and severe migraine-related disability: An observational study in a tertiary headache center. *Headache, 57*(1), 21–34.
Schubiner, H., & Betzold, L. (2021). *Unlearn your pain: A 28-day process to reprogram your brain*. Mindbody Publishing.
Sullivan, M. J., Thorn, B., Haythornthwaite, J. A., Keefe, F., Martin, M., Bradley, L. A., & Lefebvre, J. C. (2001). Theoretical perspectives on the relation between catastrophizing and pain. *The Clinical Journal of Pain, 17*(1), 52–64. https://doi.org/10.1097/00002508-200103000-00008
Trawalter, S., Hoffman, K. M., & Waytz, A. (2012). Racial bias in perceptions of others' pain. *PLoS One, 7*(11), e48546. https://doi.org/10.1371/journal.pone.0048546
Unruh, A. M. (1996). Gender variations in clinical pain experience. *Pain, 65*(2–3), 123–167. https://doi.org/10.1016/0304-3959(95)00214-6
Vetvik, K. G., & MacGregor, E. A. (2017). Sex differences in the epidemiology, clinical features, and pathophysiology of migraine. *The Lancet Neurology, 16*(1), 76–87. https://doi.org/10.1016/S1474-4422(16)30293-9
Vlaeyen, J. W. S., & Linton, S. J. (2000). Fear-avoidance and its consequences in chronic musculoskeletal pain: A state of the art. *Pain, 85*(3), 317–332. https://doi.org/10.1016/S0304-3959(99)00242-0
Vlaeyen, J. W. S., & Linton, S. J. (2012). Fear-avoidance model of chronic musculoskeletal pain: 12 years on. *Pain, 153*(6), 1144–1147. https://doi.org/10.1016/j.pain.2011.12.009
Woolf, C. J. (2011). Central sensitization: Implications for the diagnosis and treatment of pain. *Pain, 152*(3 Suppl), S2–S15. https://doi.org/10.1016/j.pain.2010.09.030
Yoga for Migraine. (2022, June 27). *Language and pain: How subtle shifts impact migraine recovery [Video]*. YouTube. https://youtu.be/FjQrCPK00I8

Chapter 5
Acceptance and Commitment Therapy Intervention for Individuals with Endometriosis and Persistent Pelvic Pain

Leesa Van Niekerk, Suiyin Cheah, Antonina Mikocka-Walus, Brad Mertens, and Subhadra Evans

An Overview of Endometriosis

Endometriosis is a persistent inflammatory disease where endometrium-like tissue is located outside of the uterine cavity (Tomassetti et al., 2021). This endometrium-like tissue may be found in the ovaries, intestines, bowel, and bladder, with the exact cause of endometriosis remaining uncertain (Lamceva et al., 2023). Endometriosis-related symptoms can include dysmenorrhea (painful periods), dyspareunia (painful sexual intercourse), cyclic and noncyclic pelvic pain, dysuria (painful urination), dyschezia (painful bowel movements), heavy menstrual bleeding, lower back pain, abdominal pain when not menstruating, and fatigue (Allaire et al., 2023). The presence of endometriosis-related pain contributes to lowered levels of physical, psychological, and social functioning (Wang et al., 2021; Marinho et al., 2018). While persistent cyclical and noncyclical pain and fertility-related concerns are cited as common endometriosis-related symptoms, symptom profiles vary in terms of the number of symptoms experienced (symptom burden) and the distress associated with the presence of symptoms (symptom distress) (Van Niekerk et al., 2022a,

Leesa Van Niekerk & Suiyin Cheah are Joint First Authors.

L. Van Niekerk (✉) · B. Mertens
School of Psychological Sciences, University of Tasmania, Hobart, TAS, Australia
e-mail: leesa.vanniekerk@utas.edu.au

S. Cheah · A. Mikocka-Walus · S. Evans
School of Psychology, Deakin University, Burwood, VIC, Australia

L. A. Payne (ed.), *Psychosocial Interventions for Chronic Pain in Women and Girls*, CBT: Science Into Practice, https://doi.org/10.1007/978-3-031-98876-9_5

2022b, 2022c). Individuals with endometriosis are more likely to experience symptoms of depressed mood and anxiety than those without the condition (Rees et al., 2022).

The Importance of Biopsychosocial Healthcare for Endometriosis Management

Although traditional biomedical treatments (e.g., hormonal pill) are necessary for managing endometriosis disease progression and symptom burden, the pervasive nature of the condition extends beyond physical symptoms, and a holistic biopsychosocial approach is required to fully address endometriosis-related psychosocial impacts. A biopsychosocial model within endometriosis-related healthcare acknowledges that health-related quality of life (HRQoL) is determined by complex interactions between biological, psychological, environmental, and social factors associated with the condition (Engel, 1977; Armour et al., 2022). The assessment and management of endometriosis-related symptoms and their associated impacts may be better conceptualised through the lens of an extended model of health (Van Niekerk et al., 2019). This model emphasises the reciprocal interaction between biological, psychological, and social components, which vary across time due to the cyclical aspects of endometriosis (Lehman et al., 2017).

More recently, the perception of endometriosis as a gynaecological disease has shifted to one of a *whole of person* condition, with the need for psychological assessment and treatment to move beyond pain management, to include assessment and management of other aspects of wellbeing, including self-perception, body image, and sexual wellbeing (Mazalin et al., 2024; Sullivan-Myers et al., 2023). Acknowledging the impacts of endometriosis-related symptom burden and symptom distress on HRQoL and psychological wellbeing (including self-image, body image, sexual wellbeing), individuals with endometriosis and healthcare providers have called for increased research and access to psychological interventions tailored to endometriosis (Armour et al., 2023; Dowding et al., 2024). Given the findings that endometriosis-related symptoms are associated with impaired interpersonal and occupational functioning, reduced self-image and concept, and increased self-criticism (Armour et al., 2022; Mazalin et al., 2024), approaches focused on enhancing acceptance and counteracting self-blame are warranted.

Acceptance and Commitment Therapy and Endometriosis

Acceptance and Commitment Therapy (ACT) is a therapeutic approach, underpinned by core components of cognitive behaviour therapy (CBT), with a focus on cognitive processes and related behaviours (Hayes et al., 1999). However, unlike the focus on symptom reduction and amelioration noted in traditional CBT frameworks, the general premise of ACT is to foster engagement in meaningful value-guided life activities, even in the presence of negative physical, emotional, or cognitive inner events (Hayes et al., 2012). This shifts the focus away from symptom reduction, control, or suppression, which is likely to lead to a process of experiential avoidance and distress, and instead toward engagement in fulfilling and meaningful activities. While experiential avoidance provides a buffer against the experience of painful internal experiences in the short term, repeated patterns of avoidance can result in reduced psychological and physical well-being in the longer term, maintaining and heightening distress (Hayes et al., 1999).

As ACT does not specifically focus on symptom reduction, improvements in symptoms are viewed as resulting from enhanced psychological flexibility rather than as a core goal of therapeutic engagement (Hayes et al., 2006). Rather than trying to live a life avoiding negative internal or external experiences, ACT acknowledges that negative experiences are an unavoidable component of the human experience and promotes the use of psychological flexibility to manage the interaction of behavioural responses to inner events (McCracken & Morley, 2014). Psychological flexibility is the willingness to connect with the present moment, experiencing both positive and negative inner experiences, while maintaining engagement in value-based activities and behaviours (Hayes et al., 2012). Enhanced psychological flexibility may increase acceptance of persistent endometriosis-related symptoms (e.g., pain, fatigue, gastrointestinal concerns) and difficulties (e.g., impaired intimate relationships), promoting engagement in value-driven health-based behaviours, over-engaging in short-term experiential avoidance, which is likely to lead to increased symptomatic distress and lowered HRQoL in the longer term (Bernini et al., 2022). Within the context of endometriosis-related pain, like that of psychological distress, ACT techniques are not used to diminish, avoid, or treat pain (Hayes et al., 1999) but rather to mitigate the influence of endometriosis-related pain on the individual's behaviour and engagement in value-guided actions.

ACT-based interventions are efficacious in enhancing pain acceptance and subsequent pain adjustment, leading to increased levels of physical function and decreased reliance on traditional biomedical treatment approaches (Trindade et al., 2021). A systematic review of 25 randomised control trials of ACT for chronic pain by McCracken et al. (2022) noted small to large effect sizes for improving pain interference, depression, and HRQoL, with some support for ACT as a cost-effective intervention for chronic pain. The persistent nature of endometriosis places the individual in a position of having to navigate intersecting internal experiences (cognitions, emotions, physical sensations) and external stressors (interpersonal relationships, role changes, social expectations, engagement in healthcare), emphasising the important role that psychological (and pain) acceptance has in addressing experiential avoidance and lowered HRQoL.

Accordingly, ACT-based mental health interventions, with a focus on enhancing psychological flexibility and acceptance, may assist in reducing the overall biopsychosocial impacts associated with endometriosis. Although published clinical trials assessing the efficacy of acceptance- and mindfulness-based psychological therapies are in their infancy, preliminary findings are promising (Hansen et al., 2023), with the additional support for their inclusion in endometriosis-related treatment based on their efficacy with other forms of persistent pelvic pain (Bittelbrunn et al., 2023; Buhrman et al., 2024) and comorbid symptoms such as gastrointestinal concerns (Qian & Zhang, 2024), fatigue (Yu et al. 2020), and sexual wellbeing (Hess Engström et al., 2022).

While ACT-based interventions have demonstrated efficacy in the management of health-based conditions and psychological presentations, including anxiety and depression, it is not recommended as a primary intervention for clients experiencing crisis situations, acute suicidal ideation, or deliberate self-harm (Tighe et al., 2018). ACT may also be contraindicated for individuals with impaired cognitive functioning, resulting in difficulties with comprehending and responding to therapist-led discussions (Smout, 2012). Engagement in ACT-based interventions for individuals experiencing domestic or family violence is not recommended, as the focus on acceptance of current difficulties or distress may result in a risk to the safety and well-being of the client.

An Example of ACT for Endometriosis

A case example will guide readers on the use of ACT for endometriosis and is based on a therapeutic protocol originally developed for individuals diagnosed with inflammatory bowel disease (ACTforIBD; Evans et al., 2022). The ACTforIBD program (Evans et al., 2022; Wilkin et al., 2024) provides an ideal basis for understanding important ACT-based techniques that may benefit endometriosis, given the strong association between the two health conditions (e.g., their inflammatory origin). The modified program incorporates endometriosis-specific examples and a greater emphasis on the *choice point* (Ciarrochi et al., 2015; Harris, 2017a, 2017b). The choice point refers to the moment where we are required to make a choice in the face of a challenging situation, emotion, or physical sensation, and is an important construct in ACT-based programs and an effective tool in explaining and reinforcing the process of psychological flexibility. The modified program exercises, metaphors, and worksheets have been adapted from the ACTforIBD program and the work of Hayes et al. (1999, 2006, 2012) and Harris (2017a, 2017b), with the adaptations based on the clinical and research findings of the current authors.

Consistent with the aim of many ACT programs, the program outlined here is designed to increase psychological flexibility and enhance engagement in value-based, meaningful, and enriching activities, and to decrease the use of experiential avoidance. The program will be useful for individuals seeking to increase their understanding, insight, and awareness of endometriosis-related experiences (including thoughts, emotions, physical symptoms, memories), for those who would like to incorporate therapeutic techniques into their traditional endometriosis biomedical management, and/or for individuals who feel their experience of endometriosis is overwhelming and has led to a sense of loss or disconnection from other important life domains. The modified program described here is a guide for mental health care providers, and its application should be varied to suit the client's individual case formulation.

Case Example: Maeve

Maeve, a 29-year-old female, has experienced endometriosis-related symptoms from the age of 12 but only received a formal diagnosis approximately 12 months ago. Maeve advises that her mother and maternal grandmother experienced menstrual irregularities as adolescents and that heavy menstrual bleeding and painful periods were considered a 'normal' part of the female experience. Maeve indicated that she would often request time away from school during her periods due to the experience of pain, nausea, and fatigue, but that this was mostly refused, and she would have to attend school. Maeve indicated that her first sexual relationship occurred at 16 years of age, and that while she and her male partner were not very knowledgeable about sex, sex was always consensual and respectful. Penetrative intercourse has always been painful, and Maeve attributed this to the breakdown of her first, and subsequent three, relationships. Based on the messages she received regarding 'normal' female experiences, her interactions with medical professionals, and her early sexual experiences, Maeve formed the belief during adolescence that she was 'different from others', unable to tolerate 'normal pain', 'attention-seeking', 'lazy', and 'sexually broken', and she continues to hold this perception of herself. Discussion of Maeve's medical history reveals engagement with several general practitioners (GPs) to find answers for her symptoms and 'inability to cope'. She had been advised by different GPs that her symptoms were due to 'irritable bowel syndrome', 'unlucky genes', and 'an anxious personality'. The ongoing experience of physical symptoms acts to reinforce Maeve's negative self-beliefs and labels, leading to feelings of anxiousness, low mood, and fear of sexual intimacy. Maeve is caught in a cycle of experiential avoidance that reinforces her negative self-perception and belief that she is 'broken'.

A Shared Understanding of Maeve's Endometriosis-Related Symptoms and Her Broader Life Domains

Maeve's psychologist introduces her to the *Pain and Symptom Web* as a collaborative in-session exercise. This collaborative formulation assists Maeve and her psychologist in understanding how the experience of endometriosis-related pain and symptoms connects with Maeve's broader life domains. The *Pain and Symptom Web* also increases Maeve's understanding of the bidirectional relationship between her psychosocial well-being and her endometriosis-related pain and symptoms, and shifts the focus away from a belief that therapy is only effective if it results in being pain or symptom-free. Maeve's psychologist uses a whiteboard and different coloured markers to work with Maeve to draw out her personal *Pain and Symptom Web* (see Fig. 5.1). The psychologist explains that the experience of endometriosis-related pain and symptoms interacts with a person's life in complex ways, impacting mood, relationships, activity, and/or sleep, and commences the activity by writing *Pain/Symptoms* in a circle in the centre of the board.

Through discussion with Maeve, the psychologist adds each area of concern to the board in separate circles around the *Pain/Symptoms*, with a directional arrow pointing outward from the word *Pain/Symptoms.* Maeve lists the following areas of concern or endometriosis-related impacts: *Stress, Sleep, Anxiousness, Energy, Sadness, Intimacy and Sex, Work,* and *Fertility.* The psychologist explains that the arrow indicates that the *Pain/Symptoms* is impacting these identified life domains or activities. Maeve and the psychologist discuss some of the other impacts that Maeve has shared including the way she sees herself (*Self Image*), her view of her body (*Body Image*), her ability to concentrate at work (*Concentration*), her level of social connection (*Friendships*), her relationship with her mother (*Mum*), and avoidance of endometriosis-related treatments (*Pelvic Physiotherapy*), adding these to the whiteboard with a directional arrow pointing outward from the word *Pain/Symptoms.*

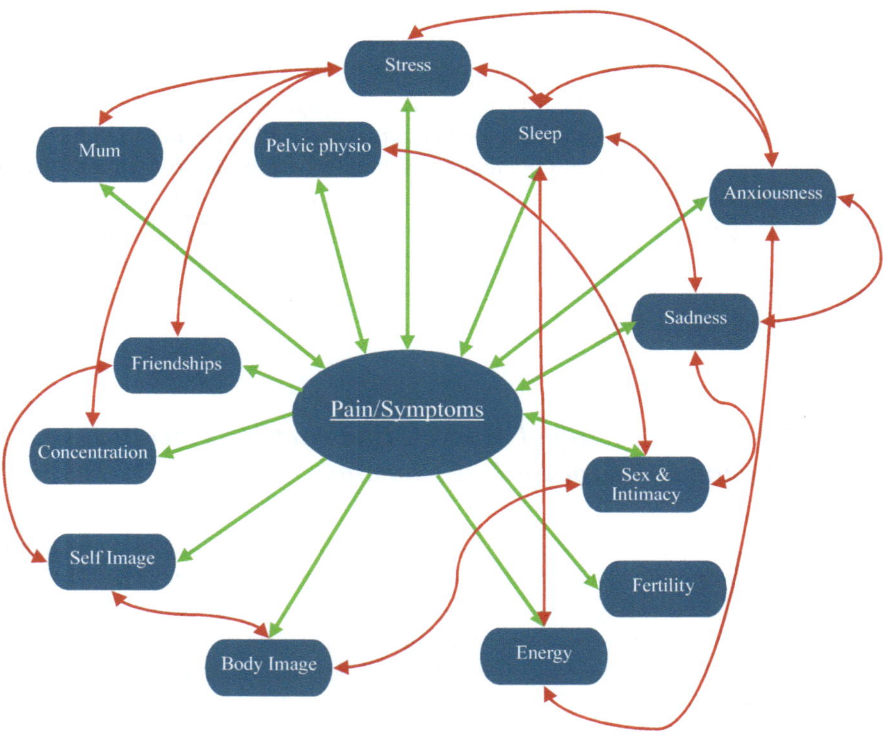

Fig. 5.1 Maeve's pain and symptom web

> As we look at the image we have drawn together here, we can see the different domains and areas that your endometriosis-related pain and symptoms have influenced, and I'm wondering if perhaps some of these domains or areas also influence your endometriosis-related pain and symptoms? I wonder if changes in some of these domains or areas alter your experience of endometriosis-related pain and symptoms, either seeming to increase or decrease them, or make them seem easier or more difficult to cope with?

As Maeve notes, the domains and areas that influence her experience of, and perceived ability to cope with, endometriosis-related pain and symptoms, the psychologist draws a directional arrow pointing inwards towards the *Pain/Symptom* circle. Maeve and the psychologist discuss that the abdominal pain she experiences, even outside of her menstrual cycle, impacts her ability to sleep, and that this, in turn, makes it more difficult to cope with the pain during the day. Maeve and the psychologist discuss the bidirectional nature of the experience of endometriosis-related pain and symptoms and the different domains and areas of Maeve's life. The collaborative discussion highlights multiple connections between the experience of endometriosis-related pain and symptoms, life domains and areas, and the interconnections between these life domains and areas. For example, Maeve and the psychologist note the bidirectional arrow between the *Pain/Symptoms* circle and the *Sex and Intimacy* circle, which also has a bidirectional arrow connecting it to the *Self-Image* and *Body Image* circles. The psychologist also shares with Maeve that many of these connections can occur for other people (such as disrupted sleep influencing mood and energy levels), with a view to gently providing an alternative viewpoint to Maeve's current perception that these difficulties are due to her 'inability to cope' or 'being broken'.

> Let's take a moment to look at the board. Is there anything coming to mind as you look at this pain and symptom web on the whiteboard? Something that I am noticing is that now that we have laid it out like this, the web looks quite complex. The different ways that endometriosis-related pain and symptoms influence life domains and areas can be complicated and sometimes we may not always be aware of how these symptoms, areas, and domains are interconnected. Is there an area of this web that you think it would be best to focus on together first? We can use this web to start to set some goals that you would like to focus on.

Maeve and the psychologist collaboratively arrive at the following therapeutic goals:

- To increase and maintain connections with my friends rather than cancelling out of fear that they will judge me (*Value-Guided Decision Making and Committed Action; Cognitive Defusion*)
- To learn how to manage my thoughts and feelings so that they do not feel so overwhelming (*Cognitive Defusion, Mindfulness of Emotions*)
- Feeling more emotionally connected to my partner when we are together rather than getting lost in my thoughts (*Present Moment Awareness, Self-As-Context*)
- To experience a greater level of physical intimacy with my partner rather than avoiding all forms of contact due to fear of pain (*Value-Guided Decision Making and Committed Action; Present Moment Awareness; Mindfulness*)

Introducing the Foundations of ACT

Clients must have a sound rationale for the use of ACT techniques for the management of their endometriosis-related symptoms and associated distress. The psychologist introduces Maeve to the foundations of ACT, with an emphasis on the *choice point* and the concept of *towards* and *away* moves (Harris, 2017a, 2017b). Here, Maeve is also introduced to the concept of *dropping anchor* (Harris, 2019) to *connect to the present moment* and engage in meaningful value-directed actions. Dropping anchor is a technique designed to bring awareness to the present moment, allowing the individual to connect with the current situation, rather than getting caught in difficult thoughts or emotions. It follows a process of acknowledging the thoughts or feelings that are occurring, connecting awareness to the body, and engaging with the present moment (Harris, 2019). The psychologist explains that ACT is a therapeutic approach that allows people to develop the skills to accept and manage the difficult thoughts, emotions, physical sensations, symptoms, or circumstances associated with endometriosis, ensuring that any discussion links to Maeve's individual experiences.

> *Through the use of ACT techniques, we can learn to shift our focus away from struggling with our endometriosis-related experiences, such as struggling with pain and fatigue* (Maeve's symptoms)*, thoughts of feeling broken or lazy* (Maeve's thoughts)*, or avoiding engaging in care such as pelvic physiotherapy* (one example of experiential avoidance described by Maeve) *so that we can connect with the things that matter to us most.*

The psychologist explains that ACT is particularly beneficial for addressing the impacts of persistent health conditions, as, over time, the physical and emotional symptoms of enduring health difficulties can negatively impact a person's quality of life. The psychologist emphasises the 'experiential' foundation of ACT, highlighting that Maeve's understanding of ACT will increase the more she engages in the techniques and applies the in-session practices outside of the therapy room. Maeve and the psychologist engage in an in-session experiential activity as an introduction to *cognitive fusion* (i.e., becoming absorbed or attached to one's thoughts, beliefs, or self-judgements) using the Hands as Thoughts and Feelings metaphor (Harris, 2017a, 2017b, 2019), with the psychologist using examples of Maeve's experiences (e.g., struggling with the pain, thoughts of not being good enough or broken, avoiding all forms of emotional and physical intimacy with her partner). The Hands as Thoughts and Feelings metaphor is a common metaphor and experiential activity used in ACT to help the client understand the process of cognitive fusion. It provides a visual representation of how being fused with our thoughts limits our ability to connect with the present situation and undertake value-guided actions (see Harris, 2017a, 2017b for a guiding script).

Following this activity, the psychologist introduces Maeve to the *choice point* (Harris, 2017a, 2017b), with a focus on its relevance for endometriosis.

> Each day we make thousands of decisions, whether related to your experience of endometriosis, or life in general. When our health and life feel manageable, our everyday decisions can be straightforward and easy. However, when we are struggling physically or emotion-

ally, or are faced with difficult situations, making decisions, or being able to consider the available options, can feel overwhelming. Living with endometriosis can be especially challenging, as it can influence many areas of your life as we saw when we looked at your pain and symptom web. Sometimes, when distressing thoughts, painful emotions, or unwanted physical sensations (such as pain) are present, it can be easy to get caught up in these experiences, which in turn can influence how we respond.

The psychologist explains that a *choice point* (Harris, 2017a, 2017b) reflects a moment in time where we can choose to act or behave in ways that move us closer towards our values or the life we would like to live; Or in ways that move us away from our values and further away from the life we want to live.

When faced with endometriosis-related symptoms and associated impacts across multiple life domains, the decisions we need to make can become increasingly challenging, leading to a sense of struggle. Getting caught in the struggle can lead to us trying to avoid or get rid of difficulties or symptoms, or to make decisions that lead us further away from what matters most to us, such as avoiding your partner. In these moments, learning to acknowledge the urge to avoid or get rid of unwanted thoughts, emotions, or physical sensations allows us to reflect on what is important to us, like sharing an emotional and physical bond with your partner, and what we need to be able to make value-guided decisions.

The psychologist uses the whiteboard to draw a visual representation of the *choice point* (Harris, 2017a, 2017b), starting with a 'towards arrow' pointing in the direction of a close and loving relationship, prioritising self-care and treatments that are helpful, feeling connected with friends (i.e., the goals that Maeve set following completion of the *pain and symptom web* activity). They then draw an 'away arrow' leading away from the goals Maeve has. The psychologist indicates that the *choice point* relates to the choices that we make when challenging events occur, whether that is a physical sensation, an emotion, a painful memory, or an external event. The psychologist explains when we become caught in the struggle, we can get stuck in 'away moves' (like avoiding intimacy or self-care activities), and although this can sometimes lead us to experience relief in the short-term, this ultimately leads us further away from the things that matter most, resulting in longer-term difficulties (see Fig. 5.2).

The psychologist and Maeve discuss the process of *dropping anchor* to *connect to the present moment.* This is an important process of providing the client with a foundation to build psychological flexibility and increasing awareness of alternative choice points that the client may not have ready cognitive and emotional awareness of when they are caught in the struggle. The psychologist describes that when we experience a challenging event, such as your mind giving the thought that "*you're broken*" (Maeve's thought) or "*you receive a reminder about an appointment with your pelvic physiotherapist and feel the urge to cancel, pulling you closer to experiential avoidance*" (Maeve's experience), the first part of being able to consider and connect with towards moves is to gently bring your mind to the *present moment.* The psychologist uses the metaphor of a ship dropping anchor in the middle of a storm to help steady itself and prevent it from being swept away from the direction it is heading. It is important that the psychologist does not indicate that *dropping anchor* will stop the storm from happening, but rather it keeps the ship from being

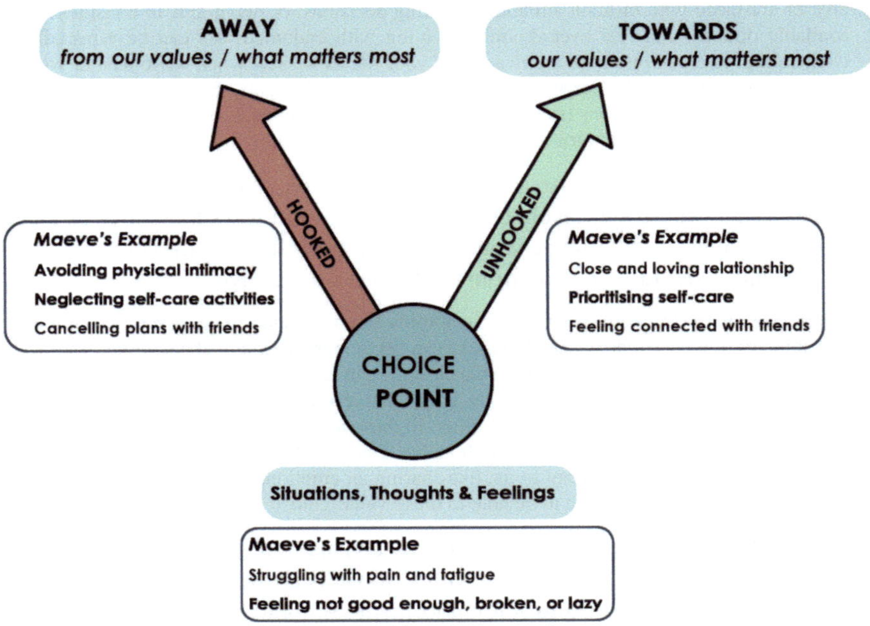

Fig. 5.2 A visual depiction of Maeve's choice point

blown off course or feeling a sense of disconnection from its destination (Harris, 2017a, 2017b). The storm can be any overwhelming event, including thoughts, intense emotions or physical sensations, a memory, an urge, etc. An anchor can be drawn from something that is part of the client's present moment, that is not part of the storm or struggle. Anchors that are commonly introduced early in ACT-based interventions often link to one or more of the five senses (i.e., taste, touch, sight, sound, smell).

Harris (2019) provides a useful acronym (ACE) that can be shared with clients to help them remember the three important components of *dropping anchor*. The first component involves an *Acknowledgment (A)* of the experience (thought, emotion, or physical sensation) at the centre of the struggle. The experience is acknowledged, observed, and the client gives themselves permission to notice rather than judge or critique the experience (or themselves) in some way. The second component encourages the client to *Connect* or *Come Back to the Body (C)*. This can include focusing attention on a certain body part (e.g., pushing feet hard into the floor, rolling your shoulders back and around). The third component connects the client to the present moment, so that they can *Engage (E)* and focus their attention on the activity they were engaged in. Here, the client is encouraged to gently focus their attention on the task at hand, or something in their environment (such as noticing sounds, smells, tastes, things they can see, or feel) (Harris, 2019). Maeve and the psychologist practice the *dropping anchor* technique in-session, allowing an opportunity to troubleshoot any difficulties that Maeve may experience and to reinforce the experiential aspect of ACT.

Introducing Experiential Avoidance

Maeve and the psychologist explore her understanding and use of *experiential avoidance* when she is faced with challenging or difficult endometriosis-related experiences. They recap on the *choice point* and discuss how experiential avoidance can lead to engagement in 'away moves' rather than 'towards moves', maintaining the struggle with painful thoughts, emotions, and bodily sensations. The psychologist explains that while experiential avoidance can appear like the only option or solution, or even like the best option from a range of possible options, our unwanted thoughts and feelings do not disappear and may unwittingly be reinforced. In the longer term, trying to control or avoid our difficult experiences does not work very well and eventually leads to more struggle, pain, and suffering (Harris, 2019; Hayes et al., 2012).

> Living with endometriosis can make everyday tasks and activities difficult and challenging, resulting in feelings of frustration, isolation, anxiety, and fear. From what you have shared with me, these feelings have led to you avoiding things that you would usually value or desire, moving you away from what really matters to you. For example, you shared that you avoid physical intimacy with your partner because you are worried that he will judge your body negatively, particularly when your stomach feels bloated. Or that you will avoid scheduling time with your friends so that you don't experience feelings of anxiousness or worry that they think you are unreliable.

Clients may express some resistance when initially exploring their current coping strategies. For example, Maeve might respond, *"But it's true! I feel terrible regardless, so it's better I just stay away from others."* The psychologist can normalise, explain, and seek collaborative consent to proceed *"These sound like ways that you have learned to cope with difficult experiences, and it makes sense why you use them. We can describe this as 'experiential avoidance'. It can lead to missing out on things that are important to us, and sometimes it makes us feel like we can't cope or are broken in some way. Would you be interested in exploring other ways to respond these feelings and thoughts when they show up to see if this allows you to reconnect with what really matters to you?"* With consent, Maeve and the psychologist complete an in-session activity identifying and reflecting on situations, emotions, thoughts, and physical sensations that she attempts to avoid. Maeve begins by noting down an event (i.e., thoughts, emotions, physical sensations, memories, urges, habits, etc.) that she has been struggling with recently. She is invited to choose any endometriosis-related, or non-endometriosis-related event. Together, they discuss how Maeve currently, and historically, has reacted to this event and how long she has been struggling with this event. Maeve indicates that she uses *distraction* (scrolling on her phone), *denial* (telling herself that she does not need friends), *projection* (telling herself that if she had a better physiotherapist, she would have less sexual pain by now), and *opting out* (avoiding physical affection, cancelling dates with friends). They identify that Maeve uses these techniques to try and avoid the fear of rejection (by partner, by friends), or the belief of being broken, from activating. They reflect that experiential avoidance has not resolved the fear of rejection or altered the belief of being broken that Maeve holds, but rather has prevented her from having the connected and loving relationships she values and has reinforced her belief of being broken.

Introducing Value-Guided Actions

Maeve is feeling stuck and despondent about her progress toward her goals, and advises that she is attempting to cope with these feelings by engaging in some of her previous patterns of experiential avoidance, including *denial* and *opting out*. The psychologist introduces the concepts of value-based decision making and committed action.

> Sometimes pain can get in the way of living our lives in the way we would ideally like to. The life that we would like to live is underpinned by our values—the principles and qualities which we seek in ourselves and others. Values can be confused with goals; however, they differ in some important ways. Values are like signposts that help direct us toward our goals and they continue to be important even when we reach our goals. Goals on the other hand are the things that you aim for or are wanting to achieve. Goals can connect us to our values, like your goal of spending more time with your friends because you value a sense of connection with others. Understanding what we value can help us to consider goals that are consistent with these values and assist us when we arrive at a choice point and need to take some form of action.

The psychologist and Maeve complete a value clarification task together to gain a greater understanding of what matters most to Maeve. Value clarification activities include value-card sort (Miller et al., 2001) or through a series of questions exploring different life domains (Harris, 2022), or client-led reflections such as "*If I'm honest with myself, what is truly important to me? What do I care most about? What do I (want to) stand for?*" The psychologist explores the goals that Maeve has set to determine how in line they are with her values.

> *One of the goals that you set for yourself is to increase the level of physical intimacy with your partner, but your mind gives you the thought that 'he doesn't want me'* (Maeve's language), *and the fear of being rejected shows up. What does intimacy with your partner mean to you? When you avoid spending time with him as a means of avoiding those negative self-labels and fear, what values does it disconnect you from?*

Maeve indicates that, to her, intimacy means a feeling of closeness and security, of being loved, and is linked to feelings of warmth, pleasure, and fun. When Maeve avoids spending time with her partner, she notes feelings of loneliness, distance, and self-criticalness. For Maeve, intimacy connects with her values of *Connection*, *Love (being loving and being loved)*, *Care*, and *Fun*. Together, they review the goal of increasing intimacy and consider moves towards and away from this goal. Maeve indicates that actions such as holding hands, hugging, and touching as they pass each other are towards moves that connect her with the goal of increasing intimacy and are consistent with her values of connection, love, and care. She acknowledges that her partner is kind, respectful, and loving, and that when she is connected to the *present moment*, she is aware of this.

> Within ACT, committed action involves the promise you make with yourself to take a specific action, in a particular situation, regardless of the thoughts, feelings, and sensations that show up. Whilst our minds may try to convince us to not take certain action and might try to come up with compelling reasons why we shouldn't make value-based decisions, committed action is a choice to do what matters most to us and helps us discover what works best for us in our life.

Maeve and the psychologist consider different actions she can commit to that will bring her closer to the goal of a more intimate relationship, in line with her identified values. The psychologist discusses Maeve's goal of increased intimacy –*"Maeve, I'd like us to consider the goal of improving intimacy in your relationship, and how making valued choices can help move you closer to this goal. Can you think of a value that you move away from when you become overwhelmed by your thoughts of not being good enough?"* Maeve replies, *"Connection. I really feel disconnected from my partner."* The psychologist continues, *"If you were to act in way in which the value of 'connection' was at the forefront of your mind, are there any different choices you would make in the way you approach intimacy?"* Confused, Maeve seeks clarification *"But it's not just up to me, my partner also does things that make me feel less connected. Are we trying to come up with idea of what we can change together?"* The psychologist clarifies, *"Not exactly. We are going to try and find way that your choices can be more 'value-led' or 'value-informed'. Imagine if the value 'Connection' was a person. Imagine this person embodied 'Connection' to the fullest. They would seek to connect with others, feel more connected, and they would try to encourage an environment around them in which connection was fostered. They would work toward goals with 'Connection' in mind. What is something you could change that would help you bring the value to Connection more into focus in your pursuit of a more intimate relationship?"*

Maeve decides that instead of sitting apart from her partner when they watch their favourite show, she will cuddle up to him. The psychologist introduces Maeve to mindfulness and mindful moments as a means of connecting to the present moment when her mind gives her the thought that "he doesn't want me," and the fear of rejection shows up. When Maeve can connect to the present moment, through mindfulness, she is able to connect to the knowledge that her partner is kind and loving and that, rather than rejecting her touch, he values this means of connection too.

Introducing Mindfulness and Mindful Moments

Maeve is introduced to the benefits of mindfulness and mindful moments as a mechanism for increasing psychological flexibility and as an alternative to experiential avoidance activities such as distraction (e.g., scrolling on her phone) or avoidance of painful emotions or physical sensations. The application of mindfulness to enhance the mind-body connection for individuals with endometriosis is important as research findings have indicated that endometriosis is linked to a lack of body familiarity and dissociation (Van Niekerk et al., 2022a, 2022b, 2022c), which can lead to impaired body image and sexual wellbeing (Melis et al., 2015). It is important to emphasise that *being mindful* takes practice and that the mind needs assistance to stay connected to the *present moment* rather than slipping into *automatic pilot* mode (Mace, 2007). Maintaining a connection to the present moment can be difficult because our mind will move between its connection to the present, to recalling past events, and/or to making predictions about future events. We say that we are in *automatic pilot mode* when our mind disconnects from the present, but we physically go through the motions of the activity we are engaged in. Mindfulness practices, even small mindful moments, increase our awareness of where our attention is focused, as well as allowing us to be more in tune with what our mind is focused on. Mindfulness can provide some cognitive and emotional distance from endometriosis-related struggles, opening up awareness of the pull of experiential avoidance and potential towards moves.

The psychologist and Maeve engage in an experiential exercise to understand where Maeve's mind travels when she is caught in an endometriosis-related struggle. Maeve is invited to tune into her mind and reflect on her experience of endometriosis for a minute or two. As she is thinking about her experiences with endometriosis, the psychologist asks Maeve to notice where her mind takes her and how it presents information to her.

> Your mind might float back to something from your past connected to endometriosis. This can be like having your own personal collection of stories that chronicle all your endometriosis-related experiences. Here in the present, our body often remembers or experiences the emotions and physical sensations that may have been present when those events occurred. Although we might replay these stories repeatedly in our mind, and this often occurs when we are in automatic pilot mode, we don't have the ability to travel back in time to change an aspect of the story. This can leave us feeling overwhelmed, exhausted, or frustrated.

The psychologist explains that perhaps Maeve's mind may have floated to the future, where it tries to make predictions about what will occur. They reflect that, like being unable to travel back in time, we are not able to travel forward in time to directly control or predict exactly what is going to happen. When our mind travels forward, it can lead us to try and fill in 'missing pieces' of information with stories, detailing how something will or should be. Here in the present, our body often experiences the emotions (e.g., anxiousness) and physical sensations (e.g., pain or tension) associated with our predictions.

> When our mind is in the present, we can be aware of difficult or distressing endometriosis-related experiences, and we can have a desire or hope for future situations to play out in a certain way, but we do not get lost in these. When difficult emotions, physical sensations, or even pain, occur, we can acknowledge the reason for their presence, while deciding what we need to help us to cope in the current moment or what decisions we may need to make to take care of ourselves in the nearer future.

The psychologist encourages Maeve to notice how her mind presents information to her.

> As you thought about endometriosis, where did your mind take you? Did it take you to the past, the present, or the future? Perhaps it took you to the past and then bypassed the present altogether and swung to your future and what living with endometriosis will mean? Perhaps you worked hard to keep your mind connected to the present because it feels too overwhelming to think about the past or future? As we have already discussed, trying to stop or supress your thoughts or feelings hasn't worked for you either. So, how did your mind give you this information? Was the information presented as images like on a TV screen, or are they voices like on a radio? Let's write down the thoughts that popped into your mind during that exercise.

The psychologist and Maeve note down the thoughts her mind presented during the experiential exercise and reflect on where Maeve's mind tends to spend most of its time. Maeve identifies that she often gets hooked into memories of the invalidation she experienced during adolescence, when she would experience intense menstrual pain (*past*), and recalls feelings of embarrassment and shame when she first tried to talk to a GP about painful sex (*past*). She notices that her mind jumps from these memories to the thoughts of being lazy and broken (*negative self-labels*), and the next thing she finds herself thinking is that it will just be a matter of time before her partner leaves (*future*). Here in the present, Maeve notices a tightness in her chest, a stabbing feeling in her abdomen, and sadness. She is surprised by how easily her mind 'slipped' into these painful memories and feels fearful for her future self. The psychologist and Maeve discuss the influence of these negative self-labels in Maeve's use of experiential avoidance (*denial, projection, opting out*), and Maeve identifies that she has viewed herself through these labels for so long that they seem like statements of fact or like a constant hum in the background, dictating her decisions and choices.

Together, Maeve and the psychologist explore ways for Maeve to recognise when her mind has disconnected from its *present moment* focus to *automatic pilot mode*. Signs of automatic pilot mode for Maeve include recognising when her body is engaged in an activity but her mind has turned to painful memories or feeling fearful about future events; when she feels disconnected from her thoughts but notices strong emotions showing up; when she feels like she is in reaction rather than response mode to what is happening internally or externally; and when she uses distraction, such as scrolling for long periods on her phone. Maeve is invited to practice some mindful moments in-session with her psychologist. They practice connecting to the present using Maeve's senses, placing her feet flat on the floor, dropping anchor, and the 3-min breathing space (Teasdale et al., 2013). With practice, Maeve engages in longer mindfulness inductions, including a mindful body scan (Kabat-Zinn, 2018), and mindfulness of emotions (Saulsman & Nathan, 2012).

Introducing Cognitive Fusion

Engaging in towards moves or making value-guided decisions can be difficult if our mind is overwhelmed by distressing thoughts, images, or memories. This state of overwhelm may make it difficult to engage in mindfulness, or even mindful moments, and ultimately leads to away moves. When we get caught up in the content of our thoughts, our thoughts may start to dictate our actions, a process referred to as *cognitive fusion* (Hayes et al., 1999). As we fuse with our thoughts, we begin to see the thought as a statement of fact, or a statement of truth regarding the experience. Although some thoughts may be factual, others may consist of predictions or expectations and can lead to a sense of overwhelm or 'feeling stuck'.

The psychologist invites Maeve to reflect on a time when she had arranged to see her friends but felt tired, overwhelmed, and in pain, and asks her to imagine what might happen if her mind gave her thoughts such as "*What's the point? I will be too tired to do anything*," or "*what if the pain gets worse?*" or "*I'll just be a burden to my friends.*" The psychologist shares that when we get hooked by difficult thoughts like these, it can be hard to see past the thoughts themselves. Our mind may start to add more information to the initial thought, and soon we have a story that feels real and believable, even though, here in the present moment, all the story endings are occurring in our mind and not in reality. Maeve states that even though her first thought is usually "*what if my pain gets worse?*", she starts having other thoughts such as "*I'm always cancelling things,*" "*my friends think I'm unreliable,*" and by the end she is telling herself "*I never cope with anything,*" even though in reality she knows this is not the case.

The psychologist revisits the *Hands as Thoughts and Feelings* exercise (Harris, 2017a, 2017b) that Maeve was introduced to in her first session, emphasising that when we fuse with our thoughts, we start to see things from the perspective of our thoughts only, which in turn influences how we view the world around us and how we respond to challenging or difficult experiences. Maeve identifies other thoughts that she fuses with, including "*I should be able to cope better,*" "*I'll be a burden to my partner,*" and "*I can't trust my body,*" and reflects that when she is fused with these thoughts, she engages in avoidance and away moves. The psychologist introduces Maeve to the alternative to cognitive fusion—*cognitive defusion*. They explain that the process of defusion allows us to notice our thoughts or observe the experience that resulted in them without getting caught up in negative self-evaluations (Harris, 2017a, 2017b, 2019).

> When we defuse from our thoughts, we have a sense of almost being able to watch our thoughts, to be able to see them as thoughts rather than absolute truths or statements of fact—we can see them for what they are—just thoughts! Whilst fusion can maximise our

distress, defusion is about learning how to notice and observe our thoughts, emotions and physical sensations rather than getting lost in or hooked by them. Defusion is not meant to change or eliminate your thoughts or feelings. Rather it's a skill to give you some distance from your thoughts or feelings so you can make value-guided choices.

The psychologist guides Maeve through an experiential demonstration of defusion called 'Taking Time to Thank Your Mind' (Harris, 2019). They invite Maeve to recall a recent endometriosis-related thought that she has been struggling with and ask her to silently repeat the thought over and over to herself, letting it run through her mind on repeat. Next, without changing the thought itself, the psychologist invites Maeve to add some new information to the start of the thought ("I'm having the thought that... *I should be able to cope better*) and asks her to let this play on repeat in her mind. Next, the psychologist asks Maeve to try different endings to her original thought, such as 'thanks mind' or 'that's an interesting thought'." For example, "I'm having the thought that *I should be able to cope better*, that's an interesting thought." The psychologist invites Maeve to observe what is happening with the level of fusion she feels with the thought, "*Does it feel as attached to you as it did when it was just on repeat on its own?*"

The psychologist and Maeve discuss the sense of space and distance from her thoughts, the experiential activity provided. Maeve agrees that the process of defusion allows her to gain a different perspective on some of the difficult thoughts and labels her mind presents to her, and that the feelings of sadness that are normally attached to the thought "*I should be able to cope better*" also seem less intense. Maeve sets a new goal of engaging in defusion exercises between her psychology sessions, with a daily practice of a mindfulness induction that emphasises the process of defusion called 'Leaves on a Stream' (Harris, 2007).

Continuing Maeve's Journey with ACT

Maeve attends a final session with her psychologist, and they spend time recapping on the ACT skills she has acquired, her successful goal attainment, and her increased ability to engage in towards moves, even in the face of difficult endometriosis-related events (thoughts, emotions, physical sensations, memories). Maeve reports that over the course of therapy, she has increased her connection with friends and has learnt that, rather than judging her negatively, they understand that her energy levels vary and are willing to come visit her at home where she has access to self-management tools such as heat packs. Maeve also reports feeling a greater level of emotional and physical connection with her partner and advises that they are working through a graded program to assist with her experience of sexual pain. She can defuse from the negative self-label of '*being broken*' and understands that, rather than this being a personal failing, other women with endometriosis also commonly report the experience of painful sex. Maeve is also actively engaged in endometriosis-related treatments (e.g., regular appointments with her pelvic physiotherapist) and has connected with other women with endometriosis to address her previous feelings of loneliness, isolation, and failure. Maeve understands that applying the skills and tools she has learnt through therapy allows her to engage more fully in life, here in the present, and as she moves forward.

Conclusion

The benefit of ACT is that the techniques can be used to address current difficulties and concerns, but are also applicable for periods of struggle or difficulty that occur once the client has ceased therapy. ACT provides a therapeutic framework that acknowledges the whole of person impacts associated with endometriosis. We recommend that therapy commences with an introduction to the pain and symptom web to reinforce the interaction between physical symptoms and psychosocial function and wellbeing. The focus of subsequent sessions will be determined by the client's individual case formulation and therapeutic goals, with psychoeducation on the choice point, experiential avoidance, value-guided decision-making and committed action, cognitive defusion, and mindfulness recommended.

> No matter where you are in your life, and any new challenges that living with endometriosis may bring, you have learnt skills to create and pursue a value-driven life. As we have discussed, we cannot inoculate ourselves against the challenging or painful life experiences because these are a part of living a value-driven life rather than one of experiential avoidance. By developing practices that allow you to ACT, that is to Accept—what is out of your control; Choose—your valued direction; and take action in line with what is most important, you can create a life that meaningful.

References

Allaire, C., Bedaiwy, M. A., & Yong, P. J. (2023). Diagnosis and management of endometriosis. *CMAJ, 195*(10), E363–E371.

Armour, M., Avery, J., Leonardi, M., Van Niekerk, L., Druitt, M. L., Parker, M. A., Girling, J. E., McKinnon, B., Mikocka-Walus, A., Ng, C. H. M., O'Hara, R., Ciccia, D., Stanley, K., & Evans, S. (2022). Lessons from implementing the Australian National Action Plan for Endometriosis. *Reproduction and Fertility, 3*(3), C29–C39.

Armour, M., Ciccia, D., Yazdani, A., Rombauts, L., Niekerk, L. V., Schubert, R., & Abbott, J. (2023). Endometriosis research priorities in Australia. *Australian and New Zealand Journal of Obstetrics and Gynaecology, 63*(4), 594–598.

Bernini, O., Tumminaro, G., Compare, L., Belviso, C., Conforti, V., & Berrocal Montiel, C. (2022). Incremental validity of acceptance over coping in predicting adjustment to endometriosis. *Front Pain Res (Lausanne), 3*, 928985.

Bittelbrunn, C. C., de Fraga, R., Martins, C., Romano, R., Massaneiro, T., Mello, G. V. P., et al. (2023). Pelvic floor physical therapy and mindfulness: Approaches for chronic pelvic pain in women-a systematic review and meta-analysis. *Archives of Gynecology and Obstetrics, 307*, 663–672.

Buhrman, M., Hällström, H., Fridén, A., Kettis Moden, E., Grahn, G., Carlfjord, M., et al. (2024). Guided internet-based acceptance and commitment therapy for provoked vestibulodynia: A randomized controlled trial. *European Journal of Pain*.

Ciarrochi, J., Harris, R., & Bailey, A. (2015). *The weight escape: Stop fad dieting, start losing weight and reshape your life using cutting-edge psychology*. Hachette UK.

Dowding, C., Mikocka-Walus, A., Skvarc, D., O'Shea, M., Olive, L., & Evans, S. (2024). Learning to cope with the reality of endometriosis: A mixed-methods analysis of psychological therapy in women with endometriosis. *British Journal of Health Psychology*.

Engel, G. L. (1977). The need for a new medical model: A challenge for biomedicine. *Science, 196*(4286), 129–136.

Evans, S., Olive, L., Dober, M., Knowles, S., Fuller-Tyszkiewicz, M., Eric, O., et al. (2022). Acceptance commitment therapy (ACT) for psychological distress associated with inflammatory bowel disease (IBD): Protocol for a feasibility trial of the ACTforIBD programme. *BMJ Open, 12*(6), e060272.

Hansen, K. E., Brandsborg, B., Kesmodel, U. S., Forman, A., Kold, M., Pristed, R., et al. (2023). Psychological interventions improve quality of life despite persistent pain in endometriosis: Results of a 3-armed randomized controlled trial. *Quality of Life Research, 32*, 1727–1744.

Harris, R. (2007). *Acceptance and commitment therapy (ACT) advanced workshop handout*.

Harris, R. (2017a). The "hands as thoughts & feelings" exercise. *ACTMindfully*. https://www.actmindfully.com.au/upimages/Hands_as_Thoughts_and_feelings_Exercise_-_2017_version.pdf

Harris, R. (2017b). The choice point 2.0: A brief overview. *ACTMindfully*. Commitment therapy in drug-dependent https://www.actmindfully.com.au/free-stuff/worksheets-handouts-book-chapters

Harris, R. (2019). *ACT made simple: An easy-to-read primer on acceptance and commitment therapy*. New Harbinger Publications.

Harris, R. (2022). *The happiness trap: How to stop struggling and start living*. Shambhala Publications.

Hayes, S. C., Luoma, J. B., Bond, F. W., Masuda, A., & Lillis, J. (2006). Acceptance and commitment therapy: Model, processes and outcomes. *Behaviour Research and Therapy, 44*(1), 1–25.

Hayes, S. C., Strosahl, K. D., & Wilson, K. G. (1999). *Acceptance and commitment therapy*.

Hayes, S. C., Strosahl, K. D., & Wilson, K. G. (2012). *Acceptance and commitment therapy: The process and practice of mindful change* (2nd ed.). Guilford Press.

Hess Engström, A., Bohm-Starke, N., Kullinger, M., Hesselman, S., Högberg, U., Buhrman, M., & Skalkidou, A. (2022). Internet-based treatment for vulvodynia (EMBLA)–a randomized controlled study. *The Journal of Sexual Medicine, 19*(2), 319–330.

Kabat-Zinn, J. (2018). *Falling awake: How to practice mindfulness in everyday life*. Hachette UK.

Lamceva, J., Uljanovs, R., & Strumfa, I. (2023). The main theories on the pathogenesis of endometriosis. *International Journal of Molecular Sciences, 24*(5), 4254.

Lehman, B. J., David, D. M., & Gruber, J. A. (2017). Rethinking the biopsychosocial model of health: Understanding health as a dynamic system. *Social and Personality Psychology Compass, 11*(8), e12328.

Mace, C. (2007). Mindfulness in psychotherapy: An introduction. *Advances in Psychiatric Treatment, 13*(2), 147–154.

Marinho, M. C. P., Magalhaes, T. F., Fernandes, L. F. C., Augusto, K. L., Brilhante, A. V. M., & Bezerra, L. (2018). Quality of life in women with endometriosis: An integrative review. *Journal of Women's Health (Larchmt), 27*(3), 399–408.

Mazalin, K., Evans, S., & Van Niekerk, L. (2024). A template thematic analysis of self-concept and self-compassion in people living with endometriosis: Analysis of qualitative survey responses. *Journal of Advanced Nursing*.

McCracken, L. M., & Morley, S. (2014). The psychological flexibility model: A basis for integration and progress in psychological approaches to chronic pain management. *Journal of Pain, 15*(3), 221–234.

McCracken, L. M., Yu, L., & Vowles, K. E. (2022). New generation psychological treatments in chronic pain. *BMJ, 376*.

Melis, I., Litta, P., Nappi, L., Agus, M., Melis, G. B., & Angioni, S. (2015). Sexual function in women with deep endometriosis: Correlation with quality of life, intensity of pain, depression, anxiety, and body image. *International Journal of Sexual Health, 27*(2), 175–185.

Miller, W. R., C'de Baca, J., Matthews, D. B., & Wilbourne, P. L. (2001). *Personal values card sort*. University of New Mexico.

Qian, X., & Zhang, J. (2024). Mindfulness-based interventions on psychological comorbidities in patients with inflammatory bowel disease: A systematic review and Meta-analysis. *Actas Españolas de Psiquiatría, 52*, 571–582.

Rees, M., Kiemle, G., & Slade, P. (2022). Psychological variables and quality of life in women with endometriosis. *Journal of Psychosomatic Obstetrics & Gynecology, 43*(1), 58–65.

Saulsman, L., & Nathan, P. (2012). *Facing your feelings: Learning to tolerate distress*. Centre for Clinical Interventions.

Smout, M. (2012). Acceptance and commitment therapy: Pathways for general practitioners. *Australian Family Physician, 41*(9), 672–676.

Sullivan-Myers, C., Sherman, K. A., Beath, A. P., Cooper, M. J. W., & Duckworth, T. J. (2023). Body image, self-compassion, and sexual distress in individuals living with endometriosis. *Journal of Psychosomatic Research, 167*, 111197.

Teasdale, J., Williams, M., & Segal, Z. (2013). *The mindful way workbook: An 8-week program to free yourself from depression and emotional distress*. Guilford Publications.

Tighe, J., Nicholas, J., Shand, F., & Christensen, H. (2018). Efficacy of acceptance and commitment therapy in reducing suicidal ideation and deliberate self-harm: Systematic review. *JMIR Mental Health, 5*(2), e10732.

Tomassetti, C., Johnson, N. P., Petrozza, J., Abrao, M. S., Einarsson, J. I., et al. (2021). An international terminology for endometriosis, 2021. *Human Reproduction Open, 2021*(4), hoab029.

Trindade, I. A., Guiomar, R., Carvalho, S. A., Duarte, J., Lapa, T., Menezes, P., Nogueira, M. R., Patrão, B., Pinto-Gouveia, J., & Castilho, P. (2021). Efficacy of online-based acceptance and commitment therapy for chronic pain: A systematic review and meta-analysis. *The Journal of Pain, 22*(11), 1328–1342.

Van Niekerk, L., Johnstone, L., & Matthewson, M. (2022a). Health-related quality of life in endometriosis: The influence of endometriosis-related symptom presence and distress. *Journal of Health Psychology, 27*(14), 3121–3135.

Van Niekerk, L., Johnstone, L., & Matthewson, M. (2022b). Predictors of self-compassion in endometriosis: The role of psychological health and endometriosis symptom burden. *Human Reproduction, 37*(2), 264–273.

Van Niekerk, L., Steains, E., & Matthewson, M. (2022c). Correlates of health-related quality of life: The influence of endometriosis, body image and psychological wellbeing. *Journal of Psychosomatic Research, 161*, 110993.

Van Niekerk, L., Weaver-Pirie, B., & Matthewson, M. (2019). Psychological interventions for endometriosis-related symptoms: A systematic review with narrative data synthesis. *Archives of Women's Mental Health, 22*(6), 723–735.

Wang, Y., Li, B., Zhou, Y., Wang, Y., Han, X., Zhang, S., He, Z., & Ouyang, L. (2021). Does endometriosis disturb mental health and quality of life? A systematic review and meta-analysis. *Gynecologic and Obstetric Investigation, 86*(4), 315–335.

Wilkin, K., Evans, S., Van Niekerk, L., Romano, D., Fuller-Tyszkiewicz, M., Knowles, S., et al. (2024). Moving towards acceptance and values: A qualitative study of ACTforIBD compared to IBD psychoeducation. *Journal of Clinical Psychology in Medical Settings*, 1–13.

Yu, L., Scott, W., & McCracken, L. M. (2020). Change in fatigue in acceptance and commitment therapy-based treatment for chronic pain and its association with enhanced psychological flexibility. *European Journal of Pain, 24*(1), 234–247.

Chapter 6
Hypersexual or Hypersensitive? Understanding and Treating the Bigger Picture of Persistent Genital Arousal Disorder (PGAD)

Alexandra T. Milspaw

Introduction

Chronic pelvic pain (CPP) and associated dysfunctions and chronic illnesses are poorly understood and significantly underfunded compared to other diseases, such as cancer (Lamvu et al., 2021). CPP is rarely included within the curriculum of health care providers, including gynecologists, who are the most common specialists sought out for medical treatment of these symptoms (Castellanos et al., 2024). This creates a major disservice for both providers and patients, as they lack the appropriate understanding to both assess and treat the overlapping conditions that contribute to CPP (Castellanos et al., 2024). One of the most misunderstood of these conditions is Persistent Genital Arousal Disorder (PGAD). PGAD is a physiological condition where patients perceive prolonged genital arousal without any sexual desire, intent, or physical or mental stimulation, which eventually leads to experiences of mental and physical pain and discomfort. Current literature, while limited in quantity and scope, reports a significant lack of effective assessment and treatment protocols for PGAD (Goldstein et al., 2021; Magana et al., 2024; Merwin & Brotto, 2023). It is estimated that PGAD affects anywhere from 0.6 to 4.3% individuals globally. However, that number is most likely significantly higher due to the etiology of PGAD not being well understood (Merwin & Brotto, 2023).

PGAD is a term that was hidden in the online blogs of anonymous patients desperate to find answers to their silent suffering (Kapuśniak & Piegza, 2022). Until recently, patients reporting symptoms of PGAD were perceived as potential "sex addicts"—people who were deemed hypersexual, with an obsessive focus on experiencing sexual stimuli, arousal, and orgasm (van Tuijl et al., 2020). They were sent

A. T. Milspaw (✉)
Private Practice, Macungie, PA, USA
e-mail: Alex@dralexmilspaw.com

L. A. Payne (ed.), *Psychosocial Interventions for Chronic Pain in Women and Girls*, CBT: Science Into Practice, https://doi.org/10.1007/978-3-031-98876-9_6

to counselors, psychologists, or sex therapists for treatment of their mental "obsession" only to be met with another field of healthcare providers who, once again, focused on their thoughts and beliefs and behaviors around sexual satisfaction, rather than exploring an underlying physiological phenomenon (Kumpers et al., 2023). Today, even providers willing to discuss PGAD as a medical concern often leave patients with less than satisfactory answers and treatments (Kapuśniak & Piegza, 2022; Magana et al., 2024). The majority of both medical healthcare providers and mental health clinicians lack the education and skills necessary to adequately assess and treat PGAD and the underlying associated conditions (Martín-Vivar et al., 2022). This chapter will provide an overview of the physiology related to PGAD's epidemiology and maintenance, as well as the psychological interventions necessary for effective and sustainable treatment. Furthermore, the case study will demonstrate how to take healing beyond the elimination of symptoms to the creation of pleasure, satisfaction, and connection with self and partner(s).

The Trauma of Misdiagnosis

Patients navigating symptoms of PGAD report feeling lost at sea, with nowhere to turn and nowhere to go for an accurate assessment, understanding, diagnosis, and treatment plan. Due to a lack of education, in addition to the miseducation, around sexual health and pelvic pain within the curricula of healthcare providers, pathologizing physical pain as a mental health problem is often the result (Castellanos et al., 2024; Lamvu et al., 2021; Orlando et al., 2021). This experience of medical gaslighting—blaming the patient's mental and emotional status for their physical symptoms, rather than searching for the cause of the physical symptoms—adds to the trauma and upregulation of both the central nervous system and autonomic nervous system (ANS) (Milspaw, 2022; Pease et al., 2022). The maze of confusion amongst providers and patients alike around the symptoms of PGAD results in a delay in diagnosis, which serves only to intensify the underlying problem based in the neuro-muscular system (Lamvu et al., 2018).

Upregulation of the ANS is directly correlated with the activation of the vagus nerve and its role in the ANS's fight/flight response (Hutton et al., 2022; Milspaw, 2022). The vagus nerve is the tenth cranial nerve, which controls all organ functions, including immune function and the inflammatory response. It is responsible for everything in the body that is on "autopilot," such as digestion, sweat glands, heart rate, blood pressure, pupil dilation, and respiration. There are two main phases of the ANS: sympathetic ("fight-flight-freeze-faint") and parasympathetic ("rest-digest-heal"). When the sympathetic phase of the ANS is triggered, the vagus nerve, which is rooted in the pelvic floor muscles, creates muscle tension and spasm in the pelvic floor as well as increases the visceral nerve sensitivity throughout the pelvis and genital region (Lamvu et al., 2018). Due to the location of this increase in sensitivity and reactivity in the genital region, the sensory-motor cortex in the brain is receiving similar signals that are involved in genital stimulation and consequential perception of sexual arousal. Therefore, the patient is experiencing spontaneous, nonconsensual genital arousal due to the upregulation of the ANS and consequential sensitivity and reactivity of the neuromuscular structures in the pelvis and genital region (Klifto & Dellon, 2020). This creates extreme confusion and anxiety in the patient, which unfortunately, serves only to increase the cyclical nature of the physical experience.

Therefore, it is necessary to recognize the difference between someone with a cognitive-based hypersexual focus versus someone with a physical-based hypersensitive neuromuscular system whose symptoms are manifesting in the pelvic floor and genital region of the body. A key feature of the diagnostic criteria and the experience of patients with PGAD is the urge to satisfy the arousal through sex or masturbation with the hope, and sometimes the experience, of a temporary relief in symptoms, such as the relaxation of the muscles due to the expression of oxytocin in the brain during orgasm (Pease et al., 2022). While this has been reported by patients experiencing PGAD as a helpful coping skill in the beginning, the duration of relief shrinks quickly, and the experience of pain both before, during, and after orgasm increases. The pain is also mixed with feelings of shame around their attempts to decrease the arousal through orgasm (Pease et al., 2022). Furthermore, patients with PGAD report feeling violated by their own bodies due to the nonconsensual nature of the arousal experience. This, of course, is amplified in patients with a history of sexual abuse and assault.

Consequently, it is necessary for healthcare providers to have a full understanding of the epidemiology of hypersensitivity within the pelvic and genital region of the body so they can adequately assess the underlying causes of PGAD symptoms and provide effective and sustainable treatment approaches for the patient.

The Biology of Hypersensitivity: It Is All Connected

Hypersensitivity, also known as central sensitization, is an increase in neuromuscular reactivity and the brain's perception of these incoming signals (Moseley et al., 2024; Lamvu et al., 2021). It is a physiological manifestation resulting from trauma, pain, chronic stress, and systemic inflammation (Moseley et al., 2024; Lamvu et al., 2021). The quantity and frequency of nociception (the perception of pain, resulting from information sent to the brain through the nervous system), mixed with the brain's perception of threat or danger of those signals equals the intensity of the brain's reaction within the nervous system (Moseley et al., 2024; Moseley, 2003). This is why the experience of pain is actually an output of the brain, not an input. The source location of these signals, and the brain's perception and memory of the importance of that part of the body, the survival risk of that part of the body, the memory of past experiences in that location, and what the neuromatrix of knowledge our brain has "downloaded" from education and experience about that part of the body (and therefore what is "normal and safe" versus "not normal and dangerous") all play a role in the reaction to the incoming signals from the body (Moseley et al., 2024; Moseley, 2003). This process happens outside of conscious awareness and explains why someone with a severe injury may lack awareness of it if their brain is focused on something more important. On the opposite side of the spectrum, someone can experience extreme pain if they perceive they have had a grave injury, even if there has been no actual tissue damage (Moseley et al., 2024; Moseley, 2003).

The Vagus Nerve

Polyvagal Theory (Porges, 2022) brings attention to the role of the vagus nerve in trauma and trauma release therapies. The vagus nerve plays an important role in the expression and management of emotions, particularly fear. When the mind is triggered into an arousal state, the body is alerted through stored connections, and this information is relayed by the vagus nerve (Porges, 2022; Pohl & Ketcham, 2015). The vagus nerve is also the connection between the genitals and the brain. When the nerves in the pelvis are inflamed and agitated, the local muscles and ligaments react with muscle tension and spasm (Klifto & Dellon, 2020). Chronically, this leads to pelvic floor dysfunction (PFD), which is when the pelvic floor muscles are in a chronic hypertonic state and are unable to relax without interventional treatment approaches (Lamvu et al., 2018; Laycock & Jerwood, 2001). It is important to note, again, that the vagus nerve, which is the main nerve involved in the ANS, is rooted in the pelvic floor muscles (Klifto & Dellon, 2020). Consequently, when the pelvic floor muscles are in a hypertonic state, this triggers reactivity of the vagus nerve, which in turn engages the sympathetic state of the ANS and creates the subjective experience of anxiety. Furthermore, any nerves that navigate through or in proximity to these muscles and pelvic organs can begin to fire and send signals to the brain, which can confuse and overwhelm the brain. This causes an inaccurate perception of danger and the location of the potential danger within the brain. This is demonstrated when a patient reports "radiating" or "moving" sensations, and sometimes a "cascade" of symptoms such as the combination of urinary urgency, genital burning and arousal, abdominal cramping, and the feeling of hard stool in their rectum. Due to ANS and vagus nerve involvement, it is common for a patient with PGAD to experience symptoms in multiple genitopelvic areas, including the gastrointestinal system, the bladder, and reproductive organs (Merwin & Brotto, 2023).

Comprehensive Assessment

The main assessment tools to utilize for a comprehensive assessment for patients navigating symptoms of PGAD include a comprehensive questionnaire, such as the International Pelvic Pain Society (IPPS) Pelvic Pain Questionnaire, which is available to members only (www.pelvicpain.org), and the 4-D Wheel of Sexual

Experience (Ogden, 2018). Additional questions to ask will also be provided to add to the comprehensive assessment.

The IPPS Pelvic Pain Questionnaire

The IPPS Pelvic Pain Questionnaire provides an array of quantitative and qualitative questions that span all the major ingredients for the development and sustainability of PGAD. This includes exploring all areas of the patient's experience with pain, all symptoms related to their pelvic organ systems (gastrointestinal, bladder, reproductive organs), and the patient's perception of their pain experience and how it affects their mood and quality of life. The questionnaire invites the patient to make a timeline of the onset of their symptoms, their medical surgeries and interventions (i.e., injections, medication, physical therapy), and when their pain began to spread or increase. As you review the answers to the questionnaire with your patient, you can guide the patient on how it is all connected within their anatomy and physiology, especially if you place the development of their symptoms and their past physical injuries or surgeries on a timeline. When placed on a timeline, both provider and patient can see the build-up of stress and trauma and consequential upregulation of the nervous system over time.

Additional questions to ask:

- Do you experience sensations of arousal with a full bladder?
- Do you have frequent urination? Do you experience pain or urgency with a full bladder sensation?
- Do you experience painful or uncomfortable sensations with arousal? Orgasm? After orgasm?
- Do you strain with passing bowels? Do you have a history of hemorrhoids?
- Do you masturbate in an effort to relieve the PGAD symptoms? If so, how long do you masturbate? Does it help? (NOTE: The longer the masturbation practice, the more intense the pelvic floor muscle spasms will become and the more sensitive the visceral nerves will become. If they report a practice of longer duration masturbation—longer than 20 min, such as in the practice of "edging" (Gillman & Gillman, 2019)—prior to the PGAD symptoms, it is important to educate the client on how prolonged arousal and pelvic floor tension can lead to PFD and PGAD symptoms.

If they answered yes to any or all of the above additional questions, refer them to a pelvic floor physical therapist for further evaluation of the pelvic floor muscles. These muscles, which are like three bowls inside of each other that hold the pelvic organs, can become hypertonic and tense, resulting in these symptoms and are a main variable in CPP, including PGAD (Castellanos et al., 2024).

The 4-D Wheel of Sexual Experience

The 4-D Wheel of Sexual Experience was created by Gina Ogden, PhD. The Four-Dimensional Wheel approach to body, mind, heart, and spirit is an embodied practice. It springs from spiritual principles that honor all people, all diversity, all life. It is grounded in systems theory and sex survey research and has been developed through decades of clinical practice. Its healing effects are affirmed by findings of contemporary neuroscience (Ogden, 2018). Unfortunately, clinical research does not yet exist on applying the 4-D Wheel specifically to clients with PGAD. Therefore, the visual map of Dr. Ogden's approach will be described as it provides a map for psychoeducation of PGAD as well as for assessing the client's biopsychosocial variables around PGAD. As such, the 4-D Wheel of Sexual Experience looks like a circle divided into four quadrants: mind, body, heart, and spirit. At the center of the circle is a space of "integration" and represents when a client's perspective shifts based on their increased awareness of how "it's all connected." The case study below will provide examples.

Mind

The mind quadrant stands for the mental story, the mental narrative, aka "the monkey mind." Questions to explore in this quadrant include: What are your thoughts? What are your beliefs? What do you know? What don't you know? What's happening in your mind? What thoughts or beliefs do you wish you experienced less or more?

Body

The body quadrant is the physical story, the physical sensations, the physical experiences. Questions in this quadrant include: Where do you sense pain, tension, or resistance? Where do you sense pleasure, relaxation, flow? Where is their function? Where is their dysfunction? When you're thinking a specific thought, where do you feel your body reacting? For example, do you feel your throat contract? Do you feel a ball of anxiety in your chest? Do you feel your stomach turn? You feel your emotions through physical sensations. *Note:* Trauma teaches the body to shut down emotional responses that feel overwhelming and unsafe, and so the body tries to release this energy through physical manifestations.

Heart

The heart quadrant is the emotional story. Inviting your client into this quadrant may sound like this: "notice all of the emotions that feel present for you. Emotions are e-motions = energy in motion. All emotions are energetic or nervous system responses (electromagnetic frequencies that can be measured) to your thoughts and surroundings. What's your emotional story? What emotions are you feeling?" You can even invite your client to stand in both the body and the heart at the same time, as emotions are commonly felt physically in the body. They can lean back and forth towards the quadrant they are speaking from to identify the sensation and the emotion that occur at the same time. This not only incorporates bilateral stimulation through swaying, but also provides an opening to becoming an observer of their experience, as is trained in the techniques of Mindfulness-Based Cognitive Therapy, which will be discussed later. You can do this with any of the quadrants.

Spirit
Introduce this quadrant to your client by stating: "the spirit quadrant is the experience of connection and disconnection. This is the quadrant of all relationships and whether you feel connected or disconnected to yourself, your partner(s), your friends, your social life, your family, and to a higher power, depending on your belief system." Pain is a common trigger for existential crises, depending on your cultural, ethnic, and religious backgrounds. (See *The Pain Chronicles* by Melanie Thernstrom for a more detailed review of historical and religious teachings on the meaning of pain.) "The spirit quadrant is where you explore your relationships, memories, and interactive experiences. The spirit quadrant is where you can identify feeling grounded or feeling dissociated." Questions to include in this quadrant may be: What memories or relationships come to mind as you pay attention to your physical sensations? What memories or relationships come to mind as you tune into your thoughts and beliefs about those sensations? What memories or relationships come to mind when you imagine being free of the uncomfortable sensations—when you're feeling calm and safe?

Center
The center of the 4-D Wheel is the space to acknowledge the moments of insight, shifts in perspectives, and increased awareness the client has about their story and the interconnectedness of their thoughts, sensations, emotions, memories, and relationships. This is the "ah-ha" quadrant when the client realizes "it's all connected." Often, when a client reaches this moment, they enter a deeper level of awareness and other layers of their experience and story are revealed. Encourage them to continue walking the 4-D Wheel or exploring each quadrant on their own between sessions, such as through journaling or listening to the recorded guided process available via "Guided Meditations for 4-D Healing" by Dr. Alexandra Milspaw.

Psychological Interventions

Calming the nervous system and balancing the brain activity for optimal well-being is not a linear process. It is important to help the patient understand that they will practice more of a pendulation process between the sympathetic and parasympathetic state of the ANS. Safety is the ultimate priority before, during, and after every intervention. Likewise, calming and balancing the brain activity must be done in a systematic, step-wise process so as not to "shock the system." For example, when the nervous system has been upregulated for a prolonged time (more than 3 weeks) and therefore the brain activity has been imbalanced during that time, the nervous system can experience an abreaction to calming the system too quickly. The therapist should only guide the client through the technique when the client reports feeling a sense of trust in the intervention's ability to establish a sense of safety and feeling grounded. Therefore, therapists should describe and demonstrate each technique during the session before asking their client to participate, being sure to answer any questions about the technique prior to practice. Examples on how to do this are offered within each section. As always, establish a word or signal to allow the client to stop the technique at any time.

Case Study: Background and Review of the IPPS Pelvic Pain Questionnaire

Before meeting with the client, review their questionnaire so you can be prepared with the basic background of their medical, social, and emotional status, as well as read their written statements on how the pain is affecting them today. During the first session, go through the questionnaire with them, asking any questions you may have about their answers, or clarifying anything they chose not to answer. You also want to gain an idea of the timeline and duration of past medical and psychological treatments and how these overlap with their social, family, work, and other life events. You can create a visual timeline of major life events and the onset of symptoms, as well as build on the image demonstrated in Fig. 6.1. This allows for a fluid process of both reviewing the client's history and providing pain science education. Below is a summary of what the client wrote in her IPPS Pelvic Pain Questionnaire.

Case study: Veronica is a 27-year-old cisgender female referred by her pelvic floor physical therapist (PT) for the treatment of her anxiety and panic attacks, which the PT believes is a contributing variable to her PGAD. Veronica is currently diagnosed by the PT with PFD, and holds the medical diagnoses of vulvodynia, PGAD, migraines, and irritable bowel syndrome (IBS), constipation dominant. Upon review of her IPPS pelvic pain questionnaire, Veronica reports experiencing constipation since middle school and reports that the vulvodynia started in college. Her PGAD symptoms started 18 months ago. Her pelvic pain questionnaire also demonstrates a Pelvic Pain Urgency and Frequency (PUF) Symptom Scale score of 21, demonstrating symptoms of Painful Bladder Syndrome, which causes urgency, frequency, and pain with a full bladder (Parsons et al., 2002). Veronica reports

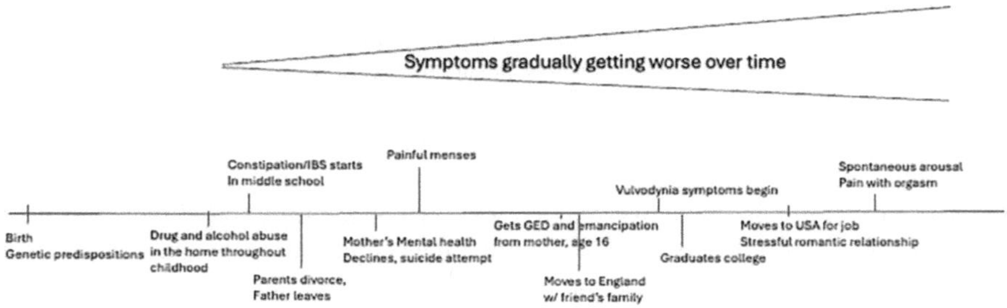

Fig. 6.1 An example of Veronica's timeline after reviewing her questionnaire

needing to void 2–3 times per hour or more, depending on her pain and stress level. She also notes painful periods since the beginning of menses at age 12. She reports low quality of life in every area and scores 28 on the Beck Depression Inventory, which is borderline for severe depression (Beck et al., 1961, 1988).

Veronica reports counseling in college but states it "did nothing," and she found running and intensive exercise to be more beneficial in managing stress. She states she made this appointment as a "last resort but doesn't believe it's going to help her." Veronica denies a trauma history, but notes her last sexual relationship was "stressful." Her history also notes that she moved to a different continent when she was 16 years old, lived there through college, then moved to the United States when she was 24 years old. She has been residing in a major city where she found employment since that time. Upon initial consultation, she reports that when she moved at age 16, she did so without parental accompaniment, claiming she had lived independently since the age of 15. She works remotely and reports enjoying her job, which includes sitting long hours in front of her computer. She reports working with people around the world, so her hours vary greatly and sometimes require her to be awake in the middle of the night for meetings. She reports having several panic attacks daily, which are brought on by the intensity of the PGAD symptoms, which she says can last for hours. Veronica states that in the beginning, she found masturbation and orgasm helpful in giving her relief for 4–6 h, but that time of relief slowly decreased. She now reports persistent burning pain with arousal, which intensifies after orgasm.

She reports she is "desperate" for relief and has contemplated suicide because "many doctors" told her this was a permanent condition, and she would have to "learn to live with it." She also reports being told by physicians to "have a glass of wine" and "try to relax and enjoy life." She was once told by her gynecologist that she was "lucky to experience arousal and orgasm so easily" and "maybe she should talk to someone about her hypersexuality." Veronica reports it being increasingly difficult to concentrate on her work, and she is currently on probation at work due to her submitting reports late and needing to take off for doctor appointments. She reports being afraid to lose her job due to her high financial needs and living in the big city, and not having any family or other outside financial support. She is currently living alone and has tried living with roommates but found it challenging to cohabitate with someone due to her "need to be in a quiet space" to manage her pain and migraines.

She reports trying meditation and breathing exercises, but "attention to her body increases her anxiety and PGAD symptoms." Due to exercise increasing her symptoms, she now watches hours of Netflix and scrolls social media to distract herself. Her current medications are diazepam (5 mg) and baclofen (muscle relaxant) suppositories at night, three 1 mg lorazepam daily, gabapentin 1800 mg, and duloxetine 120 mg. She reports being on this medication for 15 months. She reports finding the meditation helpful at first, and now "feels like it does nothing."

Figure 6.1 demonstrates how Veronica's timeline may look at the end of reviewing her questionnaire. This is important to utilize during the pain science education portion of your first session.

Education in Pain Science and Fear Avoidance Model

Pain science education is the first step when treating any chronic pain or chronic illness. The more a patient understands how the mind and body are connected and the physiological processes that are involved in their experience, the more the "mystery" is decreased. Consequently, the fear of their sensory experience decreases, which serves to decrease pain (Moseley et al., 2024). You cannot treat pain without treating the fear that goes with it. Therefore, a clinician can also present the client with the Fear Avoidance Model of PGAD, as it helps make sense of her increase in symptoms that parallels the increase in her fear of the symptoms over time (Dewitte & Meulders, 2023; Merwin & Brotto, 2023).

It is ideal to provide this education during the assessment process, as described above. Highlight for the patient the importance of helping the brain perceive the incoming stimuli from the body as a "baby lion instead of a big scary daddy lion" (Milspaw, 2022). This is accomplished through teaching clients about their bodies and how pain is processed in the brain. Begin by drawing a simple picture of the brain and spinal cord. Draw "red flags" in the brain, which include emotions, experiences, beliefs, and thoughts about the physical sensations. Next, draw circles where the body would be, and inside each circle, note all the incoming stimuli that are sending signals up the spine. Next, draw arrows from the circles up the spine to the brain, and from the red flags down to the body. This visually demonstrates the cycle of pain and fear and sensory reactivity (Fig. 6.2), which will parallel smoothly

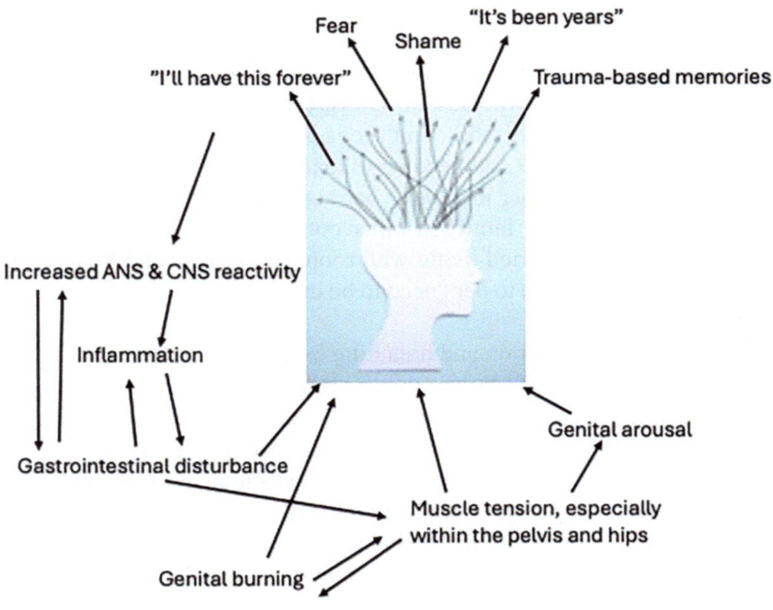

Fig. 6.2 Example of the cycle between the brain/mind and the body

with the clinical diagram of the Fear Avoidance Model for PGAD. Utilize the details in their IPPS Pelvic Pain Questionnaire to personalize the drawing, identifying their history, symptoms, and their beliefs about their experience. Personalizing the drawings helps the client make sense of the theoretical models behind pain and fear. Be sure to emphasize how the duration of this cycle changes the hardware of the brain, which in turn serves to both create and amplify the neural habit of this process. This basic understanding will serve as the foundation from which to explain the following interventions as to the how and why they will be useful in downregulating their nervous systems, reprogramming their brain, and creating a healing environment for the body.

By the end of the first session, the provider will have reviewed in detail the client's history, utilizing the Pelvic Pain Questionnaire, and provided two drawings: (1) the cycle shown in Fig. 6.1 as it demonstrates how her body triggers her mind and how her mind triggers her body, and (2) the timeline of her life experiences and the onset, and crescendo, of her physical symptoms as shown in Fig. 6.2. Combined, this allows the client to walk away with the understanding of how the body holds on to stress and trauma and the importance of providing a multidisciplinary, simultaneous treatment plan that addresses her mind and body. Furthermore, this is the first step in providing them a tool to utilize for the training you will guide them through in Mindfulness-Based Cognitive Therapy (MBCT; Segal et al., 2002), as this image reminds them to be the observer of this cycle within their physical, mental, and emotional self.

Case study: After Veronica's first session, which also included a visual walk-through of her anatomy, including organs, muscles, and nerves, she reported feeling, "heard for the first time. Someone actually listened to my whole story and put the pieces of my life's jigsaw puzzle together. It all finally makes sense."

Mindfulness-Based Cognitive Therapy

MBCT combines the best of both worlds between cognitive behavioral therapy (CBT) and Mindfulness-Based Stress Reduction (MBSR; Kabat-Zinn & Hanh, 2009). In fact, when MBSR is added to CBT practices, relapse rates significantly decrease at the six-month follow-up (MacKenzie, et al. 2018). Merwin and Brotto (2023) examined the efficacy of combining Mindfulness with CBT for a female suffering from PGAD. They reported significant decreases in rumination and helplessness as well as an improvement in quality of social interactions when combined with education on pain science and the Fear Avoidance Model (Merwin & Brotto, 2023).

As will be discussed below in regard to utilizing bilateral stimulation music, mindfulness techniques are best introduced to chronic pain and PGAD clients in a slow, systematic way, as introducing the client to body-awareness exercises prior to the establishment of trust with the clinician and trust with an emotional regulation exercise can lead to adverse reactions. The client may benefit more from *active*-based MBSR practices before beginning more *meditation*-based MBSR. Active-based MBSR techniques include mindful eating, mindful movement, and other *actions* that can be done in a mindful way, requiring the client's attention in the present moment and practicing being the compassionate observer of their experience. Meditation-based MBSR techniques include listening to guided meditations, such as breath awareness, body scans, or visualizations. Explaining the difference between these two types of MBSR techniques with PGAD and chronic pelvic pain clients is important because if they "tried mindfulness" in the past, it most likely was too much too fast, which commonly leads this population to conclude "it doesn't work" or "it makes things worse."

Utilizing the 4-D Wheel of Sexual Experience offers an ideal tool to apply MBCT and active-based MBSR techniques, while at the same time gathering more information to apply to the pain science education and Fear Avoidance Model. As you guide the client through the following process, ask them if they wish to take notes during the process, or if you may take notes for them.

Walk the Wheel

You can have the client hold an image of the 4-D Wheel, which is a circle with the four quadrants, or you can place the image on the floor and invite the client to walk around the 4-D Wheel. This can be done in either an in-person or virtual telehealth session. The more the client moves and involves their body, the more they have an opportunity to embody this experience, which can lead to a deeper sense of exploration and understanding (Biondo, 2023). If the client is open to walking around the image of the 4-D Wheel, invite the client to stand next to the quadrant they wish to start on. Ask them to think about one of their therapeutic goals. As they focus on the aspect of that intention within that quadrant (i.e., the pain within the Body quadrant), ask any of the following questions: (1) "What else do you notice *in this moment* that's happening in your body?" (2) "What are the other sensations that you experience when you tune into what you want to release or invite in?" (3) "Do you become aware of an emotion, memory, relationship, or thought when you are focused on those sensations?" (4) "When you do, move to that quadrant and notice what you become aware of."

Continue this process for as long as the client desires or as long as time allows, noting all the connections that they may not have noticed or acknowledged in session before this exercise. Invite the client to take a moment to write down what stood out to them about that process. You can add encouragement, such as, "notice how when you walk around the 4-D Wheel, this helps you connect with and observe the various aspects of your experience (past, present, and future) you may not have noticed before. As you walk the 4-D Wheel, this helps your mind shift perspective and go deeper into your experience."

Case study: For Veronica, she chose to walk around a picture of the 4-D Wheel while being guided during a telehealth session. She chose to start in the physical quadrant. As she walked, she verbalized her observations: "(stepping into the body quadrant) When I notice the pressure, and burning, and arousal, (stepping into the heart quadrant) I feel humiliated, rageful, and terrified, (stepping into the spirit quadrant) and the past 2 years of doctor appointments and painful injections and so many medications flash through my mind like a nightmare and feeling abandoned by God, (stepping into the mind quadrant) and I'm left with the thought that this is my life and I'll be alone forever." Once she walked a few more rounds, her body began to relax, and she took a deep breath. At this time, the clinician invited her to walk the 4-D Wheel and state at least one word in each quadrant that she wants to invite into her experience. She said "(body quadrant) calm and still, (heart quadrant) free and loveable, (spirit quadrant) dreaming of a joyful, healthy future, (mind quadrant) and believing there's a path to get there." This provides an example of how many different layers can come up using the 4-D Wheel as a map to explore the client's biopsychosocial influences, as well as their treatment goals.

Bilateral Stimulation and Hemispheric Synchronization

Bilateral stimulation via eye movements, tapping, sound, or movement (swaying or walking/marching) manually engages the communication between the left and right hemispheres of the brain, as we see in the hundreds of studies on Eye-Movement Desensitization and Reprocessing (EMDR) (Scelles & Bulnes, 2021; Lancioni et al., 2021). Bilateral stimulation music is considered to be a highly valuable form of intervention for people with complex trauma, brain injuries, and other disabilities related to imbalances in brain activity, including chronic pain, anxiety, and depression (Lancioni et al., 2021). The therapist may recommend starting with music, as that is easily accessible to most clients, although any form of bilateral stimulation can be used. This type of bilateral stimulation music is only effective when listened to through headphones, as it provides different sounds in the left and right speakers.

Case study: For clients like Veronica who experience daily anxiety and panic attacks, it is critical to calm their nervous system slowly and methodically. If they relax too quickly, this can cause the "shock" or surprise to their nervous system, as mentioned earlier, due to the contrast of their experience going from intense levels of fight-or-flight to relaxed. Consequently, for someone like Veronica, they might listen to the music while doing another activity, rather than lying quietly and listening to it. Otherwise, clients may sometimes report an increase in the severity of their pain or anxiety symptoms the first time they listen to the bilateral stimulation music. As an example, they can listen to music while engaging in their pelvic floor stretches or going for a walk. Once the client reports feeling calm while listening to the music, you can recommend that they listen to it while falling asleep. The music can be especially helpful to deepen a client's level of sleep into a more restorative, peaceful sleep cycle (Kanzler et al., 2023).

Emotional Freedom Techniques

Emotional Freedom Techniques (EFT; Craig, 2011) is a meridian tapping method where you tap (or rub) specific acupressure points on the body. There are more than 250 clinical trials to date on the effects of tapping, and it is truly the new "magic wand" in the trauma healing community. EFT decreases amygdala and cortisol activity, resulting in a state of calm, which is contradictory to that of distress or trauma—a common state for those experiencing PGAD. In one study, 83 adults were randomly assigned to either an hour of EFT, a psychotherapy support group, or no treatment (Church et al., 2012). All adults had their cortisol levels tested via saliva immediately before and 30 min after the intervention. The EFT group showed a 58% decrease in anxiety and a 49% decrease in depression, with their cortisol dropping by 24%.

In a review of 51 peer-reviewed papers investigating clinical outcomes following the EFT process, there were 18 randomized controlled trials identified (Feinstein, 2012). Feinstein reported they consistently demonstrated strong effect sizes and other positive statistical results that far exceeded chance (Stapleton, 2019, p. 42). EFT has resulted in relief for some clients after a single session (Church, 2013), and often an absence of diagnosis for post-traumatic stress disorder after six hours of EFT treatment (Church et al., 2009; Geronilla et al., 2016).

The recent science on EFT demonstrates that it directly stimulates the amygdala to shift out of the fight-or-flight mode and aids in creating over 72 genetic changes. Over 72 different genes—particularly those related to trauma and fear-based experiences—are changing within 1 h of tapping (Church et al., 2018). Research demonstrates that tapping can eliminate phobias and trauma-related symptoms in as little as 30 min without any relapse, even six months later (Church et al., 2018). For example, Ortner et al. (2014) completed the first study of EFT for chronic pain patients. His study consisted of including 50 adults with chronic pain in a three-day workshop. Pain was measured using the Pain Catastrophizing Scale and the Multidimensional Pain Inventory immediately before and after treatment, and at the 1-month and 6-month follow-ups (Ortner et al., 2014). Eighty-six percent of the participants were women with an age range of 35–27 years, and their average pain rating was 8, indicating severe pain. Following treatment, the average Pain Catastrophizing Scale score decreased by 43%. These scores were maintained at both follow-ups.

This adds to the body of literature demonstrating that the body will match what you feel and what you say. As you tap on what you feel and what you are thinking, you help your brain process out the old and invite in the new. This method is the perfect tool to utilize alongside MBCT due to its focus on thoughts, beliefs, and behaviors that are undesirable and unhelpful while creating thoughts, beliefs, and behaviors that are desirable and helpful. However, while MBCT relies mostly on mental processing, willpower, motivation, and repetition, EFT provides a manual tool that directly disengages the sympathetic state of the ANS and helps shift the nervous system's fear-based reaction to those unwanted thoughts, beliefs, and behaviors, which opens the pathway for the brain to more easily create new neural connections by shifting the state of the amygdala (Church et al., 2018). When EFT is compared to the effectiveness of a more generalized CBT approach (without the mindfulness practice), research finds a significant difference in remission rates as well as the speed of improvement. In a large-scale study of 5000 patients seeking treatment for anxiety, complete remission was reported by 76% of the patients in the EFT group and 51% of the CBT group (Andrade & Feinstein, 2004). "Some improvement to complete remission was reported by 90% of the patients in the [EFT] group and 63% of the CBT group ($p < 0.0002$). Those 90% of [EFT] patients improved in an average of three sessions, compared with an average of 15 sessions for the CBT patients" (Stapleton, 2019, p. 43).

It is important to remember that any fear-based learning can only be unlearned experientially. One cannot talk themselves out of being afraid of being in pain. Rather, they must have a physical shift of the nervous system moving into the parasympathetic state for the brain to "click save" on the new thoughts, new beliefs, and new behaviors the client is seeking to obtain (Jungwon et al., 2022). This includes supporting the client's goals of neuromuscular relaxation and neutralizing the fear response to the unwanted symptoms of PGAD.

When practicing this technique with a client, you can begin by taking their subjective units of distress (SUDS) score (0–10 scale; 0 = none, 10 = maximum distress) before and after a couple of rounds of tapping through the points. The first time you guide a client through tapping, invite them to observe their thoughts, emotions, and sensations without trying to make anything happen. Encourage them to speak these observations aloud, even if they feel it is "focusing on the negative." This is called the "negative round." Notice how the SUDs score changed simply by going through the tapping points. Then, when the SUDs score is below a five (5/10), guide them through the tapping points while they state out loud the thought, feeling, or sensation they wish to experience. This is called the "positive round." Finally, end with listening and following along to a guided tapping sequence via one of the tapping sequences or apps (Ortner, 2016). Encourage the client to download and utilize the app at home daily.

Case Study: Veronica found the tapping "distracting" and initially thought that was the main point of the intervention. She found herself tapping a lot because it "calmed" her. After a few weeks of tapping daily using different scripts from the app and personalized ones created in session, she noticed it was "easier to redirect [her] thoughts away from beliefs [she] had previously ruminated on incessantly."

MBCT Exercise: Mindful Breathing Exercise

The most common form of breath work prescribed to clients with pelvic pain, PFD, and high stress in general is diaphragmatic breathing, which focuses on expanding the breath down into the abdomen and pelvic region. Unfortunately, PFD can make this challenging in how it restricts the movement of the diaphragm, and the client can report feeling more stressed trying to "perform" this specific type of breathing exercise. Do not instruct the client to "take a deep breath" because this can also trigger a performance-based stress response. Rather, encourage them to "inhale completely" or to simply "breathe in." It is also recommended that they focus on breathing out to the sides rather than down towards the pelvis. This can not only aid in rib expansion and stretching the diaphragm, but it can also distract the mind's attention away from the pelvic area.

Case study: Veronica initially found breathwork "annoying," but when mixed with tapping, she discovered it was easier to take a deeper breath and started enjoying the rhythmic circular breathing.

MBCT Exercise: Mindful Journaling

There are many approaches to the technique of journaling, such as writing the current narrative, and then rewriting the narrative in a way that feels more empowering and filled with positive potential. Another option that engages the bilateral stimulation concept by initiating activity of the left and right hemispheres of the brain in a pendulating manner is called Mindful Journaling. Below is a script for how to instruct clients to engage in Mindful Journaling:

> To begin, write the numbers 1 through 20 down the side of a sheet of paper. On the odd numbers, you're going to notice your thoughts and label them in one or a few words. Imagine you could put all the thoughts into a file folder—what would you label the folder? That's what you're writing down. Short and sweet is the goal. Sometimes it takes me to number 40 to start feeling relief, but even so, this works every time. The bilateral stimulation comes from utilizing different hemispheres of your brain for each awareness. Your right brain is for your awareness of physical sensations, and your left brain is used for your awareness of your thoughts. On the even numbers, you're going to notice a physical sensation and write it down.

It may look like this:

1. I'm doomed
2. Tense and painful neck
3. Fears and doubts
4. Tight chest
5. Self-care to-do list
6. Headache and pressure
7. Judgments and shame
8. Deeper breath
9. Loneliness
10. Tearful
11. Doctor appointments
12. Pursed lips
13. Medical healing team
14. Chest relaxed

15. It's all coming together
16. Relaxed shoulders
17. I'm going to be okay
18. Deep breath
19. Peaceful nature scenes
20. Comfort/calm/peaceful

Self-Hypnosis and the Utilization of Metaphors

In Adam Grant's book, *Think Again* (2021), he discusses the research behind the nervous system's response to unfamiliar thoughts, behaviors, perspectives, and movements. He demonstrates how offering a different perspective can create a fight/flight response in the ANS as it triggers the brain to recognize that something "different" or "strange" is happening. When working solely with CBT approaches, this can play out in clinical practice, appearing as if the client was "being difficult" or "resistant" to the treatment approach. This creates a dilemma for both clinician and client. The truth of what is happening is that the client's amygdala is being triggered by the new perspective, and their fight/flight response is taking over their brain's ability to be open to creating new neural pathways. Therefore, utilizing an approach that can slip past the brain's "guard dogs" can be especially helpful when working with clients who already have a sensitive ANS trigger. Metaphors are the answer to this dilemma. Metaphors are the back door to the subconscious mind.

Self-hypnosis offers a variety of techniques that guide clients through this process. The most simplified version is teaching the client to imagine a metaphor of their current symptoms, and then transform that image into something that represents the resolution of their problem (in this case, the PGAD symptoms), which can be referred to as the "transforming energy" technique (Milspaw, 2022). For example, if their pelvic and genital region feels like a black, hot, spiky, heavy ball that can vibrate out of control, creating intense pressure and pain, then they may want to imagine that image transforming into a still, white, soft, light, fluffy cloud gently floating in the sky. With this technique, it is important *not* to offer any leading words or images in an effort for the client to identify the most authentic, intuitive-based images that come into their mind, free of influence from the clinician's subconscious projections.

To maximize the effectiveness and sustainability of this technique, you can either record talking them through this process, guide them to audio recordings where they can listen to this process, or they can draw, paint, or color the before and after images on a piece of paper. This allows them to rehearse this image transformation daily. Examples of audio recordings are available at www.dralexmilspaw.com/books/hellodownthere/exercises.

Conclusion

PGAD is a commonly misunderstood, underrecognized, under-researched, and painful physiological experience that causes a myriad of emotional, mental, sexual, and spiritual chaos for the patient. Those navigating the involuntary, chronic sensations of arousal and associated pain, muscle spasms, nerve sensitivity, and autonomic nervous system dysregulation find it extremely difficult to find a healthcare provider in both the medical and psychological worlds who can help them. PGAD involves the autonomic nervous system, central nervous system, peripheral nerves, pelvic floor muscles, and abdominal organ systems, as well as the brain and mind's perception of subjective experience. To effectively and sustainably assess and treat PGAD, a comprehensive, multidisciplinary, simultaneous team approach is necessary.

Behavioral health treatments for PGAD include education in pain science and the fear-avoidance model, bilateral stimulation, nervous system (and emotional) regulation exercises, and MBCT. As practitioners who can spend more time with these patients, it is our ethical responsibility to provide them with the time and care they deserve to fully understand the physiology, anatomy, and holistic approach to PGAD. Utilizing the 4-D Wheel offers a map that both client and clinician can interweave these treatments with the story of the client's healing journey. Returning to the concept that "it's all connected" when the client hits a plateau or experiences resistance to treatment provides a compassionate perspective and a safe, therapeutic environment. It reminds the clinician that the best answers and best next steps are within the client—they are the expert in the room. As they walk the Wheel, the connections will reveal themselves and offer new content to address, utilizing the techniques discussed in this chapter.

The most important thing to remember about PGAD and all chronic pain and illness is that it is all connected. When in doubt, step back and look at the bigger picture. Try not to get lost in the weeds and the details of the diagnoses and individual muscles, nerves, organs, etc. Step back and remember there is a complex interplay of emotion, neural networks of thoughts and memories, and cellular memory and reactivity all happening on a greater scale that can be positively influenced by supporting the nervous system and creating a sense of safety and resourcefulness. The body knows how to heal, and healing happens faster when the mind-body feels safe and secure and can exist in a calm, restorative state.

References

Andrade, J., & Feinstein, D. (2004). Energy psychology: Theory, indications, evidence. In D. Feinstein, *Energy psychology interactive* (Appendix 199–214). Innersource.

Beck, A. T., Ward, C. H., Mendelson, M., Mock, J., & Erbaugh, J. (1961). An inventory for measuring depression. *Archives of General Psychiatry, 4*, 561–571.

Beck, A. T., Steer, R. A., & Garbin, M. G. (1988). Psychometric properties of the Beck depression inventory: Twenty-five years of evaluation. *Clinical Psychology Review, 8*(1), 77–100.

Biondo, J. (2023). Dance/movement therapy as a holistic approach to diminish health discrepancies and promote wellness for people with schizophrenia: A review of the literature. *F1000Res, 12*, 33. https://doi.org/10.12688/f1000research.127377.2

Castellanos, M. E., Carrillo, J., Green, I., Lamvu, G., & Milspaw, A. (2024). Identifying gaps in pelvic pain education: A scoping review and structured analysis of obstetrics and gynecology training milestones. *Journal of Minimally Invasive Gynecology, 31*(3), 180–192. https://doi.org/10.1016/j.jmig.2023.12.002

Church, D. (2013). Clinical EFT (Emotional Freedom Techniques) as single session therapy: Cases, research, indications, and cautions. In M. Hoyt & M. Talmon (Eds.), *Capturing the moment: Single session therapy and walk-in service*. Crown House.

Church, D., Geronilla, L., & Dinter, I. (2009). Psychological symptom change in veterans after six sessions of EFT (emotional freedom techniques): An observational study. *International Journal of Healing and Caring, 9*(1), 1–13.

Church, D., Yount, G., & Brooks, A. (2012). The effect of emotional freedom techniques on stress biochemistry: A randomized controlled trial. *Journal of Nervous and Mental Disease., 200*, 89–896.

Church, D., Stapleton, P., Yang, A., & Gallo, F. (2018). Is tapping on acupuncture points an active ingredient in emotional freedom techniques? A systematic review and meta-analysis of comparative studies. *The Journal of Nervous and Mental Disease, 206*(10), 783–789. https://doi.org/10.1097/NMD.0000000000000878

Craig, G. (2011). *The EFT manual*. Elite Books.

Dewitte, M., & Meulders, A. (2023). Fear learning in genital pain: Toward a biopsychosocial, ecologically valid research and treatment model. *Journal of Sex Research*. Advance online.

Feinstein, D. (2012). Acupoint stimulation in treating psychological disorders: Evidence of efficacy. *Review of General Psychology, 16*(4), 364–380. https://doi.org/10.1037/a0028602

Geronilla, L., Minewiser, L., Mollon, P., McWilliams, M., & Clond, M. (2016). EFT (emotional freedom techniques) remediates PTSD and psychological symptoms in veterans: A randomized controlled replication trial. *Energy Psychology, 8*, 29–41. https://doi.org/10.9769/EPJ.2016.8.2.LG

Gillman, N., & Gillman, M. (2019). Premature ejaculation: Aetiology and treatment strategies. *Med Sci (Basel), 7*(11), 102. https://doi.org/10.3390/medsci7110102

Goldstein, I., Komisaruk, B. R., Pukall, C. F., Kim, N. N., Goldstein, A. T., Goldstein, S. W., Hartzell-Cushanick, R., Kellogg-Spadt, S., Kim, C. W., Jackowich, R. A., Parish, S. J., Patterson, A., Peters, K. M., & Pfaus, J. G. (2021). International Society for the Study of women's sexual health (ISSWSH) review of epidemiology and pathophysiology, and a consensus nomenclature and process of Care for the management of persistent genital arousal disorder/genito-pelvic dysesthesia (PGAD/GPD). *The Journal of Sexual Medicine, 18*(4), 665–697. https://doi.org/10.1016/j.jsxm.2021.01.172

Grant, A. (2021). *Think again: The power of knowing what you don't know*. Ebury Publishing.

Hutton, D., Mustafa, A., Patil, S., Rathod, S., Shrikhande, G., Advincula, A., Drummond, J., Gregersen, P., Hall, J., Metz, C., Milspaw, A., Orbuch, I. K., Stahl, P., Stein, A., & Shrikhande, A. (2022). The burden of chronic pelvic pain (CPP): Costs and quality of life of women and men with CPP treated in outpatient referral centers. *PLoS One, 18*(2), e0269828. https://doi.org/10.1371/journal.pone.0269828

Jungwon Min, Nashiro, K., Yoo, H. J., Cho, C., Nasseri, P., Bachman, S. L., Porat, S., Thayer, J. F., Chang, C., Lee, T.-H., & Mather, M. (2022). Emotion downregulation targets interoceptive brain regions while emotion upregulation targets other affective brain regions. *Journal of Neuroscience, 42*(14), 2973–2985. https://doi.org/10.1523/JNEUROSCI.1865-21.2022

Kabat-Zinn, J., & Hanh, T. N. (2009). *Full catastrophe living: Using the wisdom of your body and mind to face stress, pain, and illness*. Delta.

Kanzler, S. A., Cidral-Filho, F. J., Kuerten, B., & Prediger, R. D. (2023). Effects of acoustic neurostimulation in healthy adults on symptoms of depression, anxiety, stress and sleep quality: A randomized clinical study. *Explor Neuroprot Ther., 3*, 481–496. https://doi.org/10.37349/ent.2023.00064

Kapuśniak, N. E., & Piegza, M. (2022). Persistent genital arousal disorder - The present knowledge. *Psychiatry Pol., 56*(6), 1203–1219. https://doi.org/10.12740/PP/OnlineFirst/135253

Klifto, K. M., & Dellon, A. L. (2020). Persistent genital arousal disorder: Review of pertinent peripheral nerves. *Sexual Medicine Reviews, 8*(2), 265–273. https://doi.org/10.1016/j.sxmr.2019.10.001

Kumpers, F. M. L. M., Sinke, C., Schippert, C., Kollewe, K., Korner, S., Raab, P., Meyer, B., Maschke, S., Karst, M., Sperling, C., Dalkeranidis, E., & Kruger, T. (2023). Characterization of women with persistent genital arousal disorder: The iPGAD-study. *Scientific Reports, 13*, 22814. ISSN 2045-2322 (online). https://doi.org/10.1038/s41598-023-48790-2

Lamvu, G., Carrillo, J., Witzeman, K., & Alappattu, M. (2018). Musculoskeletal considerations in female patients with chronic pelvic pain. *Seminars in Reproductive Medicine, 36*(2), 107–115. https://doi.org/10.1055/s-0038-1676085

Lamvu, G., Carrillo, J., Ouyang, C., & Rapkin, A. (2021). Chronic pelvic pain in women: A review. *Journal of the American Medical Association, 325*(23), 2381–2391. https://doi.org/10.1001/jama.2021.2631

Lancioni, G. E., Singh, N. N., O'Reilly, M. F., Sigafoos, J., & Desideri, L. (2021). Music stimulation for people with disorders of consciousness: A scoping review. *Brain Sciences, 11*(7), 858. https://doi.org/10.3390/brainsci11070858

Laycock, J., & Jerwood, D. (2001). Pelvic floor muscle assessment: The PERFECT scheme. *Physiotherapy, 87*(12), 631–642. https://doi.org/10.1016/S0031-9406(05)61108-X

MacKenzie, M. B., Abbott, K. A., & Kocovski, N. L. (2018 Jun). Mindfulness-based cognitive therapy in patients with depression: Current perspectives. *Neuropsychiatric Disease and Treatment, 18*(14), 1599–1605. https://doi.org/10.2147/NDT.S160761

Magana, K., Howard, H., Fitzgerald, K., Hemmerich, C., Babb, C., & Vassar, M. (2024). Treatment in persistent genital arousal disorder: A scoping review. *Proc (Bayl Univ Med Cent)., 37*(6), 970–975. https://doi.org/10.1080/08998280.2024.2402159

Martín-Vivar, M., Villena-Moya, A., Mestre-Bach, G., Hurtado-Murillo, F., & Chiclana-Actis, C. (2022). Treatments for persistent genital arousal disorder in women: A scoping review. *The Journal of Sexual Medicine, 19*(6), 961–974. https://doi.org/10.1016/j.jsxm.2022.03.220

Merwin, K. E., & Brotto, L. A. (2023). Psychological treatment of persistent genital arousal disorder/genitopelvic dysesthesia using an integrative approach. *Archives of Sexual Behavior, 52*(5), 2249–2260. https://doi.org/10.1007/s10508-023-02617-3

Milspaw, A. (2022). *Hello down there: A guide to healing chronic pelvic and sexual pain*. Bright Communications Publishing.

Moseley, G. L. (2003). A pain neuromatrix approach to patients with chronic pain. *Manual Therapy, 8*(3), 130–140. https://doi.org/10.1016/s1356-689x(03)00051-1

Moseley, G. L., Leake, H., Beetsma, A., Palermo, T., Meeus, M., Watson, J., Butler, D., van der Mee, A., Stinson, J., Harvie, D., & Ryan, C. (2024). Teaching patients about pain: The emergency of pain science education, its learning frameworks and delivery strategies. *The Journal of Pain, 25*(5). https://doi.org/10.1016/j.jpain.2023.11.008

Ogden, G. (2018). *Expanding the practice of sex therapy: The neuro* (update ed.). Routledge.

Orlando, M. S., Moulder, J. K., Carrillo, J. F., Carey, E. T., Findley, A. D., Atashroo, D., & Dassel, M. (2021). Chronic pelvic pain educational experience among minimally invasive gynecologic surgery fellows and recent graduates: A needs assessment. *Journal of Minimally Invasive Gynecology, 28*(11), 1903–1911. https://doi.org/10.1016/j.jmig.2021.04.021

Ortner, N. (2016). *The tapping solution for pain relief: A step-by-step guide to reducing and eliminating chronic pain*. Hay House.

Ortner, N., Palmer-Hoffman, J., & Clond, M. A. (2014). Effects of emotional freedom techniques (EFT) on the reduction of chronic pain in adults: A pilot study. *Energy Psychology: Theory, Research, and Treatment, 6*(2), 14–21. https://doi.org/10.9769/EPJ.2014.6.2.NO

Parsons, C. L., Dell, J., Stanford, E. J., Bullen, M., Kahn, B. S., Waxell, T., & Koziol, J. A. (2002). Increased prevalence of interstitial cystitis: Previously unrecognized urologic and gynecologic cases identified using a new symptom questionnaire and intravesical potassium sensitivity. *Urology, 60*(4), 573–578. https://doi.org/10.1016/s0090-4295(02)01829-0

Pease, E. R., Ziegelmann, M., Vencill, J. A., Kok, S. N., Collins, C. S., & Betcher, H. K. (2022). Persistent genital arousal disorder (PGAD): A clinical review and case series in support of multidisciplinary management. *Sex Med Rev., 10*(1), 53–70. https://doi.org/10.1016/j.sxmr.2021.05.001

Pohl, M., & Ketcham, K. (2015). *The pain antidote: The proven program to help you stop suffering from chronic pain, avoid addiction to painkillers, and reclaim your life*. Hachette Books.

Porges, S. W. (2022). Polyvagal theory: A science of safety. *Frontiers in Integrative Neuroscience, 16*, 871227. https://doi.org/10.3389/fnint.2022.871227

Scelles, C., & Bulnes, L. C. (2021). EMDR as treatment option for conditions other than PTSD: A systematic review. *Frontiers in Psychology, 12*, 644369. https://doi.org/10.3389/fpsyg.2021.644369

Segal, Z. V., Williams, J. M. G., & Teasdale, J. D. (2002). *Mindfulness-based cognitive therapy for depression: A new approach to preventing relapse*. Guilford Press.

Stapleton, P. (2019). *The science behind tapping: A proven stress management technique for the mind and body*. Hay House.

Thernstrom, M. (2010). *The pain chronicles*. Farrer, Straus, and Giroux.

van Tuijl, P., Tamminga, A., Meerkerk, G. J., Verboon, P., Leontjevas, R., & van Lankveld, J. (2020). Three diagnoses for problematic hypersexuality; which criteria predict help-seeking behavior? *International Journal of Environmental Research and Public Health, 17*(18), 6907. https://doi.org/10.3390/ijerph17186907

Chapter 7
A Mind-Body Approach for the Treatment of Dysmenorrhea

Laura C. Seidman and Laura A. Payne

Dysmenorrhea is defined as pain occurring during menstruation and is categorized as either primary (i.e., pain occurring in the absence of identified pelvic pathology) or secondary (i.e., attributed to the presence of medical conditions such as endometriosis, adenomyosis, uterine fibroids, etc.). Dysmenorrhea is the most common gynecological complaint among reproductive-age girls and women, with prevalence estimates ranging anywhere from 45 to 95% (Iacovides et al., 2015). Around a quarter of reproductive-age girls and women experience moderate to severe pain, which can have a significant impact on quality of life and productivity (Armour et al., 2019).

Current treatment approaches for dysmenorrhea include both pharmacological and non-pharmacological options. Despite being first-line treatments for dysmenorrhea that are generally considered safe and efficacious, non-steroidal anti-inflammatory drugs (NSAIDs) and hormonal contraceptives are ineffective for a small but substantial portion—about 20%—of the population (Oladosu et al., 2018; Owen, 1984; Schroll et al., 2023). Even women who demonstrate a response to NSAIDs may still have substantial residual pain (Iacovides et al., 2014). Furthermore, both NSAIDs and hormonal treatments often have side effects and carry a risk of adverse events; hormonal contraception is also undesirable for many individuals due to personal preference/ethical reasons. Non-pharmacological approaches, such as transcranial electrical nerve stimulation (TENS; a device that uses electrical impulses to stimulate sensory and motor nerves, triggering mechanisms of pain

L. C. Seidman (✉)
McLean Hospital, Belmont, MA, USA
e-mail: LCSeidman@mclean.harvard.edu

L. A. Payne
McLean Hospital, Belmont, MA, USA

Department of Psychiatry, Harvard Medical School, Boston, MA, USA
e-mail: LPayne@mclean.harvard.edu

L. A. Payne (ed.), *Psychosocial Interventions for Chronic Pain in Women and Girls*, CBT: Science Into Practice, https://doi.org/10.1007/978-3-031-98876-9_7

relief), acupuncture and acupressure, herbal supplements, hypnotherapy, etc., are commonly used to treat dysmenorrhea, though evidence for their efficacy is mixed.

There is also some support for behavioral and psychological approaches for treating dysmenorrhea. A recent systematic review of exercise for primary dysmenorrhea (PD) evaluated studies using both low- and high-intensity exercise regimens and found that exercise had a significant effect in reducing menstrual pain intensity and duration in the treatment groups compared to control groups at a level that was deemed likely to be clinically meaningful (Matthewman et al., 2018). Results held for both low- and high-intensity regimens, which may increase the appeal of exercise interventions to a wider population of individuals with PD. Acupuncture (stimulating specific body points using needles) and acupressure (stimulating specific body points using pressure) have also emerged as potentially promising interventions for dysmenorrhea, though additional research is needed. A recent review found significant effects of acupuncture on pain and response rates (i.e., likelihood of an individual in the treatment group responding to the treatment as compared to those in the control group) for individuals with endometriosis-associated dysmenorrhea (Chen et al., 2024). Psychological interventions, including cognitive behavioral therapy (CBT), biofeedback, hypnosis, relaxation, pain management training, psychoeducation, and eye movement desensitization reprocessing (EMDR) also demonstrate significant reductions in menstrual pain intensity and interference (see Rogers et al., 2023 for a comprehensive review and meta-analysis). Evidence supporting each of these behavioral and psychological approaches is mixed and limited by methodological issues, though it is clear that they are effective in at least a subset of individuals.

Biopsychosocial Model of Pain Applied to Dysmenorrhea

The biopsychosocial model of pain posits that biological, psychological, and environmental factors influence the pain experience (Gatchel et al., 2007), and this model is particularly relevant for dysmenorrhea. The experience of dysmenorrhea certainly encompasses biological phenomena in the physiological process of the shedding of the uterine lining; pain in the abdomen, head, lower back, and other body parts; sleep disturbance and fatigue, but psychological and social factors are also largely involved in the condition (Gagnon et al., 2022). Psychologically, an individual with dysmenorrhea may experience mood fluctuations, distorted body image, increased concern about menstrual symptoms, and anxiety about their ability to conduct their regular daily activities when menstruating. Many have considerable worries about being prepared for upcoming periods (i.e., availability of hygiene products and pain medication) due to the unpredictable nature of menstruation. Socially, dysmenorrhea impacts relationships via its effect on intimacy, interpersonal relational disturbances caused by irritability and mood changes, stigma/taboo, and the reclusiveness that many people with dysmenorrhea report experiencing (Allyn et al., 2020). By understanding dysmenorrhea in this context, it warrants consideration of a psychosocial intervention for addressing a number of factors that contribute to this disabling condition.

Pain Catastrophizing in Dysmenorrhea

One potential mechanism that may play a significant role in dysmenorrhea is pain catastrophizing (PC). PC is a psychological factor that has been associated with a variety of chronic and acute pain experiences, including menstrual pain. PC is defined as the tendency to experience negative cognitive and emotional responses to pain (Quartana et al., 2009; Sullivan et al., 1995). Higher levels of pain catastrophizing are associated with higher levels of menstrual pain intensity both in women with PD and in those with endometriosis (Evans et al., 2022; Walsh et al., 2003), and over one third of women with PD and half of women with endometriosis show clinically relevant levels of PC (Evans et al., 2022). Young women with higher PC scores also demonstrate more affective impact of menstrual pain (e.g., descriptions of menstrual pain as "fearful," "punishing," etc.), lower perceived efficacy of pain medication, and greater disability than those with lower PC scores (Walsh et al., 2003). Notably, these analyses control for pain intensity, indicating that PC likely plays a role in dysmenorrhea-related impairment above and beyond pain intensity.

A number of interventions have been developed to specifically target PC for a variety of pain conditions. A 10-session group CBT intervention for individuals with headaches demonstrated reductions in PC and anxiety and improvements in pain management self-efficacy (Thorn et al., 2007). Even single-session interventions have demonstrated improvements in pain catastrophizing, pain intensity, interference, bothersomeness, and self-efficacy in patients with chronic low back pain (Darnall et al., 2021).

For menstrual pain specifically, Payne et al. (2020) developed a group-based intervention to target pain catastrophizing in individuals with moderate to severe dysmenorrhea. In this pilot study, small cohorts of between three and eight young adult women completed five group sessions that involved psychoeducation about pain and the menstrual cycle, mindfulness practice, de-catastrophizing skills, and coping skills. Results demonstrated a significant reduction in both menstrual pain and pain catastrophizing up to 12 months following treatment (Payne et al., 2020). The case of Lena, described below, illustrates an adaptation of this intervention for individual patients.

Case Presentation

Case Description

Lena was a 26-year-old, single, Hispanic White woman who was a graduate student at a large urban university. While generally considering herself "healthy," Lena had always experienced significant pain during menstruation, which she remembered as starting around a year or two after menarche (around age 12). Lena typically had short (1–2 min) episodes of lower abdominal pain on and off in the day or two before her period started, with intense lower abdominal and pelvic pain starting a few hours after the onset of bleeding and lasting for several days. She also reported experiencing moderate headaches beginning the day prior to menstruation onset, which continued into the first day of her period. Lena reported taking over-the-counter pain medication (usually ibuprofen) but only when she felt like she "really needed it." Usually, she would wait until the pain became very bothersome, and then she would take the medication at the recommended dose on the bottle.

Lena had mentioned her menstrual pain to her primary care physician, who had expressed that Lena's experience was typical and that there was not much that could be done apart from continuing to use NSAIDs or trying hormonal birth control. Lena reported never truly considering hormonal birth control as an option because nobody in her family had used it as a treatment for menstrual pain, and she did not like the idea of "messing with" her hormones at this life stage. Lena reported having friends and colleagues who had sought follow-up specialty care specifically for menstrual pain, but it was not a step that she had pursued yet. Lena had decided to continue with her NSAID regimen because it "took the edge off" of the pain enough to allow her to function (though at a low level), although she still experienced significant activity interference. However, she did ask her physician for a referral to a therapist to help her learn new ways of coping with menstrual pain.

Treatment Approach

Lena was referred to a therapist who had experience administering CBT for dysmenorrhea. Lena's initial meeting with the therapist included providing a background of her experiences with menstruation, menstrual pain and symptoms, and the impact of menstrual pain on her daily life, particularly on her graduate studies and her part-time work in the school's library. Lena's graduate advisor was understanding of her limitations, but Lena expressed that she struggled with accepting accommodations for days missed due to menstrual pain because she felt like it was "normal" and that others were not receiving, or in need of, similar accommodations. One aspect of her menstrual cycle that Lena found particularly challenging was its unpredictability. She reports that while her cycle was generally "regular," there could still be several days' fluctuation in length from cycle to cycle. As a result,

Lena never felt fully prepared for her period to start. Though there was a trend for how long after bleeding onset the pain would start, she did report variation in that element as well, making it hard to have a consistent approach to managing her dysmenorrhea. Furthermore, the effectiveness of pain medication varied from cycle to cycle.

Module 1: Psychoeducation and Introduction to Mindfulness (Approximately Two Sessions)

At the first session after the assessment, the therapist introduced the treatment, including its rationale, empirical evidence supporting CBT for pain conditions, and what Lena could expect from the upcoming sessions. Then the first part of Session 1 was spent providing psychoeducation on (1) the anatomy of the reproductive system; (2) how hormones change across the menstrual cycle and how those regulate menstruation; (3) dysmenorrhea, including definitions, prevalence, and potential impact; (4) the differences between primary and secondary dysmenorrhea; (5) causes of and treatments for dysmenorrhea; and (6) an introduction to how pain is experienced and processed in the body and central nervous system.

Lena reported that the information about pain processing was new to her, and she expressed surprise at the complexity of pain, thinking previously that the experience of physical pain was in direct proportion to only changes in her body. She also noted that understanding what was happening in her body, not only during menstruation but also across the entire menstrual cycle, was helpful and therapeutic in and of itself. This information allowed Lena to consider that she could change aspects of her thinking and her emotions that might help her pain.

In this first session, the therapist also identified and challenged a few common myths related to pain, especially because they are relevant to dysmenorrhea. The first myth about pain that the therapist presented to Lena was the idea that if a doctor cannot cure your pain or find out what is causing it, then the pain must be in your imagination. Lena mentioned that she had heard the phrase "it's all in your head," which the therapist affirmed as both common and unhelpful. The therapist expounded that technically, pain is "in your head" due to the role of the brain in pain processing, but this does not mean the pain is "made up" or due to some mental deficit, or means that she is "weak." Lena's therapist added that in cases of dysmenorrhea without a clearly identified cause, or for individuals who seek care for dysmenorrhea and have their problems minimized or dismissed by providers, this myth can be particularly harmful because it can isolate and discourage the individual, which in turn makes it harder for them to persist in seeking treatment. The second myth about pain covered during this session is that if you can make your pain improve by using behavioral techniques, then the pain was "all in your head" to begin with. The therapist emphasized to Lena that there is a lot of evidence supporting behavioral interventions for pain and that behavioral changes can impact many different aspects of our functioning and perception of pain. The third myth about pain is that if you look like you are doing fine, then you must be "exaggerating" or "making up" the pain. This myth is especially insidious in cases of dysmenorrhea because of the lack of outwardly observable symptoms. The therapist explained that there are numerous medical conditions, including dysmenorrhea, for which there is no definitive diagnostic test like there is for diabetes or heart disease, for example. That does not mean that pain problems without such diagnostic tests are any less real or impactful in people's lives. Lena found it helpful to challenge these myths that even she had believed were true.

After completing the psychoeducation component and answering Lena's questions, additional sessions in this module focused on an introduction to a mindfulness practice. Mindfulness is the practice of paying attention to the present moment with curiosity but without judgment and is a common component of behavioral treatments for many conditions, including pain (Ludwig & Kabat-Zinn, 2008; McClintock et al., 2019). The therapist probed Lena's experience with mindfulness, meditation, yoga, or similar practice, and Lena reported that she had gone to a few yoga classes at the gym where they did some type of breathing exercise and what she thinks was something called mindfulness, but it was not an especially salient part of the class for her, and she only ended up going a few times. She also mentioned that she has a friend who uses a meditation app, but it is not something they have discussed in depth. Other than that, she reported hearing about "mindfulness" on social media and online but did not know much about it. The therapist explained that the purpose of mindful awareness is to focus on the present moment, without getting caught in thoughts about the past or the future. The therapist emphasized that, like any skill, mindfulness skills take practice, and that Lena would be asked to practice the mindfulness exercises at home in between sessions. The therapist then proceeded to read a script of a gentle breathing meditation, guiding Lena through the exercise. After Lena had opened her eyes and was alert to the room, the therapist asked her to report on her experience, emphasizing that there is no "wrong" answer.

Therapist: What was that like for you?

Lena: I felt a little uncomfortable at first, but I ended up settling into the practice after a little while.

Therapist: What physical feelings did you notice?

Lena: The first thing I noticed was a feeling of fatigue. I had a busy shift yesterday that continued right into a long study session. Then I woke up early this morning and had classes back-to-back right before coming here. So, this is the first time in a while that I've just sat and felt how tired all of that made me. But then I also felt a sense of rest and relaxation too. Like sitting here was letting my body start the recovery process.

Therapist: Those are great observations; what about thoughts—did you notice any thoughts pop up during the practice?

Lena: Definitely, I feel like thoughts are always swirling around in my head. Most of the thoughts I noticed were related to school. I kept thinking back to a confrontation I had with a study partner recently and immediately felt bad about it, like I might've been the one who was wrong, but I'm not really sure. Then I also noticed my thoughts going to an assignment I have due next week—different ideas for how I could approach it, resources I'll need to gather, stuff like that.

Therapist: Notice how you also described having an emotional reaction to your thought about the confrontation with your study partner. You mentioned feeling bad about the interaction and having uncertainty about how you handled it. Were there any other emotions related to that thought?

Lena: Yeah, I felt disappointed in myself, that I didn't handle the situation better.

Therapist: And what about the thoughts related to your assignment, what emotions did those thoughts evoke?

Lena: Anxiety. Each time I thought about it, I realized how big a project it is and how much work will be involved, which makes me worried that I won't be able to get it all done or do it at a high quality.

Therapist: And do you feel like you were able to observe these thoughts and emotions without judgment as they occurred? What was your experience guiding yourself back to the present moment?

Lena: It was really hard, but I can see how doing it might get easier over time. The emotional part came really fast after having each thought. I guess I hadn't noticed that before, just how quickly the judgment comes into my head.

Therapist: Exactly, and that is something that we'll work on during our sessions. It takes practice, but being able to notice thoughts without assigning meaning or judgment is beneficial when it comes to approaching our pain experiences.

To close the session, the therapist provided Lena with an audio recording of the same meditation and encouraged her to do the practice a few times over the upcoming week and record her experiences on a practice form, which included places to record when and where she practiced the exercise, pain ratings before and after, and the physical sensations, thoughts, and emotions she noticed during the practice.

Module 2: Introduction to Thoughts and Interpretations (Approximately One Session)

The next session began with a review of the meditation practice form from the previous week—Lena had not gotten her period during the prior week, but she was able to do the awareness practice two times. She liked that she could play the audio file from her phone, enabling her to do the practice wherever she was. She found the practice uncomfortable at first, similar to how she felt doing it in-person at the previous session, though the second time felt more comfortable than the first. When asked if there were any obstacles to doing the mindfulness practice, Lena reported that, because of her busy schedule, she had just forgotten about it for several days.

Lena and the therapist decided that in the upcoming week, Lena could try setting a few reminders on her phone to prompt her to do the exercise.

The session then moved to the introduction of thoughts and interpretations, and cognitive reappraisal strategies to help support more balanced interpretations. First, Lena needed to begin to understand what kinds of thoughts or interpretations she makes, given that in any situation, there are many different aspects (or stimuli) that individuals can attend to or focus on. Given Lena's status as a graduate student and part-time employee at the library, her therapist used the following example: "Imagine having a conversation with your advisor where they are discussing your performance on a presentation in class or at work. During the conversation, your advisor begins by praising you for doing well on the presentation. Imagine that later in the conversation, your advisor also tells you about an aspect of your performance where you could improve. What do you think you would mostly focus on when walking away from the conversation?" Lena reported that her first instinct is that she would probably focus on the negative, even though she thinks that, in that moment, she would be able to acknowledge that her advisor had included positive aspects as well.

The therapist continued by explaining that, in addition to what aspect of the situation she focused on, there are also different ways for that aspect to be interpreted or appraised. In the example with her advisor, the therapist explained that Lena could have interpreted her advisor's pointing out areas for improvement as indicating failure. Alternatively, she could interpret this as constructive criticism or an opportunity for improvement. The therapist clarified that these types of focus are not inherently bad in all situations—they are the way our brain serves as a filter to focus on certain aspects of a situation and assign meaning to those aspects, which helps to increase the efficiency and speed with which we can respond to a given situation. But these assessments are not helpful in *all* situations. The therapist concluded this portion of the session by explaining that individuals also tend to draw on their experiences from the past to help interpret or appraise current situations and will often use these interpretations to project what might happen in the future.

Sessions in Module 2 concluded with another mindfulness practice—this time a body scan. Body scan practices are a way to notice sensations in the body (e.g., contact between the chair and the person's back, abdominal sensations caused by breathing, etc.) and approach those sensations with curiosity but without attaching emotion or judgment to the observations. Lena was encouraged to use the practice, particularly if she experienced sensations related to her upcoming period.

Module 3: Automatic Thoughts, Catastrophizing, and Pain Catastrophizing (Three Sessions)

The therapist began Module 3 by explaining that many thoughts and interpretations pass through our minds every day. As discussed in the previous session, we automatically latch onto certain ways of understanding things to help us filter our experience and respond to situations quickly and efficiently. Over time, individuals often develop a particular way or style of thinking about situations. The therapist asked Lena if she noticed that she or someone she knew tended to have a particular style of thinking. Lena mentioned that her mom often noticed and commented on flaws or problems (e.g., ill-fitting clothes, minor mistakes made by a waiter, etc.); relatively minor things, but now, on reflection, Lena realized that they represented a pattern in her mother's thinking. The therapist affirmed this experience and explained that sometimes this process can be very helpful, and sometimes it can keep us stuck so that we are not able to get new information and change the way we think about it.

The therapist next reviewed one particular style of thinking, called *catastrophizing*. Catastrophic thinking refers to the tendency to think that the worst possible outcome is going to happen, and when it does, that an individual will be unable to cope with it. The therapist emphasized to Lena that pain catastrophizing does not mean the pain is "made up" or "not real." Instead, it is a natural product of being in pain—the mind starts to think more and more negatively about the pain, which then adds the burden of suffering. The therapist explained that the goal of this treatment was to help Lena find ways of (1) trying to teach her mind to think in a more balanced way about pain, and (2) developing specific, helpful, and useful ways of coping or managing the pain so it feels more controllable.

Lena's therapist pointed out that she might notice that she sometimes judges or blames herself for her thoughts. The therapist emphasized that this is common, but that it also makes it hard to think flexibly because the more we blame ourselves, the more we try to control those thoughts, and the more rigid our thought patterns become. It is also important to practice being aware of thoughts in a non-judgmental way, and the mindfulness practice, done at the end of the session, was designed exactly for this purpose.

The therapist then explained that there are specific techniques for helping challenge and "de-catastrophize" pain thoughts.

Therapist: Let's take a look at some of your catastrophic or "worst" thoughts about pain when you have menstrual pain.

Lena: Okay, well, when I start to feel some pain in my stomach, I think this pain means my period could come today, but I have a busy day, and I don't remember if I have my medication with me. If I go un-medicated, I'm not going to be able to concentrate in class and I won't learn the information I need for the exam next week.

Therapist: One way we can create an alternate thought is to think about what we would expect based on past experiences. Based on your past experiences, what alternate thought could you apply to this situation?

Lena: Usually, my PMS symptoms last a full 2–3 days, so the likelihood of bleeding starting within a few hours is low.

Therapist: Yes, that's a great alternate thought. Another approach is to consider what we are *actually* afraid of happening. What would it happen if you weren't able to concentrate in class and didn't learn the information you needed for the exam?

Lena: I'd fail the exam and therefore end up failing the class.

Therapist: Yes, and what would that mean?

Lena: That I'm not a good student and that my family would be disappointed in me.

Therapist: Okay, good, now let's examine evidence for that fear. What evidence do you have supporting either of those thoughts—that you're not a good student or that your family would be disappointed in you if you failed a class?

Lena: In college, I got mostly As and Bs in my classes, so that's evidence that I'm a good student. I did get two Cs so that's evidence of struggling in a class, although I guess that doesn't make me a "bad" student. And my parents have been disappointed with some choices I've made in the past, but they've never been disappointed with how I do in school or with me as a person.

Therapist: Okay, and now that you've presented the evidence, let's revisit the thoughts. If you did end up failing the test and observed yourself having the thought "I'm a bad student, my parents are going to be disappointed in me," what alternate thoughts you could propose to yourself?

Lena: That I can be displeased with my performance on this one test, but that I know from past experience that I'm able to overcome it and still have the potential to do well in the class overall. And that my parents have been proud of me in the past when I do my best, and their love for me is not based on how I do in school.

Therapist: Yes, those are great alternate thoughts for that situation.

In addition to the catastrophic thoughts regarding her period starting soon, Lena was able to use and document her use of de-catastrophizing skills in a few other situations in the prior week. Lena and her therapist reviewed each automatic thought and associated emotions, and the therapist affirmed the alternative thoughts that Lena had documented and helped her generate a few additional alternative thoughts for each situation.

The therapist gave Lena a monitoring form for helping her practice de-catastrophizing pain thoughts and instructed her to take note of pain-related catastrophic thoughts she had over the coming week and come up with at least one alternative thought for each one.

Sessions in Module 3 concluded with a practice of getting used to physical sensations and discomfort. This exercise begins similarly to the body scan mentioned above by instructing the patient to notice physical sensations and breath. However, this exercise then directs the individual to notice uncomfortable sensations (an itch, the urge to move, etc.) and encourages them to observe the discomfort without acting on it. Similarly, the individual is encouraged to observe associated thoughts (e.g., "I have to scratch this itch") without acting on them. The individual is prompted to notice how these sensations come and go or change in intensity level. After repeating the process with a few other areas of discomfort, the individual is told to focus back on their breath and the exercise is ended.

Module 4: Identifying and Applying Coping Skills (Approximately Three Sessions)

The fourth module began with Lena writing down coping skills that she currently uses with some amount of regularity. The therapist then prompted Lena to think of coping skills that she had heard about either from others or from the media, but that she had not used herself. Lastly, the therapist and Lena brainstormed other possible coping skills and looked online to fill in a complete brainstorm of ideas (see Fig. 7.1 for an example, which may be used as an inspiration for prompting patients during the exercise). One important aspect of this exercise is to actually write down all of the coping skills—in addition to helping commit the skills to memory, having a written brainstorm of coping skills provides proof to confront the potential automatic thought that there is nothing that can be done to treat menstrual pain.

After creating the brainstorm, Lena was given a worksheet and worked with the therapist in-session to complete it. This worksheet is divided into three sections: things Lena could do to prevent pain from escalating, things she could do to cope with pain when it is present, and things she could do to handle the worst-case scenario. Lena started with the second section, expressing that it was the section that felt like where she would put most of her current coping skills. Into this section for coping with pain when it is present, Lena wrote taking a shower or bath, taking

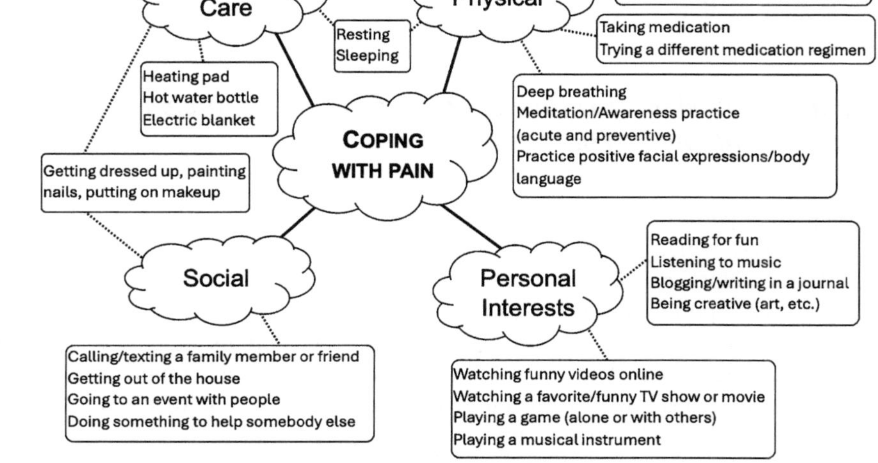

Fig. 7.1 Example of Lena's brainstorming of coping skills exercise

medication, and watching a funny video. She also added two ideas from the brainstorm that she had not previously considered: using a heating pad and taking a walk. Lena expressed that the other two sections were more difficult for her to complete—she was not sure anything could help prevent pain from escalating, and she felt like the only thing she could see herself doing in the worst-case scenario was to spiral into catastrophic thoughts and just go to bed. Lena's therapist reminded her that these are just places to start, and that she can move on if they do not end up working for her. Furthermore, the therapist affirmed that going to bed could be a valid coping skill that is part of her toolkit. When the worksheet was complete, Lena's therapist observed that none of the coping skills were present in multiple sections. She clarified with Lena that a coping skill can be applicable in two (or even three) of these sections. Lena admitted that she had not even considered that and was able to see that even her approach to coping skills lacked flexibility. Lena was given another worksheet and asked to record any coping skills she used over the coming week.

The awareness exercises for Module 4 focused on progressive muscle relaxation (PMR) skills. The therapist introduced the idea of PMR to Lena as a method where the individual learns to systematically go through major muscle groups and first tense the muscle group and then relax in order to induce the "relaxation response." This method is used in many different therapies and can help with pain, anxiety, physical symptoms, and improve sleep. The therapist emphasized to Lena that it is important during this practice to not tense muscles to the point of being in pain; rather, she should tense the muscle group for approximately 5 s—tensing hard enough to certainly feel it but taking care not to "overdo" it.

[Note: Modules 3 and 4 are presented separately but may be implemented in a more overlapping fashion toward the end of Module 3 (e.g., beginning to incorporate coping skills while continuing to conduct de-catastrophizing exercises). As sessions progress, a larger portion of each session will be spent reviewing the handouts completed during the previous week.]

Module 5: Review of Information Learned and Anticipating Future Challenges (One Session)

Lena got her period in the week before the final session and reported that she used a heating pad, which was new to her. Lena was amazed that something so simple could be so helpful and was glad that the idea had come up during the brainstorming session. She reported that in addition to the heat decreasing the pain a moderate amount, she also felt less stressed, which enabled her to think more clearly about what she needed to get done. She was also able to use de-catastrophizing skills to realize that some tasks that seemed urgent could actually wait until she was feeling better, thus further reducing her stress.

The majority of the final session was spent developing a plan for how Lena would continue the skills she had learned during treatment when she was no longer meeting with the therapist. She expressed that by then she had really incorporated de-catastrophizing skills into her regular thinking habits (including when she was in pain), but that she was nervous that she would not be able to continue the coping skills. The therapist encouraged her to think of practical ways to overcome this obstacle, and Lena decided to put the coping skills brainstorm on her bulletin board as a reminder. The therapist reviewed the other skills presented over the course of treatment and identified ways to support Lena's continued practice. Lena expressed that she felt more in control of her pain, and she hoped these tools would help her better advocate for her needs, particularly when she was experiencing pain.

Treatment Outcome

Lena completed a set of standardized questionnaires immediately before the first session and again several weeks post-treatment. Lena rated her worst pain experienced during her most recent period using a 0 (no pain) to 10 (worst pain possible) numeric rating scale (Chen et al., 2015; Dworkin et al., 2005). Before treatment, Lena reported that her typical level of menstrual pain, without medication, was a 9 out of 10. Lena completed the Dysmenorrhea Symptom Interference (DSI) Scale (Chen et al., 2021), a 9-item measure assessing the impact of menstrual pain and gastrointestinal symptoms on functioning across various domains (e.g., physical activities, social activities, sleep, etc.). Responses to the nine items are averaged for a total score ranging from 1 to 5, with higher scores indicating greater interference; Lena's pre-treatment DSI score was 3.4. Lena also rated the severity of each of a set of 14 common menstrual symptoms (e.g., bloating, nausea, diarrhea, etc.) during her most recent period (Chen et al., 2018). Each item is rated from 0 (not present) to 10 (extremely severe), and the items are summed to yield a possible range of 0–140. Lena's pre-treatment score was 47. The final questionnaire Lena completed was the Pain Catastrophizing Scale (PCS; Sullivan et al., 1995), which consists of 13 items and assesses the respondent's tendency to catastrophize when experiencing pain. Scores range from 0 to 52, with higher scores indicating higher frequency of catastrophizing; Lena's pre-treatment PCS score was 35. Lastly, Lena reported that during her most recent period before starting treatment, she had taken ibuprofen for pain relief, every 6 h for the first 2 days of her period, and once on the third day for a total of approximately 6–7 doses (12–14 pills).

At post-treatment, Lena reported that the worst pain she experienced during her most recent period was a 7 out of 10. This decrease of 2 NRS points did represent a meaningful difference from the pre-treatment score (Dworkin et al., 2008), though there remained room for improvement. Her DSI score was 2.8, which represents a modest improvement in interference caused by menstrual pain and symptoms. Her symptom score was 39 due to reductions in lower back pain, nausea, and body aches. Lena's PCS score was 9, a significant decrease from the pre-treatment value of 35. Lastly, Lena reported taking pain medication only on the first day of her most recent period (two doses for a total of 4 pills), which was a considerable reduction from pre-treatment.

Skill Use

Lena reported which of the skill groups (mindfulness, de-catastrophizing, coping skills) she had used during her most recent period and separately during the prior month when not menstruating. For each skill group endorsed, she also reported on how frequently she used that skill. Lena did not report using mindfulness during her most recent period or the prior month, but she did report at least daily use of de-catastrophizing and using coping skills multiple times a day during her most recent period. She also reported using de-catastrophizing skills 2–3 times per week during the previous month when not on her period.

One Year Later

Lena scheduled an appointment with her therapist 1 year after finishing treatment for a "check-in" about how she was doing. During this follow-up visit, Lena completed the measures described above and provided written quantitative and qualitative feedback reflecting on her use of skills over the prior 12 months, and on what she attributed any observed improvement. All of Lena's scores on the measures described above remained fairly consistent with scores at the post-treatment time point (i.e., considerably lower than pre-treatment). The worst pain during her most recent period was a 6; PCS score was 12; DSI score was 2.6; symptom total score was 40; and pain medication use during her most recent period was 4 pills (2 pills once a day for the first 2 days).

With regard to skill use, Lena reported using both de-catastrophizing and coping skills, each a few times per day, during her most recent period, and reported that their effectiveness at reducing pain and increasing functioning was an 8 out of 10. Lena also reported using de-catastrophizing skills every day and coping skills 2–3 times per week during the prior month when not menstruating. The effectiveness of these skills at increasing functioning was rated a 7. These data suggest that Lena had successfully integrated the skills she learned during the treatment into her life, which offers the possibility of long-term maintenance of treatment gains. When asked to describe in her own words what she attributed her improvements in pain and functioning to, Lena said:

> Being able to reason with myself and de-catastrophize that the pain or a particular bad feeling/thought is only temporary has helped quite a bit. I find myself still taking ibuprofen during the worst part of my period (the first day or two), but a lesser dosage. De-catastrophize has become a tool I use daily to calm myself down when I think about the worst possible scenario. While the anxiety I have is still there, actively thinking about it and combating it with logical thoughts has helped me relax quicker.

Additional Guidance for Clinicians

Although dysmenorrhea is by definition a cyclic condition, the therapist using this treatment approach should consider non-bleeding days an opportunity for the patient to practice the skills so that they will be more readily employed when needed. Furthermore, the therapist can convey to the patient (or validate if already noticed by the patient) that the relationships among pain, functioning, and cognitive work are complex and that, like other pain problems, treatment for dysmenorrhea is most effective when addressing the whole person. In light of research demonstrating that PC levels are highest at the beginning of menstruation and decrease as the cycle progresses (Cosic et al., 2013), therapists should work with patients to anticipate and plan for fluctuations in PC and other cognitive and emotional factors, which may also fluctuate across the menstrual cycle.

Group Setting

Several studies have demonstrated considerable benefits to administering CBT and other behavioral interventions in a group format (Bergeron et al., 2016; Khoo et al., 2019). The intervention described above has previously been administered as a group-based intervention, and participants reported deriving benefit from the camaraderie created during the sessions and the advantage of having multiple individuals with different viewpoints, experiences, and approaches to the exercises all contributing to the discussion (Seidman et al., 2023).

The beginning of a course of group treatment should begin similarly to the first session described above, with regard to the introduction to the rationale behind the intervention. Additionally, there are a few more treatment-specific principles that the therapist should emphasize. Specifically, due to the variety of experiences that can accompany dysmenorrhea, it is important to emphasize that group members should not compare themselves to other group members. Similarly, some exercises will be more relevant for some than for others, but there are principles to be learned with each component of the treatment. Lastly, the therapist should emphasize that the active engagement of every participant is critical to gaining the maximum benefit from the group dynamic of the intervention.

Module 1

In addition to the psychoeducational content mentioned above, the therapist can also use this time to present research on the benefits of administering this type of treatment in a group setting. One benefit of conducting the intervention in a group is that it allows for the introduction of the anonymous question exercise. This allows individuals to ask questions (about menstruation, pain, anatomy) that they may have otherwise been too embarrassed to ask. The facilitator should distribute index cards and pens to all participants and ask everyone to write at least one question. All cards are collected, and the therapist reads them aloud and answers or provides additional information as applicable.

Module 3

The therapist will ask each member of the group to share at least one item from their de-catastrophizing handouts from the prior week and will work through de-catastrophizing exercises with each member. Later in the module, group members can be partnered and work through the de-catastrophizing exercises in pairs.

Module 4

Brainstorming of coping skills is done as a group with minimal input from the therapist, apart from recording the skills mentioned. Group members are able to hear ideas from peers and to generate new ideas based on what is discussed in the group.

Conclusion

Dysmenorrhea is a common condition that results in significant life interference and societal costs. The case described in this chapter—Lena—demonstrates how implementing a mind-body intervention focusing on mindfulness, de-catastrophizing, and coping skills practice can lead to a reduction in menstrual pain and medication use and an increase in functioning. As Lena noted, the skills may be utilized both during menstruation and at other times throughout the month. By practicing skills in between periods, she felt more comfortable using them during menstruation and noticed that the skills helped her overall level of anxiety, which allowed her to approach her period differently than before. Lena's case shows that individuals not only remember the skills they learned during the treatment, but that they are able to implement them even up to a year following treatment.

References

Allyn, K., Evans, S., Seidman, L. C., & Payne, L. A. (2020). "Tomorrow, I'll be fine": Impacts and coping mechanisms in adolescents and young adults with primary dysmenorrhoea. *Journal of Advanced Nursing, 76*(10), 2637–2647. https://doi.org/10.1111/jan.14460

Armour, M., Parry, K., Manohar, N., Holmes, K., Ferfolja, T., Curry, C., MacMillan, F., & Smith, C. A. (2019). The prevalence and academic impact of dysmenorrhea in 21,573 young women: A systematic review and meta-analysis. *Journal of Women's Health (2002), 28*(8), 1161–1171. https://doi.org/10.1089/jwh.2018.7615

Bergeron, S., Khalife, S., Dupuis, M. J., & McDuff, P. (2016). A randomized clinical trial comparing group cognitive-behavioral therapy and a topical steroid for women with dyspareunia. *Journal of Consulting and Clinical Psychology, 84*(3), 259–268. https://doi.org/10.1037/ccp0000072

Chen, C. X., Kwekkeboom, K. L., & Ward, S. E. (2015). Self-report pain and symptom measures for primary dysmenorrhoea: A critical review. *European Journal of Pain, 19*(3), 377–391. https://doi.org/10.1002/ejp.556

Chen, C. X., Ofner, S., Bakoyannis, G., Kwekkeboom, K. L., & Carpenter, J. S. (2018). Symptoms-based phenotypes among women with dysmenorrhea: A latent class analysis. *Western Journal of Nursing Research, 40*(10), 1452–1468. https://doi.org/10.1177/0193945917731778

Chen, C. X., Murphy, T., Ofner, S., Yahng, L., Krombach, P., LaPradd, M., Bakoyannis, G., & Carpenter, J. S. (2021). Development and testing of the dysmenorrhea symptom interference (DSI) scale. *Western Journal of Nursing Research, 43*(4), 364–373. https://doi.org/10.1177/0193945920942252

Chen, C., Li, X., Lu, S., Yang, J., & Liu, Y. (2024). Acupuncture for clinical improvement of endometriosis-related pain: A systematic review and meta-analysis. *Archives of Gynecology and Obstetrics, 310*(4), 2101–2114. https://doi.org/10.1007/s00404-024-07675-z

Cosic, A., Ferhatovic, L., Banozic, A., Kraljevic, S., Maric, A., Sapunar, D., & Puljak, L. (2013). Pain catastrophizing changes during the menstrual cycle. *Psychology, Health & Medicine, 18*(6), 735–741. https://doi.org/10.1080/13548506.2013.769609

Darnall, B. D., Roy, A., Chen, A. L., Ziadni, M. S., Keane, R. T., You, D. S., Slater, K., Poupore-King, H., Mackey, I., Kao, M. C., Cook, K. F., Lorig, K., Zhang, D., Hong, J., Tian, L., & Mackey, S. C. (2021). Comparison of a single-session pain management skills intervention with a single-session health education intervention and 8 sessions of cognitive behavioral therapy in adults with chronic low Back pain: A randomized clinical trial. *JAMA Network Open, 4*(8), e2113401. https://doi.org/10.1001/jamanetworkopen.2021.13401

Dworkin, R. H., Turk, D. C., Farrar, J. T., Haythornthwaite, J. A., Jensen, M. P., Katz, N. P., Kerns, R. D., Stucki, G., Allen, R. R., Bellamy, N., Carr, D. B., Chandler, J., Cowan, P., Dionne, R., Galer, B. S., Hertz, S., Jadad, A. R., Kramer, L. D., Manning, D. C., Immpact et al. (2005). Core outcome measures for chronic pain clinical trials: IMMPACT recommendations. *Pain, 113*(1–2), 9–19. https://doi.org/10.1016/j.pain.2004.09.012

Dworkin, R. H., Turk, D. C., Wyrwich, K. W., Beaton, D., Cleeland, C. S., Farrar, J. T., Haythornthwaite, J. A., Jensen, M. P., Kerns, R. D., Ader, D. N., Brandenburg, N., Burke, L. B., Cella, D., Chandler, J., Cowan, P., Dimitrova, R., Dionne, R., Hertz, S., Jadad, A. R., Zavisic, S. et al. (2008). Interpreting the clinical importance of treatment outcomes in chronic pain clinical trials: IMMPACT recommendations. *The Journal of Pain, 9*(2), 105–121. https://doi.org/10.1016/j.jpain.2007.09.005

Evans, S., Dowding, C., Olive, L., Payne, L. A., Druitt, M., Seidman, L. C., Skvarc, D., & Mikocka-Walus, A. (2022). Pain catastrophizing, but not mental health or social support, is associated with menstrual pain severity in women with dysmenorrhea: A cross-sectional survey. *Psychology, Health & Medicine, 27*(6), 1410–1420. https://doi.org/10.1080/13548506.2021.1948581

Gagnon, M. M., Moussaoui, D., Gordon, J. L., Alberts, N. M., & Grover, S. R. (2022). Dysmenorrhea across the lifespan: A biopsychosocial perspective to understanding the dysmenorrhea trajectory and association with comorbid pain experiences. *Pain, 163*(11), 2069–2075. https://doi.org/10.1097/j.pain.0000000000002649

Gatchel, R. J., Peng, Y. B., Peters, M. L., Fuchs, P. N., & Turk, D. C. (2007). The biopsychosocial approach to chronic pain: Scientific advances and future directions. *Psychological Bulletin, 133*(4), 581–624. https://doi.org/10.1037/0033-2909.133.4.581

Iacovides, S., Baker, F. C., & Avidon, I. (2014). The 24-h progression of menstrual pain in women with primary dysmenorrhea when given diclofenac potassium: A randomized, double-blinded, placebo-controlled crossover study. *Archives of Gynecology and Obstetrics, 289*(5), 993–1002. https://doi.org/10.1007/s00404-013-3073-8

Iacovides, S., Avidon, I., & Baker, F. C. (2015). What we know about primary dysmenorrhea today: A critical review. *Human Reproduction Update, 21*(6), 762–778. https://doi.org/10.1093/humupd/dmv039

Khoo, E. L., Small, R., Cheng, W., Hatchard, T., Glynn, B., Rice, D. B., Skidmore, B., Kenny, S., Hutton, B., & Poulin, P. A. (2019). Comparative evaluation of group-based mindfulness-based stress reduction and cognitive behavioural therapy for the treatment and management of chronic pain: A systematic review and network meta-analysis. *Evidence-Based Mental Health, 22*(1), 26–35. https://doi.org/10.1136/ebmental-2018-300062

Ludwig, D. S., & Kabat-Zinn, J. (2008). Mindfulness in medicine. *JAMA, 300*(11), 1350–1352. https://doi.org/10.1001/jama.300.11.1350

Matthewman, G., Lee, A., Kaur, J. G., & Daley, A. J. (2018). Physical activity for primary dysmenorrhea: A systematic review and meta-analysis of randomized controlled trials. *American Journal of Obstetrics and Gynecology, 219*(3), 255 e251–255 e220. https://doi.org/10.1016/j.ajog.2018.04.001

McClintock, A. S., McCarrick, S. M., Garland, E. L., Zeidan, F., & Zgierska, A. E. (2019). Brief mindfulness-based interventions for acute and chronic pain: A systematic review. *Journal of Alternative and Complementary Medicine, 25*(3), 265–278. https://doi.org/10.1089/acm.2018.0351

Oladosu, F. A., Tu, F. F., & Hellman, K. M. (2018). Nonsteroidal antiinflammatory drug resistance in dysmenorrhea: Epidemiology, causes, and treatment. *American Journal of Obstetrics and Gynecology, 218*(4), 390–400. https://doi.org/10.1016/j.ajog.2017.08.108

Owen, P. R. (1984). Prostaglandin synthetase inhibitors in the treatment of primary dysmenorrhea. Outcome trials reviewed. *American Journal of Obstetrics and Gynecology, 148*(1), 96–103. https://doi.org/10.1016/s0002-9378(84)80039-3

Payne, L. A., Seidman, L. C., Romero, T., & Sim, M. S. (2020). An open trial of a mind-body intervention for young women with moderate to severe primary dysmenorrhea. *Pain Medicine, 21*(7), 1385–1392. https://doi.org/10.1093/pm/pnz378

Quartana, P. J., Campbell, C. M., & Edwards, R. R. (2009). Pain catastrophizing: A critical review. *Expert Review of Neurotherapeutics, 9*(5), 745–758. https://doi.org/10.1586/ern.09.34

Rogers, S. K., Galloway, A., Hirsh, A. T., Zapolski, T., Chen, C. X., & Rand, K. L. (2023). Efficacy of psychological interventions for dysmenorrhea: A meta-analysis. *Pain Medicine, 24*(9), 1086–1099. https://doi.org/10.1093/pm/pnad058

Schroll, J. B., Black, A. Y., Farquhar, C., & Chen, I. (2023). Combined oral contraceptive pill for primary dysmenorrhoea. *Cochrane Database of Systematic Reviews, 7*(7), CD002120. https://doi.org/10.1002/14651858.CD002120.pub4

Seidman, L. C., Handy, A. B., Temme, C. R., Greenfield, S. F., & Payne, L. A. (2023). Reflections on the group dynamic in a group cognitive behavioral therapy intervention for young adult women with moderate to severe dysmenorrhea: A qualitative analysis. *Journal of Psychosomatic Obstetrics and Gynaecology, 44*(1), 2264486. https://doi.org/10.1080/0167482X.2023.2264486

Sullivan, M. J. L., Bishop, S. R., & Pivik, J. (1995). The pain catastrophizing scale: Development and validation. *Psychological Assessment, 7*(4), 524–532.

Thorn, B. E., Pence, L. B., Ward, L. C., Kilgo, G., Clements, K. L., Cross, T. H., Davis, A. M., & Tsui, P. W. (2007). A randomized clinical trial of targeted cognitive behavioral treatment to reduce catastrophizing in chronic headache sufferers. *The Journal of Pain, 8*(12), 938–949. https://doi.org/10.1016/j.jpain.2007.06.010

Walsh, T. M., LeBlanc, L., & McGrath, P. J. (2003). Menstrual pain intensity, coping, and disability: The role of pain catastrophizing. *Pain Medicine, 4*(4), 352–361. https://doi.org/10.1111/j.1526-4637.2003.03039.x

Chapter 8
Interstitial Cystitis/Bladder Pain Syndrome in Women: An Overview and Introduction to a Novel Cognitive-Behavioral Intervention

Valery Bodziony, Elizabeth G. Walsh, and Lindsey C. McKernan

Interstitial cystitis/bladder pain syndrome (IC/BPS or "IC") is a debilitating, chronic, costly pain condition that affects approximately three to eight million individuals in the United States alone (Berry et al., 2011; Hsieh et al., 2021; Payne et al., 2007). The American Urological Association (AUA) defines IC as unpleasant sensations that are perceived to be related to the bladder, associated with lower urinary tract symptoms of more than 6 weeks, in the absence of infection or other identifiable causes (Clemens et al., 2022). Hallmark symptoms include pain in the pelvis, urogenital floor, or external genitalia; and urinary urgency, pressure/discomfort, and/or urinary frequency. There is no single "cause" of IC, and research suggests that multiple factors may contribute to its development, which may vary from person to person. Leading researchers propose that symptoms vary on a spectrum from widespread, systemic pain (i.e., "widespread" phenotype) to pain confined to the bladder (i.e., "localized") (Nickel et al., 2009). IC symptoms can be intense and debilitating, with some individuals experiencing symptom flares that can last days to weeks and result in increased distress and limited overall functioning (Lai et al.,

V. Bodziony (✉)
Department of Outpatient Behavioral Health, St. Elizabeth Physicians,
Crestview Hills, KY, USA
e-mail: valery.bodziony@stelizabeth.com

E. G. Walsh
Department of Physical Medicine and Rehabilitation, Osher Center for Integrative Health,
Vanderbilt University Medical Center, Nashville, TN, USA

L. C. McKernan
Departments of Psychiatry & Behavioral Sciences, Physical Medicine & Rehabilitation,
Urology, Osher Center for Integrative Health, Vanderbilt University Medical Center,
Nashville, TN, USA

L. A. Payne (ed.), *Psychosocial Interventions for Chronic Pain in Women and Girls*, CBT: Science Into Practice, https://doi.org/10.1007/978-3-031-98876-9_8

2019). Additionally, sexual dysfunction is highly prevalent in women with IC (Bogart et al., 2011), with symptoms such as dyspareunia (i.e., painful intercourse), decreased sexual desire, orgasm frequency, and lubrication. Sexual dysfunction in IC is consistently associated with poor quality of life (Nickel et al., 2007; Tripp et al., 2009), with few treatments offering significant improvements in symptoms (Chen et al., 2022). Overall, IC symptoms often result in reduced physical, mental/emotional, social, and sexual functioning, which greatly impact quality of life. Given that patients often present with a variety of different symptoms and needs in treatment, it is important to conceptualize and treat IC using a biopsychosocial perspective. The AUA recommends both pharmacological and non-pharmacological interventions for IC, including self-management strategies coping skills for stress and pain (Clemens et al., 2022).

Consideration of Unique Symptom Presentations

Research has indicated that IC symptom presentations fall on a "spectrum" of disease, from "localized" symptoms to "widespread" (Akiyama & Hanno, 2019). Patients with the localized phenotype typically experience frequency, urgency, and pain that is localized to the bladder only. Some, though not all, patients with symptoms localized to the bladder may have Hunner lesions, which are ulcers in the bladder that can cause blood in the urine and are identified via cystoscopy. Patients with the widespread phenotype may have more severe urgency, frequency, and widespread pain throughout the body. These symptom presentations are often complex and are accompanied by psychological distress and comorbid symptoms, including fatigue, sleep difficulties, cognitive dysfunction, anxiety, and depression (Clemens et al., 2019). Patients with a widespread phenotype may be diagnosed with other chronic overlapping pain conditions, such as fibromyalgia, irritable bowel syndrome, migraine, low back pain, and others (Chelimsky et al., 2012) and have more polysymptomatic complaints (Lai et al., 2017). It is theorized that different symptom presentations and the spectrum of IC may be influenced by central sensitization, or amplified pain sensitivity in the body (Woolf, 2011). Additionally, IC symptoms can occur in "flare" patterns, or periods of more severe and debilitating symptoms which can be brought on by symptom triggers, including dietary factors, stress, emotional distress, menses, or sexual activity, and can have a significant impact on life and functioning, as well as increased healthcare-seeking behavior (Lai et al., 2019; Sutcliffe et al., 2023).

Interstitial Cystitis/Bladder Pain Syndrome in Women

Prevalence of IC in women may range from 3.3 to 7.9 million aged 18 years or older in the United States; however, it is likely that prevalence is much higher as symptoms are generally under-addressed and under-diagnosed (Berry et al., 2011). IC is most often diagnosed in women, with some research indicating IC is 10 times more likely to occur in women than men (Teichman & Parsons 2007). Given a wide variety of symptom presentations, women with IC commonly report difficulties and frustrations in the diagnostic process (Kirkham & Swainston, 2022). Many factors may contribute to diagnostic difficulties, including a lack of specialty providers, ruling out other diagnoses, and even broader sociocultural considerations such as invalidation and stigma surrounding women's experiences with pain.

Qualitative studies on women's experiences living with IC have found themes of invalidation from loved ones and medical providers, social withdrawal, isolation, and a perceived lack of control over symptoms, as well as studies showing a significant relationship between symptom severity/exacerbations and psychosocial stress (McKernan et al., 2020). Research highlights significant gender differences in IC treatment experiences, with women reporting a more difficult and longer path to diagnosis, trial-and-error treatment processes, experiencing gender-based stigma and negative stereotypes, and feeling dismissed by healthcare providers (Windgassen et al., 2022). Another study on women's experiences with IC found themes of diagnostic uncertainty and frustration, limitations on activities, and patients seeking self-management strategies due to dissatisfaction with medical treatments (Kirkham & Swainston, 2022). Consistently, a qualitative dissertation found themes of hopelessness, feeling "invisible," minimal symptom relief despite multiple treatments, invalidation from medical providers regarding sexual functioning and pain, and having to self-advocate for diagnostic and treatment options while navigating complex medical systems (Richardson, 2024). A study analyzing online discussion forums found that women with IC valued online community engagement and peer support for symptoms, and women reported high symptomatic burden, especially with comorbid nonurological conditions (Gonzalez et al., 2023). Together, research highlights the need for improved diagnostic processes, more validating and empathetic healthcare interactions, and effective person-centered treatments that address biopsychosocial needs through self-management.

Gender and Diversity Considerations

Chronic pain conditions are generally more prevalent in women than men (Munce & Stewart, 2007), with particularly high rates in conditions that have "invisible" or unexplained symptoms like fibromyalgia and IC. Although prevalence is typically higher in women, recent research suggests the prevalence of IC in men may be nearing that of women (Suskind et al., 2015). Similar to women's experiences with chronic pain in general, women with IC may experience distinct symptom profiles and psychosocial needs compared to men, influenced by internal factors and societal responses to pain (Rice et al., 2024). Windgassen et al. (2022) found that women reported more severe urologic symptoms, greater pain intensity, and higher levels of emotional distress than men. Women also reported more anxiety, depression, guilt, decreased assertive communication, and desired more mental health and social support. Overall, research suggests that gender health inequality may exist in treatment, which emphasizes the importance of providing validating and person-centered care to women with IC.

Research also highlights ethnic and racial disparities in chronic pain experiences, assessment, and treatment (Meints et al., 2019). Although IC is most common in White women, studies suggest similar prevalence in Black and Hispanic women (Berry et al., 2011; Dallas et al., 2022). Preliminary research indicates that individuals of minority race/ethnicity may experience longer time to diagnosis and more severe symptoms (Brownstein et al., 2023), as well as longer delays in diagnosis (Sant, 1993). Research on symptom presentations and treatment outcomes in these groups is limited, possibly due to underdiagnosis of symptoms (Gonzalez et al., 2022).

Psychological Comorbidities

Psychological comorbidities are significantly elevated in individuals with IC, with high prevalence of depression, anxiety, panic disorder, low self-esteem, post-traumatic stress disorder (PTSD), sexual abuse/childhood trauma, and increased suicidal ideation and attempts [see review by McKernan et al. (2018, 2019)]. People with IC are six times more likely to experience depression than the general population (McKernan et al., 2018), and one study found that suicidal ideation was associated with increased pain and comorbid mental health difficulties (Tripp et al., 2016). Individuals with IC may have pre-existing anxiety disorders (Chung et al., 2014) and are also at risk for developing an anxiety or panic disorder following diagnosis (Chuang et al., 2015; Weissman et al., 2004). The year after diagnosis appears to be a particularly vulnerable period for increased emotional distress, and there is some evidence to suggest that depression rates are higher in younger individuals with IC (McKernan et al., 2018). Earlier psychosocial intervention is ideal for facilitating self-management, assisting with illness adjustment, and reducing the impact of bladder pain and urinary symptoms.

Specific psychological processes that may impact disease prognosis, symptom severity, and ability to cope include negative illness perception and appraisal of symptoms, rumination and catastrophizing, poor emotion regulation, and interpersonal distress (Windgassen & McKernan, 2020). Psychosocial factors associated with chronic pain can change an individual's perceptions and behaviors, which may then lead to increased severity and maintenance of symptoms over time, and a reinforcing cycle of increased psychosocial distress and IC symptoms (McKernan et al.,

2018). One study found that the type of coping behaviors used by individuals matters to both IC symptoms and mood (Sutherland et al., 2024), with disengaged coping leading to inactivity, avoidance, and symptoms of depression. Using active coping strategies, decreasing rumination and catastrophizing, and managing emotional and interpersonal distress may buffer the negative impact of urologic and pain symptoms and improve quality of life.

Consideration of Post-Traumatic Stress, Medical Trauma, and Trauma-Informed Care

The association between exposure to abuse and IC is well-documented (Chiu et al., 2017; McKernan et al., 2019), with outcomes such as greater psychiatric dysfunction, decreased bladder capacity, and sexual dysfunction (Chiu et al., 2017; Nickel et al., 2011). A study by McKernan et al. (2019) found that nearly half of women with IC met diagnostic criteria for PTSD, a higher prevalence than in the general population and in non-IC chronic pain. Those with co-occurring PTSD and IC endorsed higher prevalence of childhood trauma and lifetime trauma (e.g., sexual trauma, physical abuse). The severity and ambiguity of IC symptoms and treatment experiences may increase the likelihood of developing post-traumatic stress symptoms (McKernan et al., 2016). The bi-directional relationship between IC and PTSD is influenced by theoretical models like HPA axis dysregulation, central sensitization, and the brain-gut-bladder axis, though exact mechanisms are unknown (Bendrick et al., 2022). PTSD symptoms, such as avoidance and hyperarousal, can exacerbate IC pain, making individuals more vulnerable to pain flares and contribute to the maintenance of IC symptoms. Women may also be at risk for experiencing medical trauma, or traumatic stress associated with medical diagnoses, treatment, or experiences within the medical system (Hall & Hall, 2013). Mental health providers need to acknowledge distressing medical experiences that may occur in individuals with IC. Open, validating, and patient-centered communication is pertinent in treatment to create a safe, supportive, and empowering environment.

Given the high prevalence of post-traumatic stress symptoms and psychological distress in women with IC, especially in those with the widespread phenotype, it is recommended to use principles of trauma-informed care for women to guide treatment (McKernan et al., 2019). Such recommendations emphasize patient-centered communication and include screening for *specific* symptoms of PTSD, encouragement of patient collaboration, providing direct information, and enhancing perceived safety during examinations and procedures. The self-management for IC treatment protocol was created with trauma-informed principles in mind, with many of the skills learned being applicable to symptoms of trauma, such as grounding techniques, decreasing avoidance, and use of relaxation strategies.

Overall, IC has a significant psychological and social impact. Anxiety and depressive disorders may both precede and follow IC diagnosis, and the relationship between mental health symptoms and physical symptoms of IC is bidirectional. Women with histories of abuse and post-traumatic stress are at risk of developing IC, and living with IC may increase post-traumatic stress and medical traumatic stress symptoms. It is paramount to assess and address these symptoms in treatment.

Biopsychosocial Assessment of Interstitial Cystitis/Bladder Pain Syndrome

It is recommended that illness-specific cognitive-behavioral interventions for pain populations use methods of symptom and outcome measurements that are sensitive to patient needs (Eccleston & Crombez, 2017). Recommendations for pelvic and urologic pain conditions stress the importance of assessing biopsychosocial factors (Landis et al., 2014). In addition to pain and urologic symptoms, comprehensive biopsychosocial pain assessment includes evaluating comorbid symptoms (e.g., sleep, cognitive difficulties, functional status), affective vulnerability (e.g., depression, anxiety, anger); beliefs and attitudes (e.g., pain self-efficacy, pain catastrophizing, coping, locus of control); and environmental and social factors (e.g.., relationship satisfaction, interference of pain in work, family, and social life) (Williams, 2013). A review by Williams (2013) highlights commonly used measures such as the Brief Pain Inventory (BPI; Cleeland & Ryan, 1994), West Haven-Yale Multidimensional Pain Inventory (WHYMPI; Kerns et al., 1985), and the Pain Catastrophizing Scale (PCS, Sullivan et al., 1995).

Psychosocial Interventions for Interstitial Cystitis/Bladder Pain Syndrome

Research consistently shows that patients with IC desire a collaborative, personalized treatment approach that addresses symptoms and their emotional and functional impact (Nickel et al., 2018; McKernan et al., 2020). A study on treatment choices in IC found that women preferred self-management strategies, guided self-care practices, reducing medications and procedural intervention, and evidence-based alternative treatments (Hassani et al., 2022). Until recently, only three small pilot studies have explored psychological interventions for IC, which include an intervention using mindfulness-based stress reduction techniques (Kanter et al., 2016, $n = 11$), a brief online video-based, self-guided self-management intervention (Lee et al., 2018, intervention group $n = 30$), and an interview and education on the physiological-affective relationship in IC (Carty et al., 2016, intervention group $n = 37$). A review of these interventions by Windgassen and McKernan (2020) found high acceptability and some symptom improvement with guided imagery

(Carrico et al., 2008, $n = 30$), but the studies had small sample sizes, variable effects, and limited follow-up.

In efforts to fill the need for an evidence-based, person-centered biopsychosocial treatment designed specifically for IC, McKernan et al. (2024a) developed a novel self-management intervention based on cognitive-behavioral and interpersonal principles. Following significant patient input, the intervention incorporated content to address the unique communication difficulties that arise from managing urinary and pelvic symptoms, intimacy concerns, condition-specific education, and sleep issues related to bladder dysfunction in addition to other well-known aspects of CBT for chronic pain (e.g., relaxation, behavioral activation). This intervention was recently piloted via telemedicine in a larger randomized trial (2024a, $n = 78$), detailed below.

Self-Management for IC/Bladder Pain Syndrome: A Cognitive-Behavioral Intervention

Self-Management for IC is a cognitive-behavioral intervention that addresses individualized patient needs and difficulties in the management of urogenital symptoms, pelvic pain, psychosocial comorbidities, and other common presenting concerns. The protocol was delivered via telemedicine by trained interventionists, occurring in 50-minute individual sessions once per week for 8 weeks (McKernan et al. 2024a, b). Telemedicine greatly increases access to mental health care, especially for patients with IC who have urinary and pain symptoms that make it hard to travel. Recent research suggests that women with IC may prefer remote or telemedicine treatment modalities for increased access to care (Hassani et al., 2022). Sessions include non-pharmacological psychoeducation and building of coping skills for pain, urologic symptoms, and psychosocial distress. Specific coping skills include strategies to enhance pain and urologic symptom control, improve sleep hygiene, manage intimacy and sexual functioning, address cognitions and beliefs related to symptoms and the IC experience, and managing affective distress to reduce vulnerability to symptom exacerbations (McKernan et al., 2024a, b). The intervention is "patient-informed," meaning treatment can be delivered in a flexible manner based on individual needs, symptom presentations, and collaboratively agreed upon goals. Figure 8.1 outlines the session title, content, and processes.

The pilot RCT of the telemedicine-delivered Self-Management for IC yielded promising results and high feasibility and acceptability (McKernan et al., 2024a, b). Patients who received the cognitive-behavioral intervention reported significantly higher global improvement of symptoms and were more likely to respond to treatment. Both the treatment and control (telephone-based monitoring) reported significant reductions in genitourinary symptoms, and though there was no significant difference between groups in those reductions, the intervention group responded to treatment at a significantly greater rate (e.g., 6×, McKernan et al., 2024a). Those

Session and Title	Process and Activities
1. Psychoeducation and Goal Setting	• Discuss symptoms and phenotypic presentations of IC/BPS • Introduce S.P.A.C.E acronym and connection to symptom patterns • Identify pain triggers and provide psychoeducation • Discuss rationale for CBT for IC/BPS • Identify 3 primary areas of need/goals for the individual's unique IC experience
2. IC/BPS Pain and Relaxation	• Provide psychoeducation on IC/BPS and the pain cycle • Discuss the body's stress and trauma response (fight or flight) and the body's relaxation response • Engage in in-session relaxation activity: guided imagery, progressive muscle relaxation, body scan) • Develop relaxation coping plan
3. Sleep, Pain, and the Bladder	• Provide psychoeducation on sleep and IC • Provide behavioral sleep hygiene education • Bladder training rationale and discuss individual motivations for bladder training • Discuss sleep record and development of adaptive sleep plan
4. Managing Painful Emotions	• Explore patterns between IC symptoms and mood • Reintroduce IC pain cycle and the role of emotions; identify emotional struggles • Teach and practice one skill for effectively managing emotions/mood: pleasant activity scheduling (depression-directed), distress tolerance (anger/stress-directed), grounding (anxiety/trauma-directed)
5. IC Thoughts and Worry	• Identify thoughts and core beliefs about IC and self • Review CBT thought model with patient-specific examples • Explore methods of softening or challenging automatic thoughts through cognitive restructuring and self-compassion techniques
6. Effective Communication with IC	• Provide psychoeducation on IC and communication • Review goals for effective communication • Review communication styles and link to IC experiences • Engage in DEARMAN or GIVE activity
7. Intimacy and Sex with IC	• Provide psychoeducation on the impact of IC on sex and intimacy • Apply effective communication skills to sexual communication • Explore alternatives to intercourse • Engage in sexual planning activity
8. Integration of Skills and Termination	• Review content of treatment, coping skills, and progress (i.e., "then and now") • Explore challenges to continued practice and symptom relapse • Brainstorm and anticipate solutions

Note. CBT (cognitive-behavioral therapy); IC/BPS (interstitial cystitis/bladder pain syndrome); IC (interstitial cystitis); SPACE (sleep, pain, affect, cognition, and energy). Adapted from McKernan et al. (2024) with permission from the lead author.

Fig. 8.1 Self-management for IC/BPS intervention summary, including session-by-session description of the treatment protocol, including session title, process, and specific exercises associated with session content

who completed the intervention reported significant reductions in genitourinary symptoms, pain interference, and pain intensity as compared to "non-responders." Nearly 40% of participants receiving the intervention reported significant and meaningful change post-treatment (McKernan et al., 2024a), which may reflect improved self-efficacy of symptom management through increased coping and decreased impact of pain on overall functioning. This chapter will outline Self-Management for IC, using a case example with session-by-session excerpts and clinician dialogue from the therapist treatment manual (McKernan et al., 2024a, b).[1]

Session-by-Session Overview of Self-Management for IC/BPS Using a Case Example

"Abby" (pseudonym) is a 42-year-old white, married, cisgender female who was referred for Self-Management for IC by her urologist. Diagnosed 3 years ago, Abby has been dealing with urologic symptoms such as frequency, urgency, and bladder pain that spreads to other areas of her body. She has also experienced symptoms of anxiety and depression related to IC, which have impacted her mood and ability to engage in enjoyable activities. Abby feels her relationships are strained due to symptoms, like pain and urgency, negatively impacting her social life. She also has difficulties with sexual intimacy with her husband due to pain during intercourse and associated anxiety and avoidance. While medications and other pharmacological interventions have led to some improvement of symptoms, Abby continues to struggle with coping with IC and its impact on her life and functioning.

Session One: Psychoeducation and Goal Setting

The first session contains a large educational component, consisting of reviewing information about IC, the disease spectrum and influences on symptom presentation, as well as unique patient experiences with symptoms and triggers. The aim is to give patients a basic understanding of their symptoms using a biopsychosocial framework. Learning about patient experiences informs treatment goals to guide the intervention.

Abby *IC has completely turned my life upside-down. I am in pain all the time and am constantly going to the bathroom or searching for a bathroom. I don't do as many social things, and my relationships with friends and my husband have been impacted. I feel like I am not myself anymore, or living the way that I want to live.*

[1] Session-by-session excerpts and clinician dialogue were adapted from the Self-Management for IC/BPS Therapist Treatment Manual (McKernan et al., 2024a, b) used with permission from the lead author.

Clinician *It sounds like IC has disrupted many aspects of your life. Recent research shows that IC can have different symptom presentations, and that symptoms can fall on a "spectrum." Some people may only have bladder pain that comes and goes and can be directly linked to a specific symptom "trigger," like eating spicy foods. Others can have constant pain in the bladder and in multiple areas of the body, and feel that symptoms worsen out of the blue. People may experience central pain, which is heightened sensitivity to pain sensations, and often widespread pain throughout the body or overlapping pain conditions like migraines or fibromyalgia. Where do you feel your symptoms fall on this spectrum?*

Abby *I really identify with having central pain. I don't just experience pain in my bladder, but I have back pain and migraines sometimes, too. When the pain hits, I feel super fatigued. It seems like anything that I do results in more pain.*

Clinician *Have you noticed any specific symptom triggers, like foods or activities?*

Abby *Well, my doctor told me to cut out acidic drinks and foods because I noticed coffee makes urgency worse. Also, pain is worse around the time of my period. I usually experience flares that can last for days. Having intercourse sometimes causes pain flares, too.*

Clinician *It sounds like you have noticed many triggers for your symptoms, and we will explore this more throughout treatment. In learning from a lot of individuals with IC, we find that managing IC has its own unique sets of challenges that arise from living with a condition with pain in a vulnerable part of the body. This can include struggles with intimacy, sexual pain and avoidance, relationship difficulties, shame, and more. In addition to working with your doctor, there are things you can do on your own, without medication, to improve your day-to-day experience living with IC. Now that we have a general idea of how IC affects you and your life, we can set up some treatment goals together.*

Session Two: Pain and Relaxation

This session provides psychoeducation on the chronic pain cycle, the body's response to pain, and the connection between pain, mood, and stress. The pain cycle model illustrates how thoughts, emotions, behaviors, and physical sensations interact, and this cycle is revisited throughout treatment, with a detailed focus on emotions and worry. By identifying aspects of their own pain cycle, patients can learn to adjust their responses to pain, improving self-management.

Psychoeducation also covers the physiology of pain and the body's "fight or flight" response. Chronic pain often prevents the body from relaxing due to constant sympathetic nervous system activation, leading to muscle tension, anxiety, and stress. Relaxation strategies, such as progressive muscle relaxation, the body scan (Kabat-Zinn, 1990), and guided imagery with safe place suggestions, are introduced to activate the parasympathetic nervous system, with the goals of reducing pain and increasing relaxation. Patients are encouraged to practice two strategies during the session and continue at home, and practices can be adapted to best fit patients' needs. The session concludes with the creation of a relaxation coping plan, which includes specific techniques for patients to use. Regular practice of these strategies, even when they seem ineffective, is essential for retraining the brain and calming the nervous system. Practicing during periods of lower stress or pain can help patients feel more confident in using these strategies when they might need them the most, such as during flares.

Clinician *How does stress impact your flares?*

Abby *When I am stressed or anxious, I notice my flares and other symptoms get worse. I feel tense all over my body, and the pain and burning in my bladder is significant. I also urinate more often when I am stressed.*

Clinician *What you are describing is the body's natural response to stress. Your sympathetic nervous system, or "fight or flight" response, is being activated, which increases feelings of stress, anxiety, muscle tension, pain, and even bladder symptoms. Learning relaxation strategies can help to "turn down" the sympathetic nervous system response to stress and pain and increase the body's "rest," or parasympathetic nervous system response. Learning how to reduce stress, tension, and pain through relaxation can also help your brain to release tension and activation in the pelvic region and bladder. Today, we are going to try a few relaxation strategies—let's start with the body scan.*

Engages in body scan practice

Clinician *How was that for you? Did you notice any changes with your pain or other symptoms?*

Abby *It was interesting to pay attention to other areas of my body and take focus away from the pain. I realized other parts of my body feel "okay." I feel more relaxed, and my pain is down.*

Clinician *Engaging in relaxation practices like the body scan can really help to break the pain cycle by increasing the parasympathetic nervous system response. It could be helpful to do these practices even when feeling better or not in pain, or when feeling a flare come on. I would like to create a relaxation plan to use on a daily basis and when in need. It can be helpful to write it down or have it easily accessible and ready. Let's think of 10 things you can do to help your mind and body to relax.*

Abby *I can use relaxation strategy recordings. Also, taking hot showers, watching a funny TV show, drinking a warm cup of tea, reading a good book… all of these things usually help me to relax!*

Clinician *Wonderful! It sounds like you already have a good set of skills and tools that you use. We will expand upon this relaxation plan as we go through treatment.*

Session Three: Sleep, Pain, and the Bladder

Sleep difficulties, such as falling asleep, staying asleep, and sleep interruptions, are common in people with IC, for reasons that may include pain, bladder pressure and discomfort, difficulty relaxation, anxiety, and nocturia (frequent nighttime urination). Chronic sleep difficulties and insomnia paired with bladder dysfunction can negatively impact the HPA-axis, leading to a cycle of impacted sleep and IC symptoms. In this session, information is gathered about the patient's sleep patterns and how IC symptoms impact their sleep and vice versa. CBT-based sleep hygiene strategies are reviewed. A sleep hygiene record can be used for recording sleep and bladder symptoms, as well as sleep hygiene and bladder training techniques used. Bladder training for nocturia, urgency, and frequency is recommended in the AUA treatment guidelines. Bladder training uses classical conditioning principles to help patients control urges and improve symptoms. This involves urinating on a set schedule instead of responding to urgency. The process starts by gradually increasing the time between voiding and continues over several weeks to improve bladder capacity and reduce urgency. Small behavior changes are emphasized, with validation of patient experiences and resistance to the process. For patients with significant urgency or pain, even brief intervals (e.g., 30 seconds) can be a starting point for retraining the bladder-brain connection. Providing information on bladder physiology and capacity may also be helpful.

Bladder Training Example

Clinician	*When you experience pain or urgency in the bladder, the normal impulse is to stop the sensation. This establishes a pattern of frequent voiding, which can be difficult to reverse, even after pain is controlled. To retrain your bladder, you have to follow a series of steps to achieve longer periods between voiding. This process is called bladder training. The objective of bladder training is to increase bladder capacity so that you can hold more urine in the bladder and will not feel that impulse to go as often. Have you tried bladder training before?*
Abby	*I have tried it before, and I found it to be hard. I have learned to urinate to try to relieve pain, though sometimes even urinating itself is painful. Sometimes I try to hold it or fight the urge, especially when I am at work. I haven't been very successful, especially since I am worried about feeling more pain.*
Clinician	*How long do you think you can last in between voids?*
Abby	*At night, it is hard to tell, but during the day, it feels like I go to the bathroom every 30 minutes. It disrupts my whole day, and I am constantly going to the bathroom.*
Clinician	*Let's start small here. If you feel you are going to the bathroom every 30 minutes, try to hold the urge to urinate for 35 minutes. Really, even if you hold it for an extra minute or so, you are helping to retrain the*

classically conditioned response your bladder has learned between the sensation of the bladder being full and needing to go immediately. It could also be helpful to take a few deep breaths when the urgency gets more intense—practicing relaxation may calm the pain and urgency down enough to hold the urge for a slightly longer period.

Session Four: Managing Painful Emotions

This session focuses on identifying emotional difficulties and relating these struggles to IC symptoms using a biopsychosocial approach. Individuals with IC may find it hard to discuss their symptoms or may even experience alexithymia, which is common in individuals who experience pain (Di Tella & Castelli, 2016). In this session, the provider and patient identify a distressing emotion and practice self-management skills, including distress tolerance techniques, grounding techniques, and behavior activation. Grounding techniques, which help to decrease physiological arousal, may be particularly helpful if a patient is feeling stressed or anxious. Grounding techniques include the sensory 5–4–3–2–1 technique, use of grounding objects, observing surroundings, and anchoring in the present moment. Behavioral activation may be used for patients who identify sadness, low mood, or depression as their primary emotional struggle, as activity engagement and motivation increase can help to improve overall mood. Distress tolerance techniques, such as distraction planning, may be helpful for anger, irritability, and acute stress as these practices can redirect emotional distress (i.e., "riding the wave of distress") and increase self-regulation.

Clinician *What have you noticed about your mood since having IC?*

Abby *Lately, I have felt really down. Everything that I used to enjoy, like going on walks or going out with friends, has been taken away from me. I can't do any of those things when I worry about having a flare or needing to use the bathroom immediately.*

Clinician *Often, when people experience pain and other IC symptoms, they limit activities due to fear of the pain or symptoms getting worse or having urinary symptoms unexpectedly. Giving up or limiting things you enjoy can really dampen mood and even disrupt your sense of self.*

Abby *I have not been feeling like myself lately. Going on daily walks was a huge part of my life and how I typically de-stressed. I know walking is helpful, but I just can't seem to get started.*

Clinician *Often, when we are in pain, we lose interest in activities we used to enjoy. They can become harder to do due to pain, fatigue, and other IC symptoms. What used to be enjoyable may seem more of a hassle. It sounds like walking may be an example for you.*

Abby *Yes, exactly! Walking feels like a huge activity, especially when I feel like I can barely get up off the couch due to pain.*

Clinician *Studies show that reconnecting with things you used to enjoy can help pain, mood, and improve quality of life. Often, we feel we need to have the energy or motivation to reconnect with activities. Surprisingly, it's actually the opposite. When we identify activities and make a plan of how we want to engage in those activities, the motivation and sense of reward returns.*

At this time, the patient and provider can brainstorm together about enjoyable and meaningful activities. When creating a plan to build up activities, it is important to help the patient set realistic and appropriate goals that align with current physical state, symptoms, and functioning.

Session Five: Thoughts and Worry

This session focuses on helping individuals identify core thought patterns and beliefs, how they relate to IC experiences, and how thoughts may impact coping behavior. Antecedents, beliefs, and consequences are explored using patient-specific examples, and psychoeducation is given on common cognitive distortions, including catastrophic and black and white thinking. Exploring specific experiences of IC sets the stage for identifying automatic negative thoughts and engaging in cognitive reframing. Such experiences may include perceptions of pain, self-efficacy in managing symptoms, and how they believe others perceive them as a person living with IC. Exercises in this session include challenging automatic negative thoughts and reframing, as well as learning self-compassion and identifying self-compassionate thoughts. Patients can fill out a thought record to aid in thought awareness and identification.

Clinician *What experiences come to mind when you think about being diagnosed and living with IC?*

Abby *Getting diagnosed with IC felt like an uphill battle. I tried many different treatments and tests without getting answers. I thought I was going crazy and that I was overreacting. It felt like no one could help me and that I was all alone.*

Clinician *It sounds like during that stressful time, you may have thought "I am crazy" or "I am all alone." Thoughts do not cause IC symptoms, but they can influence how the brain processes and perceives pain and bladder activity, as well as how you act and feel. Experiencing constant pain and urgency can be upsetting and mentally exhausting. When your brain is tired, it does not always have the energy to challenge unhelpful thinking, and these patterns can become automatic. Through learning to notice and examine thoughts, we can modify or adapt thoughts to be more helpful and ultimately increase sense of control and improve mood. For example, during your journey to diagnosis, you had the thought "I must be crazy" or "I am all alone in this." How do these thoughts make you feel?*

Abby *Pretty sad and lonely. I felt very invalidated throughout the whole process.*

Clinician *The thoughts you were having made you feel sad, lonely, and invalidated. One way to help reframe or "soften" thoughts is by using self-compassion. Our thoughts can often be very self-critical. Sometimes it is helpful to think, "What would I tell a friend who is going through this same situation?" What would you tell a friend?*

Abby *I would tell them that they are not alone. I would tell them that the journey is long, hard, and disappointing at times, but I would tell them that they are strong, and they have my support.*

Clinician *Let's explore how things might change if you respond to yourself in the same way you typically respond to a friend when you're suffering.*

Session Six: Effective Communication

Individuals with IC often experience interpersonal and relational stress due to communication challenges that arise from anxiety/stress, low mood, IC symptoms, and pain. For example, individuals may struggle to assert their needs to their medical provider if they feel medications are not helping, or they may have difficulties explaining their needs/symptoms to loved ones. In this session, psychoeducation is provided about communication styles (passive vs. assertive vs. aggressive), goals of effective communication (e.g., fostering a good relationship; improving self-respect; getting what you want/need), and interpersonal skills using DBT techniques (DEAR MAN; GIVE; Linehan, 2014) are explored.

Clinician *Today, we will discuss how IC interferes with your relationships. It is common to experience conflict within relationships, and sometimes symptoms of IC make it more challenging to communicate needs. Having open communication with others about our needs helps to maintain healthy relationships. Poor communication can lead to stress, which may exacerbate symptoms. Learning how to actively communicate needs in an assertive manner is important in managing IC. How do you talk to people about IC?*

Abby *I used to talk about IC with friends and family all the time, but now not so much. I don't want to burden anyone else with my problems.*

Clinician *When you talk about your symptoms with your husband, how does he typically respond?*

Abby *Most of the time, he is understanding and supportive. He already helps me so much that I feel bad asking him for more help when I am in pain or having a bad symptom day.*

Clinician *It sounds like you find it hard to express your needs or how you are feeling to others because you don't want to be a burden, or you don't ask for more help. How does that tend to make you feel?*

Abby *Honestly, pretty isolated. I end up getting frustrated with my husband because he isn't helping me, though I never asked for it or told him how I felt in the first place.*

Clinician *Exactly. Poor communication and not expressing needs well can lead to more stress, feelings of isolation, and even relationship difficulties. It is so important to learn how to assertively communicate needs and ask for help. There are three main communication styles—passive, assertive, and aggressive. How do you identify your general communication style?*

Abby *Definitely more passive. I always put others' needs before my own, and I find it hard to ask for help. I feel like passive communication plays out when talking to my doctor, too. There have been times when I have meant to ask for a medication change or I want to bring up a new symptom I am experiencing, though I feel like I can't ask for it in the moment.*

At this point, the therapist and patient can practice assertive communication using the acronyms DEAR MAN (Describe, Express, Assert, Reinforce, Mindfulness, Appear confident, Negotiate) or GIVE (be Gentle, act Interested, Validate, use an Easy manner) (Linehan, 2014) using specific examples from the patient's life (e.g., discussing symptom needs with the doctor or husband). Assertive communication can help the patient communicate needs in a respectful manner, which may decrease stress, improve symptoms, and lead to stronger relationships and overall support.

Session Seven: Intimacy and Sex

Many individuals with IC may experience difficulties with intimacy and sexual intercourse due to symptoms (Azevedo et al., 2005; Kirkham & Swainston, 2022). Individuals may experience increased pain with intercourse or orgasm, and in some cases, sexual intercourse may exacerbate pain or lead to flare-ups. This can lead to a cyclical pattern of low desire, anxiety about sex, avoidance of intimacy, tension in relationships, guilt, and depression (Bogart et al., 2011). Impaired sexual function and difficulties within relationships may lead to poorer quality of life in people with IC. Additionally, intimacy and intercourse are not often discussed with medical providers, leaving the topic largely unaddressed in treatment.

This session focuses on providing psychoeducation on IC symptoms and sexual intimacy, as well as relationship dysfunction in general. Sex and intimacy can be difficult for patients to talk about; therefore, the provider needs to take a validating and open stance, allowing the patient's discomfort to be addressed. In this session, it is particularly important to take a trauma-informed approach, as women with prior histories of trauma or sexual abuse may struggle to discuss or engage in intimacy or intercourse due to past experiences.

The session includes an exploration of how IC has impacted sexual intimacy and intimate relationships. The DBT-based skills learned in prior sessions (Session 6:

DEAR MAN and GIVE) can be applied to foster assertive communication about sexual intimacy. If the patient is not currently sexually active, skills learned in this session can be applied to other interpersonal relationships and topics such as emotional intimacy, closeness with others, exploring femininity, and improving communication. Alternatives to sexual intercourse are explored to foster intimacy without penetration, which is often painful for individuals with IC or pelvic pain. During this session, the patient and provider collaborate on a plan for intimate encounters and sexual activity, which may include relaxation techniques and other coping skills for stress and symptoms to use pre- and post-intercourse, taking advantage of useful IC treatments, such as physical therapy (PT), bladder installations, or medications, practicing interpersonal communication skills with their partner, and experimenting with sexual and non-sexual alternatives to penetrative sex.

Clinician	*How has IC affected your intimate relationships?*
Abby	*My sex life has gone out the window, which really impacts my relationship with my husband. I noticed that having sex often causes pain flares for me, and so I tend to avoid sex altogether, which I think frustrates both of us. But I don't want to be in more pain!*
Clinician	*It is very common for people with IC to experience disruptions in sexual intimacy, which may impact closeness within relationships. Have you told your husband about how pain has impacted your desire to have sex?*
Abby	*Not really, I avoid talking about it. It is sad and embarrassing.*
Clinician	*Many people find it hard to discuss such a vulnerable topic. Last week, we learned about using assertive communication. We can apply those same skills to communicating with your husband about sex, which may increase closeness and reduce feelings of frustration.*
Abby	*I feel guilty about not having sex. It's not that I don't love him, or that he does anything wrong, I just really don't want it to cause a flare-up.*
Clinician	*It sounds like penetrative sex has resulted in flare-ups for you in the past. There are plenty of alternatives to intercourse that can deepen intimacy without increasing pain or causing flare-ups. What are your thoughts about that?*
Abby	*I have never really thought about other options, though I would be willing to try.*
Clinician	*Are that any other intercourse alternatives that you have tried? What has worked?*
Abby	*We love cuddling and spooning, and sometimes we give each other massages.*
Clinician	*Those are all great options that can deepen sexual intimacy without penetration. Perhaps you can try more alternatives, and even non-sexual alternatives like intimate touch, hugging, or even spending time together without screens.*
Abby	*It is helpful to talk about other ways of increasing intimacy. I think my husband will be willing to try some other things out.*
Clinician	*Great! I also think it would be helpful to develop a plan for sexual intimacy when and if you feel ready. Getting prepared for intimacy can*

help to decrease anxiety and increase confidence. For example, you can try some of the relaxation strategies before or after sex, and you can even plan for sexual activity after helpful IC treatments, or even before visiting the doctor so while you are at the doctor you can get calming therapies afterward. Let's spend some time building a plan together...

Session Eight: Integration and Termination

The final session focuses on reviewing content and coping skills learned over the course of treatment. The patient and provider collaboratively reflect on patient experiences, progress, symptom changes, and the patient's perspectives of the therapeutic relationship. Discussions may include how treatment has impacted their life, how they feel about treatment concluding, a review of coping skills and how they have been useful. The patient and provider collaborate on any adjustments and barriers to the coping plan, and how coping skills may be used in the future to best fit needs and longer-term goals.

Chapter Summary

IC is a chronic, biopsychosocial pain condition that often greatly disrupts quality of life. Psychological distress and psychological comorbidities are common in individuals with IC, highlighting the need for non-pharmacological, biopsychosocial treatment options. This cognitive-behavioral protocol, supplemented with interpersonal techniques, is a promising intervention for the treatment and management of IC (McKernan et al., 2024a, b). Treatment strategies such as cognitive restructuring, emotion regulation, relaxation training, interpersonal communication, bladder training, sleep hygiene, reflect direct translation from research findings on the unique physical and mental health sequelae of symptoms and women's experiences of living with IC. Future research on cognitive-behavioral interventions for IC should consider treatment responses across varying disease presentations, phenotype, and duration, as well as different modalities including in-person, group-based, and self-guided interventions (McKernan et al., 2024a). Women with IC may benefit from group-based protocols for increased opportunity for social and emotional support, to share lived experiences, and to gain insight from those who have experienced symptom improvements. More research is needed on the effectiveness of cognitive-behavioral interventions for IC in women of minority racial and ethnic identities. The efficacy of Self-Management for IC highlights the need for mental health professionals to be fully embedded into specialty care, such as urology or gynecology clinics. Alongside medical providers, mental health providers can supplement medical intervention for IC and provide women with support, coping skills, and empowerment to live meaningful and fulfilling lives while successfully managing symptoms.

References

Akiyama, Y., & Hanno, P. (2019). Phenotyping of interstitial cystitis/bladder pain syndrome. *International Journal of Urology, 26*, 17–19.

Azevedo, K., Nguyen, A., Rowhani-Rahbar, A., Rose, A., Sirinian, E., Thotakura, A., Christopher, K., & Payne, M. D. (2005). Pain impacts sexual functioning among interstitial cystitis patients. *Sexuality and Disability, 23*, 189–208.

Bendrick, T. R., Sitenga, G. L., Booth, C., Sacco, M. P., Erie, C., Anderson, D. J., Urits, I., et al. (2022). The implications of mental health and trauma in interstitial cystitis. *Health Psychology Research, 10*(4), 40321.

Berry, S. H., Elliott, M. N., Suttorp, M., Bogart, L. M., Stoto, M. A., Eggers, P., Clemens, J. Q., et al. (2011). Prevalence of symptoms of bladder pain syndrome/interstitial cystitis among adult females in the United States. *The Journal of Urology, 186*(2), 540–544.

Bogart, L. M., Suttorp, M. J., Elliott, M. N., Clemens, J. Q., & Berry, S. H. (2011). Prevalence and correlates of sexual dysfunction among women with bladder pain syndrome/interstitial cystitis. *Urology, 77*, 576–580.

Brownstein, C., Garrett, L., Kline, E., Chandler, J., Mehall, N., Lowery, L., Smith, P., et al. (2023). MP21-02 experiences of minorities with interstitial cystitis/bladder pain syndrome. *Journal of Urology, 209*(Suppl 4), e284.

Carrico, D. J., Peters, K. M., & Diokno, A. C. (2008). Guided imagery for women with interstitial cystitis: Results of a prospective, randomized controlled pilot study. *The Journal of Alternative and Complementary Medicine, 14*(1), 53–60.

Carty, J., Lumley, M., Holmes, H., Tomakowsky, J., Schubiner, H., Dove-Medows, E., & Peters, K. (2016). (516) the effects of a stress and emotion interview for women with urogenital pain: A randomized trial. *The Journal of Pain, 17*(4), S103.

Chelimsky, G., Heller, E., Buffington, C. T., Rackley, R., Zhang, D., & Chelimsky, T. (2012). Co-morbidities of interstitial cystitis. *Frontiers in Neuroscience, 6*, 114.

Chen, A., Shahiyan, R. H., & Anger, J. T. (2022). Interstitial cystitis/bladder pain syndrome treatment: A systematic review of sexual health outcomes. *Sexual Medicine Reviews, 10*(1), 71–76.

Chiu, C. D., Lee, M. H., Chen, W. C., Ho, H. L., & Wu, H. C. (2017). Childhood trauma perpetrated by close others, psychiatric dysfunction, and urological symptoms in patients with interstitial cystitis/bladder pain syndrome. *Journal of Psychosomatic Research, 93*, 90–95.

Chuang, Y. C., Weng, S. F., Hsu, Y. W., Huang, C. L. C., & Wu, M. P. (2015). Increased risks of healthcare-seeking behaviors of anxiety, depression and insomnia among patients with bladder pain syndrome/interstitial cystitis: A nationwide population-based study. *International Urology and Nephrology, 47*, 275–281.

Chung, K. H., Liu, S. P., Lin, H. C., & Chung, S. D. (2014). Bladder pain syndrome/interstitial cystitis is associated with anxiety disorder. *Neurourology and Urodynamics, 33*(1), 101–105.

Cleeland, C. S., & Ryan, K. M. (1994). Pain assessment: Global use of the brief pain inventory. *Annals of the Academy of Medicine, Singapore, 23*(2), 129–138.

Clemens, J. Q., Mullins, C., Ackerman, A. L., Bavendam, T., van Bokhoven, A., Ellingson, B. M., MAPP Research Network Study Group, et al. (2019). Urologic chronic pelvic pain syndrome: Insights from the MAPP research network. *Nature Reviews Urology, 16*(3), 187–200.

Clemens, J. Q., Erickson, D. R., Varela, N. P., & Lai, H. H. (2022). Diagnosis and treatment of interstitial cystitis/bladder pain syndrome. *Journal of Urology, 208*(1), 34–42.

Dallas, K. B., Bresee, C., De Hoedt, A., Senechal, J. F., Barbour, K. E., Kim, J., Anger, J. T., et al. (2022). Demographic differences and disparities in the misdiagnosis of interstitial cystitis/bladder pain syndrome in a national cohort of VA patients. *Urology, 163*, 22–28.

Di Tella, M., & Castelli, L. (2016). Alexithymia in chronic pain disorders. *Current Rheumatology Reports, 18*, 1–9.

Eccleston, C., & Crombez, G. (2017). Advancing psychological therapies for chronic pain. *F1000Research, 6*.

Gonzalez, D. C., Khorsandi, S., Mathew, M., Enemchukwu, E., & Syan, R. (2022). A systematic review of racial/ethnic disparities in female pelvic floor disorders. *Urology, 163*, 8–15.

Gonzalez, G., Vaculik, K., Khalil, C., Zektser, Y., Arnold, C. W., Almario, C. V., Anger, J. T., et al. (2023). Experiences of women with interstitial cystitis/bladder pain syndrome: What can we learn from women's online discussions? *Journal of Urology, 209*(1), 208–215.

Hall, M. F., & Hall, S. E. (2013). When treatment becomes trauma: Defining, preventing, and transforming medical trauma. *VISTAS Online, 73*(1), 1–15.

Hassani, D., Flick, L., Sangha, H., Brown, L. A., Andy, U., & Arya, L. (2022). How do women with interstitial cystitis/bladder pain syndrome make treatment choices? *International Urogynecology Journal*, 1–11.

Hsieh, K. L., Chin, H. Y., Lo, T. S., Long, C. Y., Ho, C. H., Huang, S. K. H., Wu, M. P., et al. (2021). Interstitial cystitis/bladder pain syndrome patient is associated with subsequent increased risks of outpatient visits and hospitalizations: A population-based study. *PLoS One, 16*(9), e0256800.

Kabat-Zinn, J. (1990). Mindfulness-based stress reduction. *Using the wisdom of your body and mind to face stress, pain, and illness*, *467*.

Kanter, G., Komesu, Y. M., Qaedan, F., Jeppson, P. C., Dunivan, G. C., Cichowski, S. B., & Rogers, R. G. (2016). Mindfulness-based stress reduction as a novel treatment for interstitial cystitis/bladder pain syndrome: A randomized controlled trial. *International Urogynecology Journal, 27*, 1705–1711.

Kerns, R. D., Turk, D. C., & Rudy, T. E. (1985). The west haven-yale multidimensional pain inventory (WHYMPI). *Pain, 23*(4), 345–356.

Kirkham, A., & Swainston, K. (2022). Women's experiences of interstitial cystitis/painful bladder syndrome. *Western Journal of Nursing Research, 44*(2), 125–132.

Lai, H. H., Jemielita, T., Sutcliffe, S., Bradley, C. S., Naliboff, B., Williams, D. A., MAPP Research Network, et al. (2017). Characterization of whole body pain in urological chronic pelvic pain syndrome at baseline: A MAPP research network study. *The Journal of Urology, 198*(3), 622–631.

Lai, H. H., Vetter, J., Song, J., Andriole, G. L., Colditz, G. A., & Sutcliffe, S. (2019). Management of symptom flares and patient-reported flare triggers in interstitial cystitis/bladder pain syndrome (IC/BPS)—Findings from one site of the MAPP research network. *Urology, 126*, 24–33.

Landis, J. R., Williams, D. A., Lucia, M. S., Clauw, D. J., Naliboff, B. D., Robinson, N. A., MAPP Research Network Study Group, et al. (2014). The MAPP research network: Design, patient characterization and operations. *BMC Urology, 14*, 1–17.

Lee, M. H., Wu, H. C., Tseng, C. M., Ko, T. L., Weng, T. J., & Chen, Y. F. (2018). Health education and symptom flare management using a video-based m-health system for caring women with IC/BPS. *Urology, 119*, 62–69.

Linehan, M. (2014). *DBT Skills training manual*. Guilford Publications.

McKernan, L. C., Nash, M., & Carr, E. R. (2016). An integrative trauma-based approach toward chronic pain: Specific applications to interstitial cystitis/bladder pain syndrome. *Journal of Psychotherapy Integration, 26*(4), 378.

McKernan, L. C., Walsh, C. G., Reynolds, W. S., Crofford, L. J., Dmochowski, R. R., & Williams, D. A. (2018). Psychosocial co-morbidities in interstitial cystitis/bladder pain syndrome (IC/BPS): A systematic review. *Neurourology and Urodynamics, 37*(3), 926–941.

McKernan, L. C., Johnson, B. N., Reynolds, W. S., Williams, D. A., Cheavens, J. S., Dmochowski, R. R., & Crofford, L. J. (2019). Posttraumatic stress disorder in interstitial cystitis/bladder pain syndrome: Relationship to patient phenotype and clinical practice implications. *Neurourology and Urodynamics, 38*(1), 353–362.

McKernan, L. C., Bonnet, K. R., Finn, M. T., Williams, D. A., Bruehl, S., Reynolds, W. S., Crofford, L. J., et al. (2020). Qualitative analysis of treatment needs in interstitial cystitis/bladder pain syndrome: Implications for intervention. *Canadian Journal of Pain, 4*(1), 181–198.

McKernan, L. C., McGonigle, T., Vandekar, S. N., Crofford, L. J., Williams, D. A., Clauw, D. J., Reynolds, W. S., et al. (2024a). A randomized-controlled pilot trial of telemedicine-delivered cognitive-behavioral therapy tailored for interstitial cystitis/bladder pain syndrome. *Pain, 165*(8), 1748–1760.

McKernan, L. C., Williams, D. A., Walsh, E. G., Connors, E., Sutherland, S., Bonnet, K., Schlundt, D., Newbury, E., & Finn, M. (2024b). *Self-management for interstitial cystitis bladder pain syndrome*. Unpublished therapist treatment manual.

Meints, S. M., Cortes, A., Morais, C. A., & Edwards, R. R. (2019). Racial and ethnic differences in the experience and treatment of noncancer pain. *Pain Management, 9*(3), 317–334.

Munce, S. E., & Stewart, D. E. (2007). Gender differences in depression and chronic pain conditions in a national epidemiologic survey. *Psychosomatics, 48*(5), 394–399.

Nickel, J. C., Tripp, D., Teal, V., Propert, K. J., Burks, D., Foster, H. E., Interstitial Cystitis Collaborative Trials Group, et al. (2007). Sexual function is a determinant of poor quality of life for women with treatment refractory interstitial cystitis. *The Journal of Urology, 177*(5), 1832–1836.

Nickel, J. C., Shoskes, D., & Irvine-Bird, K. (2009). Clinical phenotyping of women with interstitial cystitis/painful bladder syndrome: A key to classification and potentially improved management. *The Journal of Urology, 182*(1), 155–160.

Nickel, J. C., Tripp, D. A., Pontari, M., Moldwin, R., Mayer, R., Carr, L. K., Nordling, J., et al. (2011). Childhood sexual trauma in women with interstitial cystitis/bladder pain syndrome: A case control study. *Canadian Urological Association Journal, 5*(6), 410.

Nickel, J. C., Tripp, D. A., Beiko, D., Tolls, V., Herschorn, S., Carr, L. K., Golda, N., et al. (2018). The interstitial cystitis/bladder pain syndrome clinical picture: A perspective from patient life experience. *Urology Practice, 5*(4), 286–292.

Payne, C. K., Joyce, G. F., Wise, M., Clemens, J. Q., & Urologic Diseases in America Project. (2007). Interstitial cystitis and painful bladder syndrome. *The Journal of Urology, 177*(6), 2042–2049.

Rice, K., Connoy, L., & Webster, F. (2024). Gendered worlds of pain: Women, marginalization, and chronic pain. *The Journal of Pain, 25*(11), 104626.

Richardson, H. (2024). *Understanding the lived experiences of women with interstitial cystitis (IC): A qualitative study of women's sexual experience* (Doctoral dissertation, Université d'Ottawal University of Ottawa).

Sullivan, M. J., Bishop, S. R., & Pivik, J. (1995). The pain catastrophizing scale: Development and validation. *Psychological Assessment, 7*(4), 524.

Suskind, A. M., Berry, S. H., Ewing, B. A., Elliott, M. N., Suttorp, M. J., & Clemens, J. Q. (2015). Mental health disorders in bladder pain syndrome/interstitial cystitis. *Journal of Urology, 193*(2), 522–527.

Sutcliffe, S., Newcomb, C., Bradley, C. S., Clemens, J. Q., Erickson, B., Gupta, P., Stephens-Shields, A., et al. (2023). Associations between urological chronic pelvic pain syndrome symptom flares, illness impact, and health care seeking activity: Findings from the multidisciplinary approach to the study of chronic pelvic pain symptom patterns study. *The Journal of Urology, 209*(4), 719–725.

Sutherland, S., Grace Kelly, A., McKernan, L. C., Dmochowski, R. R., Reynolds, W. S., & Sebesta, E. M. (2024). Coping with interstitial cystitis/bladder pain syndrome. *Neurourology and Urodynamics, 43*(8), 1895–1902.

Teichman, J. M., & Parsons, C. L. (2007). Contemporary clinical presentation of interstitial cystitis. *Urology, 69*(4), S41–S47.

Tripp, D. A., Nickel, J. C., FitzGerald, M. P., Mayer, R., Stechyson, N., & Hsieh, A. (2009). Sexual functioning, catastrophizing, depression, and pain, as predictors of quality of life in women with interstitial cystitis/painful bladder syndrome. *Urology, 73*(5), 987–992.

Tripp, D. A., Nickel, J. C., Krsmanovic, A., Pontari, M., Moldwin, R., Mayer, R., Nordling, J., et al. (2016). Depression and catastrophizing predict suicidal ideation in tertiary care patients with interstitial cystitis/bladder pain syndrome. *Canadian Urological Association Journal, 10*(11–12), 383.

Weissman, M. M., Gross, R., Fyer, A., Heiman, G. A., Gameroff, M. J., Hodge, S. E., Kaufman, D., Kaplan, S. A., & Wickramaratne, P. J. (2004). Interstitial cystitis and panic disorder: A potential genetic syndrome. *Archives of General Psychiatry, 61*(3), 273–279.

Williams, D. A. (2013). The importance of psychological assessment in chronic pain. *Current Opinion in Urology, 23*(6), 554–559.

Windgassen, S., & McKernan, L. (2020). Cognition, emotion, and the bladder: Psychosocial factors in bladder pain syndrome and interstitial cystitis (BPS/IC). *Current Bladder Dysfunction Reports, 15*(1), 9–14.

Windgassen, S. S., Sutherland, S., Finn, M. T., Bonnet, K. R., Schlundt, D. G., Reynolds, W. S., McKernan, L. C., et al. (2022). Gender differences in the experience of interstitial cystitis/bladder pain syndrome. *Frontiers in Pain Research, 3*, 954967.

Woolf, C. J. (2011). Central sensitization: Implications for the diagnosis and treatment of pain. *Pain, 152*(3), S2–S15.

Part II
Interventions with Adolescents and Young Adults

Chapter 9
Treating Vulvodynia in Women and Adolescent Girls Using Cognitive-Behavioral Therapy

Sophie Bergeron, Natalie O. Rosen, Caroline F. Pukall, and Serena Corsini-Munt

Vulvodynia is an umbrella term referring to idiopathic chronic vulvar pain of at least 3 months' duration that encompasses numerous conditions that vary in a number of ways (e.g., pain location and temporal pattern). The pain of vulvodynia can be generalized (i.e., experienced over the entire vulvar region) or localized to a specific location (e.g., vaginal entrance, clitoris) or locations (Bornstein et al., 2016). In addition, it can be elicited by contact or pressure (i.e., provoked); present some, most, or all the time in the absence of contact (i.e., unprovoked); or mixed (e.g., unprovoked pain that worsens in response to contact). Provoked pain may occur during sexual (e.g., vaginal insertion), nonsexual (e.g., pelvic examinations), or both types of situations (Bornstein et al., 2016). Furthermore, the temporal pattern of the pain can be intermittent, persistent, constant, immediate, or delayed, and the onset may be primary (i.e., present for as long as the person can remember or

S. Bergeron (✉)
Department of Psychology, Interdisciplinary Research Center on Intimate Relationship Problems and Sexual Abuse, Université de Montréal, Montréal, QC, Canada
e-mail: sophie.bergeron.2@umontreal.ca

N. O. Rosen
Departments of Psychology and Neuroscience, Obstetrics and Gynecology, Dalhousie University, Halifax, NS, Canada

C. F. Pukall
Department of Psychology, Centre for Neuroscience Studies, School of Rehabilitation Therapy, and Department of Biomedical and Molecular Sciences, Queen's University, Kingston, ON, Canada

S. Corsini-Munt
School of Psychology, University of Ottawa, Ottawa, ON, Canada

L. A. Payne (ed.), *Psychosocial Interventions for Chronic Pain in Women and Girls*, CBT: Science Into Practice, https://doi.org/10.1007/978-3-031-98876-9_9

secondary, in which the pain appears at some point later in life) (Bornstein et al., 2016). Importantly, certain subtypes of vulvodynia, based on their pain characteristics, have emerged as distinct; examples include provoked vestibulodynia (PVD; provoked pain localized to the vaginal entrance) and generalized unprovoked vulvodynia (GUV; unprovoked pain affecting the entire vulvar region).

Epidemiology

Based on a variety of studies examining the prevalence of vulvodynia, it appears to be a common condition affecting female-assigned individuals of all ethnicities and races; the prevalence of vulvodynia in gender diverse individuals is unknown. One US-based epidemiological study reported that, by the age of 40 years, 7–8% of women will have experienced vulvodynia symptoms at some point (Harlow et al., 2014), and another found that up to 16% of women experience vulvodynia during their lives (Harlow & Stewart, 2003). Similar prevalence rates have also been reported in studies based on Spanish and Portuguese samples (lifetime prevalence rates of 13% and 16%, respectively; Gomez et al., 2019; Vieira-Baptista et al., 2014). US-based research examining the prevalence of vulvodynia stratified by race found that Hispanic women have significantly higher rates of vulvodynia incidence and prevalence than non-Hispanic white women (Reed et al., 2014).

In a study examining prevalence based on a vulvodynia diagnosis, Black women were 43% less likely to meet criteria for vulvodynia than white women, which resulted in lower prevalence rates among Black (4.2%) as compared to white (9.3%) women (Reed et al., 2012b). The difference in prevalence rates between Black and white women may be explained by biases in diagnostic criteria that are developed based on primarily white samples; one study examining racial differences in the endorsement of the fifth edition of the Diagnostic and Statistical Manual of Mental Disorders (DSM-5) (American Psychiatric Association, 2013) criteria of Genitopelvic Pain/Penetration Disorder (GPPPD, a diagnosis that includes vulvodynia as well as other genitopelvic pain conditions) found that Black women had a 2.15 times higher likelihood of reporting pain than white women (Azim et al., 2023). However, Black women's reported experiences did not align with traditional descriptors of GPPPD (e.g., burning); instead, they often reported their pain as fitting none of them (Azim et al., 2023). Another study (Brown et al., 2015) found that Black women used the adjective "aching" more frequently than white women and that white women more often used the word "burning" to describe their pain—a descriptor that is commonly used to diagnose vulvodynia.

Most studies examining the prevalence of vulvodynia have focused on adult samples. However, the existence of the primary form of vulvodynia—indicating that the pain has been present since childhood (for unprovoked pain) or since first contact with the vulva (for provoked pain)—suggests that vulvodynia can be present in female-assigned children and teenagers as well. Indeed, a Canadian study of 1425 sexually active girls aged 13–19 years found that 20% reported pain during intercourse for more than 6 months (Landry & Bergeron, 2011). Although not a specific study of vulvodynia, the most painful location reported was at the vaginal opening, which is consistent with symptoms of PVD (Bornstein et al., 2016).

Etiology

The etiology of vulvodynia is multifactorial (Pukall et al., 2016), with different biopsychosocial influences playing a role in various degrees from individual to individual. Vulvodynia has been attributed to dysfunction in the central and peripheral nervous systems, pelvic floor muscles, inflammatory processes, and hormonal factors that interact with a wide range of psychological (e.g., increased depression and anxiety symptoms, low self-esteem), cognitive-affective (e.g., pain catastrophizing), interpersonal (e.g., partner responses), and social factors (e.g., gender role expectations) (Bergeron et al., 2020; Pukall et al., 2016). In addition, vulvodynia is highly comorbid with other chronic pain conditions, such as irritable bowel syndrome and fibromyalgia [e.g., Reed et al. (2012a)], and it is considered to be one of ten chronic overlapping pain conditions (Chronic Pain Research Alliance, 2015) that predominantly affect female-assigned individuals.

Relationship Factors

Given the location of the pain, vulvodynia entails significant impacts on all aspects of sexual well-being, such as desire, arousal, frequency, pleasure, satisfaction, and one's sense of self as a sexual partner and as a woman, as well as relationship adjustment (Ayling & Ussher, 2008; Chisari et al., 2021; Groven et al., 2016). A qualitative study revealed that heterosexual couples with vulvodynia report struggling to understand the pain and to navigate their sexual and social lives, findings that underscored the difficulty in communicating about the pain; in addition, sociocultural expectations around the importance of penile-vaginal intercourse and of the relative importance of men's (as opposed to women's) sexual satisfaction contributed to difficulties in terms of how to be sexual within the context of vulvodynia (Myrtveit-Stensrud et al., 2023). However, some couples experienced personal growth and stronger relationships because of the pain, working collaboratively to find solutions (Myrtveit-Stensrud et al., 2023). Findings of struggles and strengths in relationships are echoed by other qualitative studies as well (e.g., Lountzi & Durand, 2024), and much quantitative work supports the importance of relationship dynamics in the experience of vulvodynia (for a review, see Rosen & Bergeron, 2019). Vulvodynia also has wider reaching effects in terms of psychological well-being and overall quality of life (Patla et al., 2023), with many individuals reporting symptoms of depression and anxiety as well as feelings of isolation and reduced ability to engage in social interactions and other activities, such as work and hobbies (e.g., Tribó et al., 2020).

Given the myriad factors involved in the development and maintenance of vulvodynia and the far-reaching effects of this condition, a comprehensive treatment plan is suggested (Goldstein et al., 2016). Such plans often involve medical, pelvic floor, and psychotherapy interventions; medical treatments vary in terms of success depending on specific intervention and vulvodynia subtype, but both pelvic floor physiotherapy and psychotherapy are recommended for vulvodynia (Goldstein et al., 2016).

Research on Cognitive-Behavioral Therapy (CBT) for Vulvodynia

Among psychotherapy treatment options, cognitive-behavioral therapy (CBT) is the most commonly offered and empirically-supported. It focuses on reducing pain and improving sexual function and well-being, whether in individual, couple, or group formats. Hypothesized mechanisms of change and targets of intervention include (1) reconceptualizing vulvodynia as multidimensional and multifactorial, (2) reducing pain- and sexuality-related anxiety and distress, as well as associated behavioral and experiential avoidance via skills training and behavioral activation, (3) promoting communication of sexual needs and preferences, and (4) fostering self-efficacy. Treatment studies to date have involved adult women diagnosed with PVD. They focused on both second-generation CBT, which focuses on modifying less adaptive sexuality and pain-related thoughts and behaviors to improve sexual function and satisfaction and reduce sexual distress, and third-generation CBT, which aims to foster awareness and acceptance of thoughts, emotions, and behaviors, rather than their modification (e.g., mindfulness-based CBT).

Treatment Efficacy

In a three-arm randomized clinical trial (RCT), group CBT was equivalent to vestibulectomy—a minor day surgery—and superior to biofeedback for the primary outcome of pain during intercourse at a 2.5-year follow-up (Bergeron et al., 2008). Group CBT was superior to a first-line topical corticosteroid in another RCT (Bergeron et al., 2016), whereby intent-to-treat analyses showed that participants of both groups reported significant reductions in pain measures from baseline to post-treatment and 6-month follow-up, although the CBT group reported more pain reduction at 6-month follow-up. At post-treatment, women in the CBT condition reported greater treatment satisfaction, displayed less pain catastrophizing, and reported better global improvements in sexual function than women in the topical arm. In an RCT focusing on individual treatment, CBT resulted in significantly greater reductions in pain and improvements in sexual function than supportive psychotherapy 1 year post-treatment (Masheb et al., 2009). In a pilot clinical trial comparing individual CBT to comprehensive pelvic floor physical therapy, the two groups reported significant improvements in pain during intercourse, pain catastrophizing, and perceived control over pain at post-treatment. However, sexual function only improved in the CBT group (Goldfinger et al., 2016). An RCT comparing a novel couple CBT (CBCT) to topical lidocaine for PVD showed that for women, CBCT yielded significantly more improvements than lidocaine in pain unpleasantness at 6-month follow-up, pain anxiety and pain catastrophizing at post-treatment and 6-month follow-up, and sexual distress at post-treatment, and resulted in better treatment satisfaction and global sexuality improvements at both time points. Partners in the CBCT condition reported greater treatment satisfaction at both time points and greater sexuality improvements at post-treatment relative to partners in the topical arm (Bergeron et al., 2021).

Third-generation CBT approaches also appear promising in reducing pain and sexual distress. In a partially randomized study in which 130 women with vulvodynia were assigned to either 8 weeks of group CBT or group mindfulness-based CBT (MBCT), participants reported significant reductions in pain during intercourse, pain elicited with a vulvalgesiometer, and sexual distress at 6- and 12-month follow-ups, with no group differences (Brotto et al., 2020). In a small RCT comparing 8 weeks of group MBCT to an online education support group of the same duration, participants randomized to MBCT showed significantly greater improvements in sexual function and psychological distress compared with the education support group at the 6-month follow-up. Both also reported reductions in vaginal insertion pain (i.e., tampon test), with no group differences (Guillet et al., 2019). In another RCT evaluating a 6-week guided internet-based Acceptance and Commitment Therapy (ACT) for vulvodynia compared to usual medical care, participants randomized to ACT reported significantly greater reductions in pain during intercourse at post-treatment and 10-month follow-up, yet engaged in significantly fewer intercourse attempts than those randomized to usual care. At post-treatment, women in the ACT group reported significantly greater pain acceptance relative to those receiving usual care. There were no group differences on pain elicited from the tampon test or impact of pain on sexual function (Hess Engstrom et al., 2022).

In summary, studies to date suggest that CBT is more efficacious than some medical treatments/usual care and equivalent to vestibulectomy for reducing pain during intercourse, superior to topical applications for improving pain-related distress and sexuality outcomes, equivalent to pelvic floor physical therapy on most outcomes, and superior or equivalent to other psychological treatments for improving pain and sexuality outcomes.

Moderators and Mediators of Treatment Outcome

Moderators

Few studies have examined what might inform clinicians concerning which treatment works best for whom. A first RCT showed that for group CBT, greater pre-treatment pain during the cotton-swab test of the gynecological examination predicted greater pain on this outcome 2.5 years later (Bergeron et al., 2008). No other psychological, sexual, or pain predictors were identified. Another randomized trial examined the role of fear-avoidance variables (anxiety, fear of pain, pain catastrophizing, hypervigilance to pain, and pain self-efficacy) as predictors of treatment success for group CBT. Results indicated that only higher levels of pre-treatment pain self-efficacy were significantly associated with lower pain intensity at 6-month follow-up. None of the fear-avoidance variables predicted sexual function (Desrochers et al., 2010). In the context of an RCT focusing on CBCT compared to topical lidocaine, two studies examined moderators of treatment success for women with PVD. In the first, individual-level study, findings pointed toward two important moderators of women's sexuality outcomes in the CBCT condition: those with greater pre-treatment attachment avoidance had greater sexual distress and lower satisfaction and function at 6-month follow-up, whereas those who reported higher levels of pre-treatment childhood interpersonal trauma (abuse and neglect) had lower sexual satisfaction and function at 6-month follow-up (Charbonneau-Lefebvre et al., 2022). In the second study, focusing on both women and their partners, longer pre-treatment relationship duration, lower anxiety in women, in addition to higher solicitousness and higher approach goals (being motivated for sexual activity to achieve positive outcomes) in partners, predicted lower pain for women at 6-month follow-up, independent of treatment condition. For CBCT specifically, higher partner anxiety and lower women's approach sexual goals at pre-treatment predicted women's better sexual function at post-treatment (Rosen et al., 2021). In sum, women's greater pre-treatment pain and anxiety, lower pain self-efficacy and relationship duration, as well as partners' lower solicitousness and approach goals predicted women's worse pain outcomes, whereas women's greater attachment avoidance, childhood interpersonal trauma, and lower approach sexual goals in addition to partners' lower anxiety predicted women's worse sexuality outcomes. These findings emphasize the role of relational factors in predicting CBT outcomes for vulvodynia.

Mediators

Only two studies examined mediators of treatment success, and both stemmed from the same RCT in which CBCT was compared to topical lidocaine (Bergeron et al., 2021). In a first study focusing on fear-avoidance variables, results showed that women's decreases in pain catastrophizing at post-treatment mediated improvements in their pain intensity, sexual distress, and sexual function at 6-month follow-up. Partners' decreases in pain catastrophizing at post-treatment mediated their own and women's improved sexual function, as well as women's improved sexual distress (Santerre-Baillargeon et al., 2023). In a second study in which sexual communication-related mediators were measured at four different times during treatment, women's improved collaborative communication mediated post-treatment improvements in their own and their partners' sexual satisfaction, as well as their own sexual function and distress (Rancourt et al., 2022). Hence, pain catastrophizing and sexual communication patterns should be targeted in CBT for vulvodynia.

Case Study: Luiza—A Teen Coping with PVD

Luiza just turned 18 when she presented to therapy for the first time at the suggestion of her mother who recently read an article about vulvodynia. Luiza was a cisgender woman, living in a three-generation household with her mother, grandmother, and younger brother. Her grandmother is originally from Brazil, but her mother and aunts were all born in the US. Luiza reported pain with tampon and menstrual cup insertion, so she tended to avoid their use, and her mother was aware that Luiza avoids sitting for too long in certain positions. Over the last 2 years, since Luiza quit competitive gymnastics following a minor injury and some bullying from her peers, her mother has noticed that Luiza is more anxious, moody, and more concerned about personal hygiene (e.g., washing underwear twice on high heat because she is concerned about bacteria). Her grades as a high school senior have remained stable as an A-student. Luiza's mother was very involved during the self-referral process, but once Luiza started therapy, her mother gave space to Luiza to direct her contact with the therapist. Luiza is well-spoken but shy, curious, and interested in what can be addressed with therapy.

Early during the *assessment phase*, the therapist recommended that Luiza meet with a gynecologist to confirm the presence of vulvodynia and rule out active infection. The therapist asked Luiza to share her history related to her pain, ensuring to ask specific questions about genital health and attitudes that Luiza has about her body, her genitals, and relationships. Luiza's history with vulvar pain includes repeated urinary tract infections as a child that have resolved as she aged, but that left her with a sense that it was hard to keep her genitals clean and free of infection. These concerns have been heightened again recently as she starts to be sexual with her current partner, a boyfriend of 6 months. They have attempted vaginal intercourse twice and both times, Luiza reports that her pain was an 8 out of 10 on a 0 (none) to 10 (worst possible) pain rating scale, and she asked her partner to stop after 1 min. She reported that she thinks she is experiencing orgasms with her partner and on her own with non-penetrative activities, although masturbation is rare for her. She explained that her partner is very supportive, often checking with her about her pain, but she is worried that he will grow impatient with her if she cannot eventually have penetrative vaginal sex. She has started to notice that her body tenses when her partner touches her anywhere below the shoulders or when she hears her friends talking about sex, and this is contributing to negative thoughts such as "I'm not normal" and "my body is broken." The therapist validated Luiza's disclosures and provided relevant and brief psychoeducation to contextualize Luiza's experiences. "It is understandable to feel so defeated when dealing with chronic pain like this, and the pressure to feel normal is tough to navigate. Repeated experiences of pain can start to change the way we think and interact with others. One of the things we can work on in therapy is to help reduce the distress associated with your pain."

With established trust and in offering choice, the therapist invited Luiza to speak about adverse childhood experiences and unwanted sexual experiences. Luiza reported no childhood abuse but disclosed a first sexual experience with a past boyfriend when she was 14 who attempted manual vaginal insertion, which she found extremely painful, but she did not feel she could ask him to stop because she did not know how to explain her pain. To avoid talking to him about it, she ended the relationship the next day and remembers feeling embarrassed. She said it felt consistent with her understanding that sex would be painful and would lead to bleeding, a message she remembered hearing her aunts and grandmother talk about when she was younger. Luiza was worried that while other women in her family seemed to have gotten past the pain, she would never be able to, and this would make it hard to keep a partner and eventually have a family, the latter an important expectation in her familial culture. The therapist used a gradual approach to help Luiza expand on her history, fears, and family expectations. Adolescents may not be as expansive in their responses and may have fewer sexual experiences to draw on. Therefore, therapists should be prepared with a blend of open-ended and specific questions, with transparent explanations for how this information contributes to the therapist's understanding of the client's experience and can help form treatment recommendations.

With confirmation from the gynecologist, and Luiza's history and reported symptoms, it was likely that Luiza was experiencing primary PVD, localized to the vaginal entrance and with intermittent pain. The therapist also noted symptoms consistent with Generalized Anxiety Disorder, noting worry, catastrophizing, and avoidance behaviors. These diagnoses were presented to Luiza, along with a *conceptualization framed by the biopsychosocial model*. This non-pathologizing framework complements trauma-informed and culturally sensitive practice by providing the client with a holistic and interdependent way of considering biological, social, and psychological risk factors, as well as treatment targets. It can also help reduce the stigma associated with experiencing genital pain and pain during sex. It was new to Luiza, but having the conceptualization seemed to pave the way for their work together. "So, you're saying that there is a name for what I'm feeling, and this (referring to the model) is how it all fits together. For so long, I thought it was because of the UTIs or because it ran in my family, or maybe even all in my head. I've been trying to figure it out for so long."

The therapist used the biopsychosocial model to collaborate with Luiza about which elements they could work on in therapy and to establish *realistic treatment goals*. "Your pain is real, and it's not all in your head. The biopsychosocial model helps us understand the risk factors that can contribute to your pain, but it also can help us figure out what to work on in therapy because in working on one thing we might also get some movement on another related area—like decreasing worry about your body, or decreasing worry that a future activity is going to be painful, which might help reduce the tension when with friends or your boyfriend." While Luiza wished that the pain would just disappear, she was able to verbalize the following as a goal for therapy, "I just want to feel better in my own body and not feel like I'm broken. I want to be able to sit and study without so much pain. I want to have sex with my boyfriend." With these goals in mind, the therapist recommended a concurrent referral for physiotherapy for possible pelvic floor muscle implication given Luiza's history of high-level athleticism for many years. Treatment was structured across 12 weekly sessions, drawing from empirically validated treatment manuals, and focused on acceptance-based, third-generation CBT, with one-to-two sessions made available to invite Luiza's partner to join the therapeutic work. Luiza opted not to invite her partner but preferred to relay to him the between-session exercises she felt were relevant for their shared sexual experiences. Consistent with our approach, treatment strategies focused on *psychoeducation*, *pain journaling* to better understand and track which factors contributed to Luiza's pain experiences and which of these factors could be mitigated (e.g., rest and sleep; rumination, avoidant coping); *understanding pain attributions* with the underlying goal of privileging self-compassion and acceptance; *approach and avoidance goals for sex* framed from a value-based perspective; *facilitating sexual desire and arousal* by prioritizing pleasure and no- or low-pain sexual experiences; *diaphragmatic breathing and mindfulness body scan* for anxiety reduction; *cognitive defusion* for addressing negative and catastrophizing thoughts; and addressing *partner responses to pain* to provide a framework for helpful interactions relating to pain and sex. As the therapist explained when introducing the topic of partner responses to pain, "Behaviours are something we can ultimately make efforts to change, so by exploring how your partner responds to your pain, and even how you respond to your pain, we can shift to more helpful responses that help you cope rather than make you feel bad or contribute to avoiding touching, kissing, or other sexual activity."

By the *end of treatment*, Luiza reported a reduction in her bodily tension, that she could listen to friends talk about sex without feeling distressed, and that she was enjoying kissing and other sexual activities with her boyfriend without muscle tension. She explained, "I don't feel broken anymore. I see my pain as a part of me that I have to kind of take care of, but not something that will hold me back from the things I want in life." Luiza reported that since practicing regular breathing and mindfulness exercises and continuing with her physiotherapy, she can sit for longer periods and read or study with less discomfort. She also reported that she and her partner were gradually working up to a few minutes of vaginal penetration, and that her pain is a 4 out of 10 in these instances. Together, Luiza and the therapist identified *post-treatment goals*: the importance of a gradual approach, continued practice of cognitive defusion and mindfulness to help promote anxiety reduction, and continued empowerment of Luiza with pain self-efficacy, or the confidence that she can cope with her pain.

Luiza's goals were focused on decreasing the pain and connecting with her partner sexually. Despite these understandable and common goals among our clients, therapy can offer more than improvement on outcomes related to pain reduction and improvement in sexual function. This can be particularly important for clients who see little change in these areas. In Luiza's case, therapy offered her a space to process previous negative sexual experiences, recognize the impact of the messaging about sex she had heard while growing up, and develop more confidence in her ability to face the challenges associated with her vulvar pain.

Guidance for the Practicing Clinician: CBT Treatment Strategies

Individuals and their partners can participate in empirically developed CBT programs, either in a group format, such as the manualized treatment developed by Bergeron et al. (2001), or a couple format, such as the manualized treatment developed by Corsini-Munt et al. (2014, 2021). Group treatment can reduce the isolation, shame, and stigma often felt by people with vulvodynia through connection with, and learning from, other members during treatment. It is also cost-effective. These advantages might make a group format especially appealing for younger women and more accessible to those with lower incomes. The advantage of a couple therapy format is that relationship factors can be targeted directly. Not all affected individuals are in relationships or want to involve their partners in therapy, and some partners may not wish to participate. When group or couple therapy formats are not possible or appropriate, the key elements of treatment can be delivered in individual therapy.

Cognitive-Behavioral Therapy Phases and Strategies

Initial Phase: Alliance Building, Psychoeducation, and Goal Setting

An integrated assessment coupled with psychoeducation forms the basis for a strong therapeutic alliance. It is essential to validate the myriad ways in which the pain has impacted individual and couple sexuality and relationships. Providing information about the prevalence, characteristics, etiology, and consequences of vulvodynia helps to reduce feelings of isolation while allowing clients to situate their own experience within what is known about vulvodynia. The therapist introduces a biopsychosocial and multidimensional view of pain and helps clients identify the thoughts, feelings, behaviors, and couple interactions (when relevant) that maintain and exacerbate their pain and sexual difficulties. In home practice, the individual with vulvodynia or couple explores their genitals to identify where the pain is located (and where it is not) and to consider their attitudes toward genitals. Pain and sex journaling are introduced to gather information about the connections between multidimensional factors and pain. The journal contains a numerical rating scale of pain intensity, as well as questions about menstrual cycle, and each partners' thoughts, feelings, and behaviors before, during, and after a painful and/or sexual event, how they coped with the pain, and sexual desire and arousal (Fig. 9.1). Examining journal entries can help clients recognize patterns as well as the potential ways in which they have control over the pain and its psychosexual consequences.

During this stage, the therapist also helps clients develop two or three short-term, realistic goals. Goals frequently consist of one focused on pain reduction and one related to enhanced sexual well-being; ideally, at least one goal should include the

PAIN AND SEX JOURNAL

The pain and sex journal constitutes a tool that will help you better understand your pain and the factors that influence it, as well as how you (and your partner) feel about your sexual activity. The journal will also help you measure your progress in treatment. We will use the pain and sex journal regularly in our discussions. Fill in a journal **immediately** following each event that caused you pain, or soon after a sexual experience. It's ok if you don't fill in every box in the journal at first. With practice, you will get better at identifying thoughts, feelings, and behaviors in different contexts.

1. Day: ______________________ 2. Time: ______________________
3. Time of menstrual cycle: ______________ 4. Pain intensity (0 to 10): ______________
5. Duration of the pain: ______________

6. Describe the context for the pain experience:
Outside of sexual activity (e.g., tampon insertion, dilatation exercise) __________ During sexual activity __________

7. Describe your thoughts, feelings, and behaviors before, during, and after the pain and/or sexual experience:

	Before	During	After
Thoughts			
Feelings			
Behaviors			

Fig. 9.1 Pain and sex journal. Adapted from Corsini-Munt, Rosen, and Bergeron (2021)

For painful sexual experiences:

8. *How satisfying was your sexual experience (0-10)?* ____________

9. *How much time did you spend on sexual activities other than or before trying penetration?* ____________

10. *How aroused were you (0 to 10)?* ____________

11. *How much sexual desire did you feel? (0 to 10)?* ____________

12. *How relaxed did you feel (0 to 10)?* ____________

13. *What did you (or your partner) do to try to reduce the pain?* ____________

14. *How effective was this? (Circle the appropriate number).*

0 = did not help at all 1 = helped very little 2 = helped

somewhat 3 = helped a lot 4 = stopped the pain

15. *Any additional observations about the pain/sexual experience*

____

____

Fig. 9.1 (continued)

partner, where relevant. A goal focused on eliminating the pain is not realistic and should be discouraged. Rather, clients might emphasize pain reduction as a goal, together with a focus on reducing the negative interference of the pain in their lives. Likewise, it is generally unhelpful to focus goals on sexual frequency because it can reinforce stigma, pressure, and feelings of inadequacy. Individuals and couples can instead be encouraged to set goals related to enhanced sexual satisfaction, intimacy, and expanding the sexual repertoire to less or non-painful activities. Goals should be revisited throughout treatment to monitor progress and adjust as the treatment unfolds. At this early point, we also suggest investigating motivations for sex and how these align with their values—that is, why is sex important to them (and to their relationship, if relevant)? Such discussions help to ground the individual and/or couple in what they ultimately hope to work towards in treatment.

Second Phase: CBT Treatment Strategies

The second phase of treatment aims to reduce less adaptive coping strategies (e.g., avoidance, catastrophizing, hypervigilance) and enhance more adaptive, approach behaviors as well as effective emotion regulation, communication, and self-assertiveness. This phase focuses on reconnecting with one's own sexuality and/or sexuality with a partner through non-sexual physical and emotional intimacy, expansion of the sexual repertoire, and building satisfying sexual experiences. Better management of anxiety is critical because anxiety inhibits sexual arousal, fuels avoidance, and contributes to pelvic floor muscle dysfunction, which together increase genito-pelvic pain. We therefore introduce regular practice of diaphragmatic breathing early on to target anxiety.

Communication skills training is important early in treatment. Those in relationships are taught concrete skills (e.g., use of "I" language, reflective listening) that facilitate the disclosure of thoughts and feelings, and how to respond with empathy, acceptance, and validation. They also receive psychoeducation and discuss strategies to reduce solicitous and negative partner responses to painful sex and to promote facilitative responses (Rosen et al., 2013, 2015). Clients who are not in relationships can be supported in practicing communication skills and assertiveness, particularly in the first disclosure of their vulvodynia to new partners. Additional interventions focus on non-sexual physical and emotional intimacy, expanding sexual scripts beyond penetrative activities, and facilitating experiences of desire and arousal. Many clients report feelings of shame, guilt, frustration, and inadequacy about their reduced sexual desire and frequency because of the pain. This distress, coupled with the pain itself, may make it difficult for individuals with vulvodynia to explore their sexual needs and preferences to enhance pleasure. Identifying their sexual needs with patience and validation, again with guidance in effective communication, is crucial.

Avoidance (e.g., of affection, dating, home practice) and fear of penetration are common experiences in vulvodynia treatment and should be attended to directly in a validating way. Therapists can encourage clients to notice their avoidance and explore factors beyond pain that may play a role (e.g., sexual attitudes or inhibitions). For clients who are dating or in relationships, we introduce sensate focus (non-demand touching) exercises as a behavioral approach in this context, though adaptations of this exercise can also be made for single people. Sensate focus exercises target anticipatory anxiety and avoidance of physical touch, with an emphasis on mindfulness. In addition, drawing from acceptance-based CBT, cognitive defusion teaches clients a different way of interacting with unhelpful thoughts (e.g., worry that sex will always be painful and never enjoyable) that reduces the intensity and impact of these thoughts on emotions and behavior.

Final Phase: Review and Skill Consolidation

The final phase of treatment includes a comprehensive review of the therapy content and work toward skill consolidation and maintenance of gains in the future. The therapist helps the client(s) to see the changes they have made and to identify elements that may require continued effort. Given the multidimensional nature of vulvodynia, the therapist might recommend additional treatments to target aspects that were unaddressed in the CBT approach (e.g., pelvic floor physical therapy, anesthetic medication).

Common Therapeutic Issues and Contraindications

A history of childhood maltreatment or victimization including sexual, physical or psychological abuse, neglect, witnessing interparental violence, bullying, and discrimination or marginalization in one or both partners needs to be assessed at the onset of therapy and considered in the treatment plan as these are associated with worse pain and sexuality outcomes (Charbonneau-Lefebvre et al., 2022; Corsini-Munt et al., 2017). It is important not to present childhood maltreatment as the sole cause of vulvodynia, given that this condition is complex and multifactorial. Nonetheless, the therapist must be attuned to difficulties with trust that may affect the individual's or couple's capacity to establish a working alliance with the therapist. In addition, treatment strategies should be approached from a trauma-informed perspective, particularly interventions such as sensate focus. Therapists must have sufficient experience and training in delivering culturally-competent care as well as trauma-informed psychological treatments when working with these individuals and/or couples. Therapists must be mindful of cultural influences and ask clients to share any perceived cultural factors to avoid assumptions and biases. Another common presentation with vulvodynia is co-morbid mood and anxiety disorders. When these symptoms become central or interfere with the treatment plan for vulvodynia, then the client may need treatment targeting these concerns first, such as empirically validated CBT and/or medications. Treating anxiety and depression will better prepare them to cope with vulvodynia. Finally, significant relationship difficulties, which may involve sexual, psychological, and/or physical victimization, must be assessed before initiating treatment. Without doing so first, it will not be possible to work on vulvodynia-related pain and couple sexuality, given that the treatment requires trust between partners and some level of stability.

Treatment Considerations for Adolescents and Emerging Adults

Adolescents may hold the common misconception that the first sexual activity is meant to be painful, and this belief can delay treatment-seeking and be reinforced by uninformed health care providers. As with all affected women, validation of their pain and fears related to current or future intimate relationships is critical. Adolescents may be especially vulnerable to misinformation from peers or accessed via social media about the causes and treatment of genito-pelvic pain, underscoring the importance of psychoeducation. Although adolescents may not be as elaborative as adult clients during therapy, they are frequently open to trying new exercises, and they have fewer years of avoidance and catastrophizing to contend with; these important strengths may allow them to benefit more quickly from interventions. A group format may be particularly helpful for this age group to reduce feelings of isolation, build hope through shared experiences and success, and to enhance self-efficacy for managing the pain and pursuing satisfying sexual relationships. However, the evidence-based group CBT for vulvodynia described in this chapter has not yet been tested with adolescents.

Conclusion: Gaps Between Research and Clinical Practice

Significant progress has occurred in the last two decades concerning the development and evaluation of novel psychotherapies for vulvodynia, mostly focusing on second- and third-generation CBT using group, couple, individual, and online formats. This has led to the recommendation of CBT as a first-line treatment in clinical guidelines (Goldstein et al., 2016). Nevertheless, the existing treatment literature is limited, and the certainty of the evidence remains low. First, although relationship factors are known to play a role in vulvodynia (Rosen & Bergeron, 2019), the majority of treatment studies to date have not included the partner. Second, many involved relatively short-term treatment durations—from 8 to 12 weeks—which may not be sufficient to see significant improvements in sexuality outcomes, for which it is more challenging to move the needle. Third, most follow-up periods were short, such that the long-term effects of CBT interventions for vulvodynia are not well documented. Fourth, even though many individuals presenting with vulvodynia and their partners will have at least one comorbid condition, such as another sexual dysfunction, most studies evaluated CBT in relatively homogeneous groups of patients. Fifth, no treatment study to date has focused on adolescents, whereas vulvodynia is thought to begin during that critical developmental period (Landry & Bergeron, 2009). Lastly, there remains an urgent need to better understand contextual factors contributing to the different manifestations of vulvodynia. More research among samples that account for cultural, sexual, and gender diversity is needed, as a lack thereof impacts our ability to offer culturally competent and inclusive clinical care (Pukall et al., 2025).

References

American Psychiatric Association. (2013). *Diagnostic and statistical manual of mental disorders: DSM-5* (5th ed.). American Psychiatric Publishing, Inc.

Ayling, K., & Ussher, J. M. (2008). "If sex hurts, am I still a woman?" The subjective experience of vulvodynia in hetero-sexual women. *Archives of Sexual Behavior, 37*(2), 294–304. https://doi.org/10.1007/s10508-007-9204-1

Azim, K. A., Happel-Parkins, A., Moses, A., & Haardoerfer, R. (2023). Racialized differences across experiences and measurements of pain in genitopelvic pain/penetration disorder. *The Journal of Sexual Medicine, 20*(2), 224–228. https://doi.org/10.1093/jsxmed/qdac028

Bergeron, S., Binik, Y. M., & Larouche, J. (2001). *Cognitive-behavioral pain and sex therapy (CBPST) - Treatment manual.*

Bergeron, S., Khalifé, S., Glazer, H. I., & Binik, Y. M. (2008). Surgical and behavioral treatments for vestibulodynia: Two-and-one-half year follow-up and predictors of outcome. *Obstetrics & Gynecology, 111*(1), 159–166. http://www.ncbi.nlm.nih.gov/entrez/query.fcgi?cmd=Retrieve&db=PubMed&dopt=Citation&list_uids=18165405

Bergeron, S., Khalifé, S., Dupuis, M.-J., & McDuff, P. (2016). A randomized clinical trial comparing group cognitive-behavioral therapy and a topical steroid for women with dyspareunia. *Journal of Consulting and Clinical Psychology, 84*(3), 259–268. https://doi.org/10.1037/ccp0000072

Bergeron, S., Reed, B. D., Wesselmann, U., & Bohm-Starke, N. (2020). Vulvodynia. *Nature Reviews. Disease Primers, 6*(1), 36. https://doi.org/10.1038/s41572-020-0164-2

Bergeron, S., Vaillancourt-Morel, M.-P., Corsini-Munt, S., Steben, M., Delisle, I., Mayrand, M.-H., & Rosen, N. O. (2021). Cognitive-behavioral couple therapy versus lidocaine for provoked vestibulodynia: A randomized clinical trial. *Journal of Consulting and Clinical Psychology, 89*(4), 316–326. https://doi.org/10.1037/ccp0000631

Bornstein, J., Goldstein, A. T., Stockdale, C. K., Bergeron, S., Pukall, C., Zolnoun, D., Coady, D., & consensus vulvar pain terminology committee of the ISSVD, ISSWSH, & IPPS. (2016). 2015 ISSVD, ISSWSH and IPPS consensus terminology and classification of persistent vulvar pain and vulvodynia. *Obstetrics & Gynecology, 127*(4), 745–751. https://doi.org/10.1097/aog.0000000000001359

Brotto, L. A., Bergeron, S., Zdaniuk, B., & Basson, R. (2020). Mindfulness and cognitive behavior therapy for provoked vestibulodynia: Mediators of treatment outcome and long-term effects. *Journal of Consulting and Clinical Psychology, 88*(1), 48–64. https://doi.org/10.1037/ccp0000473

Brown, C. S., Foster, D. C., Bachour, C. C., Rawlinson, L. A., Wan, J. Y., & Bachmann, G. A. (2015). Presenting symptoms among black and white women with provoked vulvodynia. *Journal of Women's Health, 24*(10), 831–836. https://doi.org/10.1089/jwh.2014.5164

Charbonneau-Lefebvre, V., Vaillancourt-Morel, M.-P., Rosen, N. O., Steben, M., & Bergeron, S. (2022). Attachment and childhood maltreatment as moderators of treatment outcome in a randomized clinical trial for provoked vestibulodynia. *The Journal of Sexual Medicine, 19*(3), 479–495. https://doi.org/10.1016/j.jsxm.2021.12.013

Chisari, C., Monajemi, M. B., Scott, W., Moss-Morris, R., & McCracken, L. M. (2021). Psychosocial factors associated with pain and sexual function in women with Vulvodynia: A systematic review. *European Journal of Pain, 25*(1), 39–50. https://doi.org/10.1002/ejp.1668

Chronic Pain Research Alliance. (2015). *Impact of chronic overlapping pain conditions on public health and the urgent need for safe and effective treatment: 2015 analysis and policy recommendations*. https://chronicpainresearch.org/wp-content/uploads/2023/05/CPRA_WhitePaper_2015-FINAL-Digital.pdf

Corsini-Munt, S., Bergeron, S., Rosen, N. O., Mayrand, M. H., & Delisle, I. (2014). Feasibility and preliminary effectiveness of a novel cognitive-behavioral couple therapy for provoked vestibulodynia: A pilot study. *The Journal of Sexual Medicine, 11*(10), 2515–2527. https://doi.org/10.1111/jsm.12646

Corsini-Munt, S., Bergeron, S., Rosen, N. O., Beaulieu, N., & Steben, M. (2017). A dyadic perspective on childhood maltreatment for women with provoked vestibulodynia and their partners: Associations with pain and sexual and psychosocial functioning. *Journal of Sex Research, 54*(3), 308–318. https://doi.org/10.1080/00224499.2016.1158229

Corsini-Munt, S., Rosen, N. O., & Bergeron, S. (2021). *Cognitive-behavioral couple therapy (CBCT) treatment manual.*

Desrochers, G., Bergeron, S., Khalifé, S., Dupuis, M.-J., & Jodoin, M. (2010). Provoked vestibulodynia: Psychological predictors of topical and cognitive-behavioral treatment outcome. *Behaviour Research and Therapy, 48*(2), 106–115. https://doi.org/10.1016/j.brat.2009.09.014

Goldfinger, C., Pukall, C. F., Thibault-Gagnon, S., McLean, L., & Chamberlain, S. (2016). Effectiveness of cognitive-behavioral therapy and physical therapy for provoked vestibulodynia: A randomized pilot study. *The Journal of Sexual Medicine, 13*(1), 88–94. https://doi.org/10.1016/j.jsxm.2015.12.003

Goldstein, A. T., Pukall, C. F., Brown, C., Bergeron, S., Stein, A., & Kellogg-Spadt, S. (2016). Vulvodynia: Assessment and treatment. *The Journal of Sexual Medicine, 13*(4), 572–590. https://doi.org/10.1016/j.jsxm.2016.01.020

Gomez, I., Coronado, P. J., Martin, C. M., Alonso, R., & Guisasola-Campa, F. J. (2019). Study on the prevalence and factors associated to vulvodynia in Spain. *European Journal of Obstetrics, Gynecology, and Reproductive Biology, 240*, 121–124. https://doi.org/10.1016/j.ejogrb.2019.06.005

Groven, K. S., Råheim, M., Håkonsen, E., & Haugstad, G. K. (2016). "Will I ever be a true woman?" An exploration of the experiences of women with vestibulodynia. *Health Care for Women International, 37*(8), 818–835. https://doi.org/10.1080/07399332.2015.1103739

Guillet, A. D., Cirino, N. H., Hart, K. D., & Leclair, C. M. (2019). Mindfulness-based group cognitive behavior therapy for provoked localized vulvodynia: A randomized controlled trial. *Journal of Lower Genital Tract Disease, 23*(2), 170–175. https://doi.org/10.1097/LGT.0000000000000456

Harlow, B. L., & Stewart, E. G. (2003). A population-based assessment of chronic unexplained vulvar pain: Have we underestimated the prevalence of vulvodynia? *Journal of the American Medical Women's Association (1972), 58*(2), 82–88. https://www.ncbi.nlm.nih.gov/pubmed/12744420

Harlow, B. L., Kunitz, C. G., Nguyen, R. H., Rydell, S. A., Turner, R. M., & MacLehose, R. F. (2014). Prevalence of symptoms consistent with a diagnosis of vulvodynia: Population-based estimates from 2 geographic regions. *American Journal of Obstetrics and Gynecology, 210*(1), 40 e41-48. https://doi.org/10.1016/j.ajog.2013.09.033

Hess Engstrom, A., Bohm-Starke, N., Kullinger, M., Hesselman, S., Hogberg, U., Buhrman, M., & Skalkidou, A. (2022). Internet-based treatment for vulvodynia (EMBLA) - A randomized controlled study. *The Journal of Sexual Medicine, 19*(2), 319–330. https://doi.org/10.1016/j.jsxm.2021.11.019

Landry, T., & Bergeron, S. (2009). How young does vulvo-vaginal pain begin? Prevalence and characteristics of dyspareunia in adolescents. *The Journal of Sexual Medicine, 6*(4), 927–935. https://doi.org/10.1111/j.1743-6109.2008.01166.x

Landry, T., & Bergeron, S. (2011). Biopsychosocial factors associated with dyspareunia in a community sample of adolescent girls. *Archives of Sexual Behavior, 40*(5), 877–889. https://doi.org/10.1007/s10508-010-9637-9

Lountzi, A. Z., & Durand, H. (2024). Help-seeking experiences and intimate partner support in vulvodynia: A qualitative exploration. *Women's Health, 20*, 17455057241241866. https://doi.org/10.1177/17455057241241866

Masheb, R. M., Kerns, R. D., Lozano, C., Minkin, M. J., & Richman, S. (2009). A randomized clinical trial for women with vulvodynia: Cognitive-behavioral therapy vs. supportive therapy. *Pain, 141*(1–2), 31–40.

Myrtveit-Stensrud, L., Haugstad, G. K., Rème, S. E., Schaller, S. L., & Groven, K. S. (2023). "it's all my fault": A qualitative study of how heterosexual couples experience living with vulvodynia. *Acta Obstetricia et Gynecologica Scandinavica, 102*(10), 1378–1389. https://doi.org/10.1111/aogs.14537

Patla, G., Mazur-Bialy, A. I., Humaj-Grysztar, M., & Bonior, J. (2023). Chronic vulvar pain and health-related quality of life in women with vulvodynia. *Life (Basel), 13*(2). https://doi.org/10.3390/life13020328

Pukall, C. F., Goldstein, A. T., Bergeron, S., Foster, D., Stein, A., Kellogg-Spadt, S., & Bachmann, G. (2016). Vulvodynia: Definition, prevalence, impact, and pathophysiological factors. *The Journal of Sexual Medicine, 13*(3), 291–304. https://doi.org/10.1016/j.jsxm.2015.12.021

Pukall, C. F., Adams, O., Garas, M., Penniston, T., & Bergeron, S. (2025). What types of genitopelvic pain studies focus on sexuality, gender, and racially minoritized samples, and what are their outcomes? A scoping review. *Annual Review of Sex Research* (in revision).

Rancourt, K. M., Bergeron, S., Vaillancourt-Morel, M.-P., Lee-Baggley, D., Delisle, I., & Rosen, N. O. (2022). Sexual communication mediates cognitive-behavioral couple therapy outcomes: A randomized clinical trial for provoked vestibulodynia. *Journal of Family Psychology, 36*(7), 1073–1083. https://doi.org/10.1037/fam0000968

Reed, B. D., Harlow, S. D., Sen, A., Edwards, R. M., Chen, D., & Haefner, H. K. (2012a). Relationship between vulvodynia and chronic comorbid pain conditions. *Obstetrics & Gynecology, 120*(1), 145–151. https://doi.org/10.1097/AOG.0b013e31825957cf

Reed, B. D., Harlow, S. D., Sen, A., Legocki, L. J., Edwards, R. M., Arato, N., & Haefner, H. K. (2012b). Prevalence and demographic characteristics of vulvodynia in a population-based sample. *American Journal of Obstetrics and Gynecology, 206*(2), 170 e171–170 e179. https://doi.org/10.1016/j.ajog.2011.08.012

Reed, B. D., Legocki, L. J., Plegue, M. A., Sen, A., Haefner, H. K., & Harlow, S. D. (2014). Factors associated with vulvodynia incidence. *Obstetrics & Gynecology, 123*(2 Pt 1), 225–231. https://doi.org/10.1097/AOG.0000000000000066

Rosen, N. O., & Bergeron, S. (2019). Genito-pelvic pain through a dyadic lens: Moving toward an interpersonal emotion regulation model of women's sexual dysfunction. *Journal of Sex Research, 56*(4–5), 440–461. https://doi.org/10.1080/00224499.2018.1513987

Rosen, N. O., Bergeron, S., Sadikaj, G., Glowacka, M., Delisle, I., & Baxter, M. (2013). Impact of partner responses on sexual function in women with vulvodynia and their partners: A dyadic daily experience study. *Health Psychology, 33*, 823–831. https://doi.org/10.1037/a0034550

Rosen, N. O., Bergeron, S., Sadikaj, G., & Delisle, I. (2015). Daily associations among male partner responses, pain during intercourse, and anxiety in women with vulvodynia and their partners. *The Journal of Pain, 16*, 1312–1320. https://doi.org/10.1016/j.jpain.2015.09.003

Rosen, N. O., Vaillancourt-Morel, M.-P., Corsini-Munt, S., Steben, M., Delisle, I., Baxter, M. L., & Bergeron, S. (2021). Predictors and moderators of provoked vestibulodynia treatment outcome following a randomized trial comparing cognitive-behavioral couple therapy to overnight lidocaine. *Behavior Therapy, 52*(6), 1502–1515. https://doi.org/10.1016/j.beth.2021.05.002

Santerre-Baillargeon, M., Rosen, N. O., Vaillancourt-Morel, M.-P., Corsini-Munt, S., Steben, M., Mayrand, M.-H., & Bergeron, S. (2023). Mediators of change in cognitive-behavioral couple therapy for genito-pelvic pain: Results of a randomized clinical trial. *Health Psychology, 42*(3), 161–171. https://doi.org/10.1037/hea0001274

Tribó, M. J., Canal, C., Baños, J. E., & Robleda, G. (2020). Pain, anxiety, depression, and quality of life in patients with vulvodynia. *Dermatology, 236*(3), 255–261. https://doi.org/10.1159/000503321

Vieira-Baptista, P., Lima-Silva, J., Cavaco-Gomes, J., & Beires, J. (2014). Prevalence of vulvodynia and risk factors for the condition in Portugal. *International Journal of Gynaecology and Obstetrics, 127*(3), 283–287. https://doi.org/10.1016/j.ijgo.2014.05.020

Chapter 10
From Screen to Session: Tailoring Digital Cognitive Behavioral Therapy for Adolescent and Young Adult Females with Chronic Pain

Caitlin B. Murray, Kaylee Yokoyama, and Tonya M. Palermo

Introduction

Chronic pain, defined as pain persisting for 3 months or longer, is a common, costly, and burdensome condition that affects approximately 12% of adolescents and young adults (AYAs; ages 18–25) worldwide (Murray et al., 2022). Chronic pain has a pervasive impact on young people's daily functioning, as evidenced by missed school and work, withdrawal from social activities, and frequent co-occurrence of insomnia and mood disorders such as anxiety and depression (King et al., 2011). If left untreated, chronic pain can result in serious long-term consequences extending into adulthood, including a higher likelihood of high school dropout and poorer vocational outcomes (Murray et al., 2020). These substantial impacts and long-term sequelae underscore the need for early intervention and effective pain management strategies for youth (Palermo et al., 2020).

Description of Clinical Implementation Material: This chapter includes a detailed case example illustrating the use of digital CBT alongside face-to-face therapy for a young adult female with chronic pelvic pain, featuring sample dialogue between the client and her psychologist.

C. B. Murray (✉) · T. M. Palermo
Center for Child Health, Behavior, and Development, Seattle Children's Research Institute, Seattle, WA, USA

Department of Anesthesiology and Pain Medicine, University of Washington School of Medicine, Seattle, WA, USA
e-mail: caitlin.murray@seattlechildrens.org

K. Yokoyama
Center for Child Health, Behavior, and Development, Seattle Children's Research Institute, Seattle, WA, USA

L. A. Payne (ed.), *Psychosocial Interventions for Chronic Pain in Women and Girls*, CBT: Science Into Practice, https://doi.org/10.1007/978-3-031-98876-9_10

Psychological interventions are a cornerstone of chronic pain management, offering a safe, effective complement or alternative to medication. Among these approaches, cognitive behavioral therapy (CBT) for chronic pain is the most widely researched. CBT is grounded in the biopsychosocial model and aims to modify behavioral and cognitive responses to pain. CBT interventions—delivered either in person or via digital platforms—teach pain self-management skills. They have been shown to significantly reduce pain intensity and disability in both youth and adults with chronic pain (Palermo et al., 2020). Such treatments typically focus on relaxation training, activity pacing, cognitive restructuring of pain-related thoughts, and goal setting to encourage a gradual return to activities.

Despite the success of CBT-based approaches for chronic pain, not all individuals respond equally. Such variability in outcomes may be partly explained by individual differences in pain experiences and their impacts. Sex and gender differences can play a crucial role in shaping pain perception and treatment response (Paller et al., 2009; Bartley & Fillingim, 2013). Women and girls report a higher prevalence and greater intensity of chronic pain across many conditions than men (e.g., musculoskeletal disorders, migraines, fibromyalgia; Osborne & Davis, 2022; Li et al., 2023; Overstreet et al., 2023). These disparities are influenced by a confluence of hormonal, neurobiological, and psychosocial factors (Rosen et al., 2017; Hashmi & Davis, 2014). For example, women are more prone to pain catastrophizing and tend to experience higher levels of pain-related distress, which can influence their pain management strategies and outcomes (Bartley & Fillingim, 2013). Overall, these differences underscore the need for personalized pain management approaches that account for gender-specific factors to optimize treatment efficacy and patient outcomes.

However, most CBT programs are manualized "one-size-fits-all" interventions that do not account for sex- or gender-related factors. Thus, there is a compelling opportunity to refine and personalize CBT to address the unique needs of AYA females. Digital health interventions such as mobile CBT applications represent a promising avenue for enhancing the personalization, accessibility, and appeal of chronic pain treatment for AYA females. Digital CBT platforms leveraging various delivery modes—websites, apps, games, even virtual reality—may be particularly suitable for this age group because of their familiarity with technology and preference for interactive content (Liverpool et al., 2020). Moreover, integrating digital CBT with traditional in-person therapy can optimize engagement and outcomes by combining the convenience and scalability of technology with the personalized guidance and support of a clinician (Wong et al., 2020).

Given these considerations, this chapter explores the current landscape of digital CBT for chronic pain, with an emphasis on gender-specific considerations for AYA females. First, we briefly review evidence on sex and gender differences in chronic pain and responses to CBT-based treatments. Next, we summarize the state of the science on digital CBT in pain management, including findings related to efficacy, accessibility, and integration into clinical practice. We then present a case study illustrating the use of a mobile CBT app alongside face-to-face therapy for a young adult female with chronic pelvic pain. Through this case, we highlight strategies for adapting digital CBT to meet the needs of AYA female patients. Finally, we conclude with practical guidance for clinicians on integrating digital behavioral interventions into practice and a discussion of future research directions to further enhance pain management for women and girls.

Sex and Gender Differences in CBT Treatment Outcomes

Individuals with chronic pain exhibit considerable variability in symptom presentation and comorbidities, and gender has emerged as an important factor that may influence treatment outcomes (Pieh et al., 2012; Pester et al., 2022). Emerging evidence suggests that while CBT for chronic pain is broadly effective across genders, females may experience greater or more rapid improvements in certain domains. For example, in adults with chronic pain, women have demonstrated larger reductions in depression and quality of life and improvements in pain acceptance from CBT and interdisciplinary pain management programs (Burns et al., 2022; Jensen et al., 2001; Pester et al., 2022; Pieh et al., 2012). Similarly, a recent meta-analysis of pediatric chronic pain (excluding headache conditions) found that girls had significantly greater reductions in pain-related disability than boys (Boerner et al., 2017). These findings highlight the potential for gender to moderate treatment effects and underscore the importance of examining sex-specific responses, particularly in AYA populations.

Several mechanisms may account for these gender differences in treatment response. Adolescent girls tend to use more emotion-focused coping strategies and report higher levels of pain catastrophizing than boys (Lynch et al., 2007; Sullivan et al., 2000)— precisely the kinds of maladaptive responses that CBT targets. Women and girls also often exhibit greater empathy and emotional insight, which may enhance engagement and the therapeutic alliance in CBT (Lim et al., 2018). Moreover, internalizing comorbidities like anxiety and depression are more common in females with chronic pain. Because CBT directly targets these conditions, this prevalence may partially explain the stronger responses observed in women (Osborne & Davis, 2022). Improvements in pain acceptance—another key mechanism in CBT—have been shown to mediate treatment gains and appear to be more robust in women. Together, these factors underscore the need to tailor CBT interventions to the unique needs of AYA females to optimize therapeutic outcomes. Acknowledging these important gender-specific factors, the following section highlights opportunities and challenges associated with digital CBT in chronic pain management.

Digital CBT for Chronic Pain: Opportunities and Challenges

Digital cognitive-behavioral therapy (digital CBT)—delivered via digital platforms such as mobile apps and web programs—has a growing body of evidence supporting its efficacy in managing chronic pain. Meta-analyses have examined digital (internet-delivered) interventions for chronic pain across age groups. For example, in pediatric chronic pain, a meta-analysis of psychological therapies found beneficial effects on pain and disability, noting that internet-based programs are effective for various conditions (Fisher et al., 2019). In adults, multiple studies of internet- or app-delivered CBT for chronic back pain have reported reductions in pain intensity and interference, along with improvements in fatigue, mood, and quality of life, relative to control groups (Gandy et al., 2022; Rosser et al., 2023). Notably, a recent review concluded that internet and mobile CBT yielded especially strong gains for patients with chronic pain (as well as those with conditions like cancer and arthritis) compared to other chronic illnesses (Tao et al., 2023). Moreover, remotely delivered pain interventions have shown efficacy comparable to in-person treatment in the few trials that have directly compared the two modalities (MacKenzie et al., 2024). Overall, these findings suggest that digital CBT can effectively teach key self-management skills and improve pain-related outcomes in both pediatric and adult populations.

Digital delivery offers several advantages for making CBT more accessible. Youth and adults with chronic pain often face numerous barriers to traditional face-to-face pain psychology care. These obstacles include geographic distance from specialty clinics, a shortage of trained pain psychologists, long waitlists, and the financial costs of frequent clinic visits. Digital CBT aims to bridge these gaps by providing therapy content remotely, on-demand, and at low cost. In doing so, it can reach patients who might otherwise not engage in psychological care. Digital formats may also appeal to AYA populations given their familiarity with technology and preference for flexible, self-paced learning.

Despite the promise of digital CBT, several challenges remain. Notably, most existing face-to-face and digital CBT programs were developed either for adolescents (typically under 18) or general adults, with very few specifically tailored to older adolescents and young adults (ages 18–29). The young adult developmental stage comes with distinct challenges (e.g., transitioning to college or work, gaining independence from parents) and potentially different treatment needs and preferences (Foy et al., 2024; Twiddy et al., 2017). Similarly, although women and girls are disproportionately affected by chronic pain, few digital programs address female-specific needs. Most current programs are "one-size-fits-all" and do not include content on issues such as menstrual cycle influences or body image—an area ripe for future innovation targeting AYA females. Furthermore, even though efficacy in controlled trials is well established, the real-world effectiveness of digital CBT can vary. Attrition and limited engagement are critical challenges in digital CBT interventions (Nahum-Shani et al., 2022a, b). Studies suggest that AYAs may prefer digital interventions that offer interactive, personalized, and relationally supportive content, aspects that are frequently lacking in generic digital CBT platforms, resulting in diminished engagement (Liverpool et al., 2020; Pretorius et al., 2019). While understudied, such issues may be particularly pronounced among AYA females. Gender-specific experiences, such as fluctuations in pain intensity linked to the menstrual cycle, social pressures, and body image concerns, may complicate consistent digital CBT usage if tailored content and strategies targeting these areas are not incorporated. If digital intervention content does not feel relevant or relatable, AYA women and girls may disengage, underscoring the importance of tailoring digital tools to their unique interests and daily life context.

Given these identified opportunities and challenges, successful integration of digital CBT into clinical practice requires thoughtful strategies. The following section provides practical recommendations for clinicians, followed by a case example demonstrating these strategies in real-world application.

Integrating Digital CBT for Chronic Pain into Practice

Integrating digital CBT for chronic pain into practice—such as mobile apps or web-based programs—can augment traditional pain management and improve patient outcomes (see Table 10.1 for examples of evidence-based digital CBT tools for chronic pain). These tools extend the reach of therapy beyond clinic walls by providing continuous support and opportunities to practice skills between sessions. For patients facing long wait times for specialty pain treatment or limited access to pain psychologists, a digital CBT program can serve as an interim intervention to prevent their condition from deteriorating. For instance, adolescents referred to a pain clinic often wait many months (6–7 months on average; Palermo et al., 2019) for their first appointment, during which time their pain and functioning may worsen. Providing a structured internet- or app-based CBT program during this waiting period can empower patients with self-management strategies and potentially improve symptoms, or at least mitigate declines. For those already in face-to-face therapy, digital interventions can reinforce and personalize care. They enable patients to monitor symptoms and interact with therapeutic content daily or as needed (for example, using a relaxation exercise in an app during a pain flare), which helps consolidate skills learned in weekly sessions.

Clinicians can incorporate digital CBT into pain management in several ways, ranging from minimal to intensive provider involvement. One approach is to prescribe a self-guided digital program to appropriate patients and then monitor their progress. For example, a psychologist might recommend a reputable pain self-management app (such as WebMAP mobile; Palermo et al., 2020) to a motivated AYA patient, who could work through the modules independently. Another approach is to use digital CBT as an adjunct to ongoing therapy. In this model, the clinician and patient collaboratively select specific app features or online modules to use between sessions (such as daily pain tracking or a cognitive reframing exercise), and then review these activities in subsequent face-to-face visits. A related strategy

Table 10.1 Examples of evidence-based digital CBT tools for chronic pain (mobile apps and web programs)

Digital tool	App or web program	Target population	Access & links
PainTRAINER (Allen et al., 2021)	Web program	Adults with chronic pain (tested so far in rheumatologic conditions, trials ongoing)	Free paintrainer.org/login-to-paintrainer/
The Pain Course (Dear et al., 2018; Dudeney et al., 2024)	Web program	Adults with chronic pain (mixed conditions)	Free https://www.ecentreclinic.org/pain-course
Goalistics Chronic Pain Management Program (Wilson et al., 2015)	Web program	Adults with chronic pain (general; often those on long-term opioids)	Free https://www.mood.goalistics.com/
ICanCope with Pain (Stinson et al., 2014)	Web program	Adolescents with chronic pain (mixed conditions)	Free https://www.icancopewithpain.com/
Curable (Thomson et al., 2024)	Mobile App (Android or iOS)	Adults with persistent pain (mixed conditions)	Free (with sign-up for clinicians, free trial period for patients) https://www.curablehealth.com/clinicians
Stanza (Gendreau et al., 2024)	Mobile App (Android or iOS)	Adults with chronic pain (fibromyalgia)	Free (with prescription from clinicians, only available in select US states) https://swingtherapeutics.com/stanza/
WebMAP Mobile (Web-Based Management of Adolescent Pain; Palermo et al., 2020)	App (Android and iOS)	Adolescents with chronic pain (mixed conditions)	Free https://www.megfoundationforpain.org/webmap-mobile/
Pain Buddy (Hunter et al., 2020)	App (Android and iOS)	Children with chronic or recurrent pain (tested in pediatric cancer patients, ages ~8–18)	Free https://health.choc.org/a-gain-against-pain/
Phendo (Urteaga et al., 2020). Note: No clinical trial data available	App (Android and iOS)	Research app that focuses on symptom tracking for adolescents and adults with chronic pelvic pain or endometriosis	Free https://citizenendo.org/phendo/

is clinician-guided digital CBT, where the patient completes a structured online CBT course (with educational lessons and homework) while the clinician provides brief weekly check-ins via secure messaging, phone, or in-person contact to support adherence and answer questions. This strategy can be especially useful for patients on waitlists or in remote areas—the clinician essentially "coaches" the patient through the digital program to ensure accountability. Indeed, a decision tree can help determine whether a patient would benefit most from a purely self-guided program, a clinician-guided program, or a blended approach (combining in-person and digital therapy), depending on their needs and context (Sundararaman et al., 2017).

One practical challenge with digital CBT programs is ensuring adherence—many users start an app or online course but fail to complete it. To boost engagement, clinicians can leverage the principle of "supportive accountability": patients are more motivated to use digital interventions when they know their provider is monitoring their progress and will follow up (Mohr et al., 2011). In addition, setting concrete expectations for digital tool use (for example, "Log your pain and mood in the app every day, and listen to the guided imagery audio at least three times this week") and tying these activities to the patient's personal goals can provide clear structure and purpose to the intervention.

In summary, effectively integrating digital CBT into practice involves selecting the right candidates (patients comfortable with technology and open to self-guided work), matching the integration method to the care context (self-help, adjunct, or clinician-guided), and actively engaging the patient to support use of the tool. When implemented thoughtfully, blending digital interventions with face-to-face care can broaden the reach of treatment and enhance its efficacy, as illustrated by the following case study.

Case Study: Tailoring Digital CBT for a Young Adult Female with Chronic Pelvic Pain

"Alexis" is a 21-year-old female college student in her third year. She has a history of chronic pelvic pain that began at age 13 during her menstrual periods. She was later diagnosed with endometriosis and underwent laparoscopic surgery as treatment. Despite surgery and other medical interventions (including hormonal therapy), Alexis continues to experience daily pelvic pain, which becomes especially intense and disabling during her menstrual periods and times of high stress.

Alexis's chronic pain significantly interferes with her life. She has difficulty sitting through long lectures due to the discomfort, causing her to miss classes. She also avoids social activities; for instance, she no longer dates because sexual activity exacerbates her pain. As a result, her most recent relationship ended last year, and she often feels lonely. Alexis used to be physically active (she ran cross-country in high school), but now she rarely exercises aside from walking to the bus because she fears triggering her pain. She has been feeling depressed about her situation and often thinks, "This is ruining my life; I'm broken." She sometimes experiences panic symptoms when her pain unpredictably increases. She worries that it signals something seriously wrong or that she will need to go to the emergency room (as happened twice in the past).

In collaboration with Alexis, her pain psychologist recommended incorporating a smartphone-based pain management app as an adjunct to weekly CBT sessions.

Together, they set specific goals for app use (for example, daily pain and mood logging and using a relaxation exercise during intense pain; see Fig. 10.1 for an example of symptom tracking in the WebMAP app) and chose app modules targeting her key concerns. For instance, they focused on cognitive restructuring exercises to challenge her negative self-talk and mindfulness techniques for her to use during pain flares. In follow-up sessions, the psychologist reviewed Alexis's progress with the app to reinforce accountability and provide support.

Over the next several weeks, Alexis engaged actively with both the app and her face-to-face therapy. Using the app's pain diary feature, she identified triggers for her symptoms—observing that stress and poor sleep worsened her pain—and practiced mindfulness techniques while reframing negative thoughts with the app's CBT exercises. She found the guided relaxation audio especially helpful at night when she would otherwise lie awake worrying. In therapy sessions, her psychologist reinforced these skills and helped troubleshoot barriers (for example, they brainstormed cues to remind her to use the app before bed). As Alexis applied these strategies in real time between sessions, she began to feel a greater sense of control over her pain.

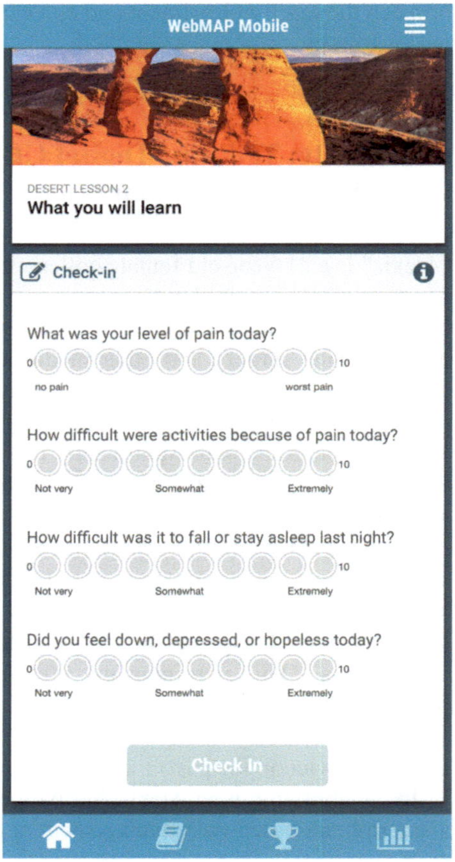

Fig. 10.1 Example of symptom tracking in the WebMAP app

Throughout treatment, integrating the app facilitated rich interactions between therapist and client and enabled more tailored adjustments to care. The following dialogue between Alexis and her therapist demonstrates how digital CBT was tailored to Alexis's needs:

Therapist: *"Looking at your pain tracker, I see your worst day was last Thursday. You recorded a pain level of 9/10 and a mood of 2/10. What was going on that day?"*

Alexis: *"That was the day I started my period and had two classes back-to-back. I was in a lot of pain and felt so tired and overwhelmed. I started having flashbacks of going to the emergency room. I couldn't breathe, and the pain was so bad I went back to my dorm."*

Therapist: *"That does sound overwhelming. And what happened after you went back to your dorm?"*

Alexis: *"Well, I tried to do what we talked about and use the app. I did the thought-challenging exercise... I'll show you what I wrote down: 'I can't handle this. I'm going to fail all my classes. There is something wrong with my body.' Then the app asked me, 'Is there evidence for this thought?' and I realized I've gotten through days like that before...I wrote an alternative thought: 'I am in pain right now, but I've managed this before, so I can try to get through it today.' It didn't make the pain vanish, but it stopped me from panicking."*

Therapist: *"That's excellent—you caught the catastrophizing and reframed it. What happened next?"*

Alexis: *"I did the box breathing exercise we practiced last week and ended up going to my next class. I was a little late, but I was proud of myself for pushing through."*

In this dialogue, the therapist and client review the app's data together and use its features (thought-challenging prompts, relaxation techniques) as a springboard for CBT intervention—specifically cognitive restructuring and positive reinforcement of gradual return to activities. This case illustrates how a digital CBT tool can be tailored and integrated into therapy to address the specific challenges faced by a young woman with chronic pain. The mobile app served as a vehicle for delivering evidence-based CBT techniques in real time, while the therapist's guidance ensured these techniques were personalized to her and that she remained engaged—thus helping to overcome potential barriers to adherence. Drawing insights from this case example, we now outline specific practical recommendations to assist clinicians in implementing digital CBT interventions into clinical care.

Summary of Practical Guidance for Clinicians

Integrating digital CBT for pain into clinical practice requires careful implementation. Below, we outline five practical recommendations and best practices for clinicians, drawn from current research and clinical experience:

1. *Select patients who are likely to benefit.* Identify patients who are likely to benefit from digital CBT interventions. Good candidates have access to necessary technology (e.g., a smartphone or computer), at least moderate digital literacy, and an openness to technology-based self-guided activities. Consider offering a self-guided digital CBT program to patients on a pain clinic waitlist to provide psychological support and coping strategies while they await face-to-face treatment.
2. *Introduce and personalize the evidence-based CBT program:* Prescribe an evidence-based app or online program and explain that it is part of the treatment plan rather than a standalone therapy. Emphasize the rationale (for example, "This app will help you practice the pain-coping skills we discuss and keep track of your progress between sessions."). Provide a brief orientation to the app and choose the first module or activity together during a session. This initial investment can increase the patient's confidence and willingness to use the tool. Many apps allow the selection of specific modules or offer other customizable features. Select the modules most relevant to the patient's issues (for instance, use a sleep module if insomnia is one of the patient's goals). Encourage the patient to personalize in-app goals or use symptom-tracking functions that address their unique stressors.
3. *Facilitate and sustain engagement:* Dedicate part of each session to reviewing the patient's use of the digital tool. This review could include looking at symptom-tracking charts, discussing which exercises the patient tried, and troubleshooting any difficulties. Incorporating app data can enrich sessions with objective measures (for example, displaying a graph of pain ratings over several weeks) and provide immediate talking points. Leverage supportive accountability by regularly checking the patient's progress and expressing continued interest in their work. Given the heightened levels of emotional insight and empathy in young women, maintaining regular supportive feedback can significantly bolster engagement and adherence. Celebrate small successes—for instance, if the app shows the patient completed exercises on 3 of 7 days, acknowledge that effort. Encourage the patient to set reminders or alerts on their device to prompt app use at routine times (e.g., a nightly reminder to do a relaxation exercise). Some programs include gamification elements (such as points, badges, or streaks); frame these as fun challenges to boost motivation. Additional strategies to improve adherence include simplifying intervention tasks (so they are not overly time-consuming), incorporating feedback (for example, in-app positive reinforcement or the clinician's personalized comments on entries), and addressing technical issues promptly so that frustration does not hinder use.
4. *Address digital health disparities.* Be mindful of disparities in access and strive for equitable implementation of digital interventions. Some AYA females may face additional barriers due to socioeconomic, cultural, or accessibility factors. Selecting digital tools that are available on multiple platforms (smartphone, tablet, computer) and free of charge to avoid economic barriers. If available, use culturally adapted or multilingual versions of digital programs.

5. *Tailor to AYA females:* Tailor interventions specifically to the unique needs of AYA females by selecting apps and content explicitly designed to address prevalent gender and developmental-related issues. For example, if a patient's pain fluctuates with her menstrual cycle, it may be useful to incorporate an app that includes menstrual cycle tracking, and/or content or face-to-face discussions centered on female-specific experiences and biopsychosocial mechanisms of pain. If the digital program does not cover body image and self-esteem issues that commonly emerge in AYA females—it may be useful to incorporate into assessment and face-to-face treatment. Similarly, as discussed earlier, young women with chronic pain may exhibit higher levels of pain catastrophizing; thus, it may be useful to ensure digital CBT content emphasizes cognitive strategies to address dysfunctional thought patterns.

It is also important to ensure the digital content is developmentally congruent with the patients' age: whenever possible, the tone, examples, and tasks should reflect AYA life experiences. For example, an adult-focused CBT app might discuss workplace pacing strategies or caring for children, which may not resonate with a 20-year-old college student and lead to disengagement from the digital app. In such cases, you might discuss ways to reframe and personalize content to ensure the intervention is personally relevant to the patient's age and stage of life (e.g., translating "workplace" to "school" pacing strategies).

By following these guidelines, clinicians can incorporate digital CBT tools into their practice in a way that complements and enhances traditional, face-to-face psychological treatments for chronic pain care. Importantly, ongoing evaluation and flexibility are key, and clinicians should solicit feedback from patients about what is and is not working with the digital component and be willing to adjust their approach.

Conclusions and Future Directions

Chronic pain in AYA females is a significant concern that demands accessible, effective interventions. CBT has a robust evidence base for improving pain-related outcomes in this population, and the advent of digital CBT tools has opened new avenues to extend these benefits to more patients.

Looking ahead, several steps are needed to further enhance the effectiveness and equity of digital pain care. Future efforts should empirically evaluate hybrid models that optimally combine digital and in-person care. This could involve "stepped care" approaches in which patients start with a digital program and step up to in-person therapy if needed, or blending in-person sessions with online modules (as in our case example). Such hybrid models may improve efficiency and outcomes by ensuring patients receive the right level of care at the right time, and they can be evaluated using innovative hybrid experimental designs (Nahum-Shani et al., 2022a, b). In addition, effectiveness-implementation hybrid trials could help identify best practices for incorporating digital CBT and other technologies into standard clinical workflows in a sustainable way (Curran et al., 2012).

Moreover, advances in artificial intelligence (AI) and related technologies (e.g., virtual reality) offer exciting opportunities to further tailor digital CBT for chronic pain. Future digital interventions might use AI to adapt content in real time based on user data—a paradigm known as personalized just-in-time adaptive interventions (JITAI; Hsu et al., 2025). For example, an app using JITAI mechanisms could detect when a user is distressed (via typing patterns or sensor data) and proactively offer a calming exercise or send an encouraging message. Research on these intelligent systems is still in its initial stages, but pilot studies in related areas (such as mental health apps) show that AI can increase user engagement and personalization (Siddals et al., 2024). However, ensuring that these technologies are accurate, safe, and used ethically—for instance, by maintaining privacy and avoiding bias—will be a key focus moving forward.

Finally, digital CBT programs must be designed to benefit diverse populations (Robinson et al., 2024). Human-centered design (HCD) is a user-centered, iterative approach that involves stakeholders such as patients, caregivers, and providers throughout the development process to ensure digital interventions are relevant and accessible. Key HCD principles include empathy building (e.g., user interviews), co-design (e.g., involving stakeholders in prototype development), and rapid iteration (e.g., refining tools based on real-time feedback) to create culturally sensitive interventions (Stiles-Shields et al., 2022). These strategies can be used to create multilingual and culturally sensitive programs as well as those that are usable across socioeconomic groups and adaptable for individuals with varying abilities (e.g., older adults or those with sensory impairments; Stiles-Shields et al., 2022). Including women and girls of color and other underrepresented groups is essential to identify unique barriers and needs and guide modifications to promote digital health equity.

Digital CBT interventions hold great promise for enhancing pain management in women and girls. Tailoring these interventions to account for gender and developmental factors, and embracing innovative tools to extend clinicians' reach, can improve outcomes for AYA females with chronic pain. As technology continues to evolve, so too must our clinical models. Integrating evidence-based digital tools into the care of young people with chronic pain can advance both individual patient outcomes and public health.

References

Allen, K. D., Beauchamp, T., Rini, C., Keefe, F. J., Bennell, K. L., Cleveland, R. J., ... & Sheikh, S. Z. (2021). Pilot study of an internet-based pain coping skills training program for patients with systemic Lupus Erythematosus. *BMC Rheumatology, 5*(1), 20.

Bartley, E. J., & Fillingim, R. B. (2013). Sex differences in pain: A brief review of clinical and experimental findings. *British Journal of Anaesthesia, 111*(1), 52–58.

Boerner, K. E., Eccleston, C., Chambers, C. T., & Keogh, E. (2017). Sex differences in the efficacy of psychological therapies for the management of chronic and recurrent pain in children and adolescents: A systematic review and meta-analysis. *Pain, 158*(4), 569–582.

Burns, J. W., Jensen, M. P., Thorn, B., Lillis, T. A., Carmody, J., Newman, A. K., & Keefe, F. (2022). Cognitive therapy, mindfulness-based stress reduction, and behavior therapy for the treatment of chronic pain: Randomized controlled trial. *Pain, 163*(2), 376–389.

Curran, G. M., Bauer, M., Mittman, B., Pyne, J. M., & Stetler, C. (2012). Effectiveness-implementation hybrid designs: Combining elements of clinical effectiveness and implementation research to enhance public health impact. *Medical Care, 50*(3), 217–226.

Dear, B. F., Gandy, M., Karin, E., Fogliati, R., Fogliati, V. J., Staples, L. G., ... & Titov, N. (2018). The pain course: 12-and 24-month outcomes from a randomized controlled trial of an internet-delivered pain management program provided with different levels of clinician support. *The Journal of Pain, 19*(12), 1491–1503.

Dudeney, J., Scott, A. J., Hathway, T., Bisby, M. A., Harte, N., Titov, N., & Dear, B. F. (2024). Internet-delivered psychological pain-management for young adults with chronic pain: an investigation of clinical trial data. *The Journal of Pain, 25*(6), 104447.

Fisher, E., Law, E., Dudeney, J., Eccleston, C., & Palermo, T. M. (2019). Psychological therapies (remotely delivered) for the management of chronic and recurrent pain in children and adolescents. *Cochrane Database of Systematic Reviews, 4*.

Foy, J. G., Kechichian, S., Foy, M. R., & Ziadni, M. (2024). Psychological/behavioral interventions for emerging adults with chronic pain. *Frontiers in Pain Research, 5*, 1253700.

Gandy, M., Pang, S. T., Scott, A. J., Heriseanu, A. I., Bisby, M. A., Dudeney, J., Dear, B. F., et al. (2022). Internet-delivered cognitive and behavioural based interventions for adults with chronic pain: A systematic review and meta-analysis of randomized controlled trials. *Pain, 163*(10), e1041–e1053.

Gendreau, R. M., McCracken, L. M., Williams, D. A., Luciano, J. V., Dai, Y., Vega, N., ... & Arnold, L. M. (2024). Self-guided digital behavioural therapy versus active control for fibromyalgia (PROSPERFM): a phase 3, multicentre, randomised controlled trial. *The Lancet, 404*(10450), 364–374.

Hashmi, J. A., & Davis, K. D. (2014). Deconstructing sex differences in pain sensitivity. *PAIN®, 155*(1), 10–13. https://doi.org/10.1016/j.pain.2013.07.039

Hsu, T. C. C., Whelan, P., Gandrup, J., Armitage, C. J., Cordingley, L., & McBeth, J. (2025). Personalized interventions for behaviour change: A scoping review of just-in-time adaptive interventions. *British Journal of Health Psychology, 30*(1), e12766.

Hunter, J. F., Acevedo, A. M., Gago-Masague, S., Kain, A., Yun, C., Torno, L., ... & Fortier, M. A. (2020). A pilot study of the preliminary efficacy of Pain Buddy: A novel intervention for the management of children's cancer-related pain. *Pediatric Blood & Cancer, 67*(10), e28278.

Jensen, I. B., Bergström, G., Ljungquist, T., Bodin, L., & Nygren, Å. L. (2001). A randomized controlled component analysis of a behavioral medicine rehabilitation program for chronic spinal pain: Are the effects dependent on gender? *Pain, 91*(1), 65–78. https://doi.org/10.1016/S0304-3959(00)00420-6

King, S., Chambers, C. T., Huguet, A., MacNevin, R. C., McGrath, P. J., Parker, L., & MacDonald, A. J. (2011). The epidemiology of chronic pain in children and adolescents revisited: A systematic review. *Pain, 152*(12), 2729–2738.

Li, J. X., Wang, X., Henry, A., Anderson, C. S., Hammond, N., Harris, K., Woodward, M., et al. (2023). Sex differences in pain expressed by patients across diverse disease states: Individual patient data meta-analysis of 33,957 participants in 10 randomized controlled trials. *Pain, 164*(8), 1666–1676.

Lim, J. A., Choi, S. H., Lee, W. J., Jang, J. H., Moon, J. Y., Kim, Y. C., & Kang, D. H. (2018). Cognitive-behavioral therapy for patients with chronic pain: Implications of gender differences in empathy. *Medicine, 97*(23), e10867.

Liverpool, S., Mota, C. P., Sales, C. M., Čuš, A., Carletto, S., Hancheva, C., Edbrooke-Childs, J., et al. (2020). Engaging children and young people in digital mental health interventions: Systematic review of modes of delivery, facilitators, and barriers. *Journal of Medical Internet Research, 22*(6), e16317.

Lynch, A. M., Kashikar-Zuck, S., Goldschneider, K. R., & Jones, B. A. (2007). Sex and age differences in coping styles among children with chronic pain. *Journal of Pain and Symptom Management, 33*(2), 208–216.

MacKenzie, N. E., Marbil, M. G., Soltani, S., Lorenzetti, D. L., & Birnie, K. A. (2024). A systematic review of in-person versus remotely delivered interventions for youth with chronic pain. *Paediatric and Neonatal Pain, 6*(2), 35–43.

Mohr, D., Cuijpers, P., & Lehman, K. (2011). Supportive accountability: A model for providing human support to enhance adherence to eHealth interventions. *Journal of Medical Internet Research, 13*(1), e1602.

Murray, C. B., de la Vega, R., Murphy, L. K., Kashikar-Zuck, S., & Palermo, T. M. (2022). The prevalence of chronic pain in young adults: A systematic review and meta-analysis. *Pain, 163*(9), e972–e984.

Murray, C. B., Groenewald, C. B., de la Vega, R., & Palermo, T. M. (2020). Long-term impact of adolescent chronic pain on young adult educational, vocational, and social outcomes. *Pain, 161*(2), 439–445.

Nahum-Shani, I., Dziak, J. J., Walton, M. A., & Dempsey, W. (2022a). Hybrid experimental designs for intervention development: What, why, and how. *Advances in Methods and Practices in Psychological Science, 5*(3), 25152459221114279.

Nahum-Shani, I., Shaw, S. D., Carpenter, S. M., Murphy, S. A., & Yoon, C. (2022b). Engagement in digital interventions. *American Psychologist, 77*(7), 836.

Osborne, N. R., & Davis, K. D. (2022). Sex and gender differences in pain. In *International review of neurobiology* (Vol. 164, pp. 277–307). Academic Press.

Overstreet, D. S., Strath, L. J., Jordan, M., Jordan, I. A., Hobson, J. M., Owens, M. A., Meints, S. M., et al. (2023). A brief overview: Sex differences in prevalent chronic musculoskeletal conditions. *International Journal of Environmental Research and Public Health, 20*(5), 4521.

Palermo, T. M. (2020). Pain prevention and management must begin in childhood: The key role of psychological interventions. *Pain, 161*, S114–S121.

Palermo, T. M., Slack, M., Zhou, C., Aaron, R., Fisher, E., & Rodriguez, S. (2019). Waiting for a pediatric chronic pain clinic evaluation: A prospective study characterizing waiting times and symptom trajectories. *The Journal of Pain, 20*(3), 339–347.

Palermo, T. M., de la Vega, R., Murray, C., Law, E., & Zhou, C. (2020). A digital health psychological intervention (WebMAP Mobile) for children and adolescents with chronic pain: Results of a hybrid effectiveness-implementation stepped-wedge cluster randomized trial. *Pain, 161*(12), 2763–2774.

Paller, C. J., Campbell, C. M., Edwards, R. R., & Dobs, A. S. (2009). Sex-based differences in pain perception and treatment. *Pain Medicine, 10*(2), 289–299.

Pester, B. D., Crouch, T. B., Christon, L., Rodes, J., Wedin, S., Kilpatrick, R., Barth, K., et al. (2022). Gender differences in multidisciplinary pain rehabilitation: The mediating role of pain acceptance. *Journal of Contextual Behavioral Science, 23*, 117–124.

Pieh, C., Altmeppen, J., Neumeier, S., Loew, T., Angerer, M., & Lahmann, C. (2012). Gender differences in outcomes of a multimodal pain management program. *Pain, 153*(1), 197–202.

Pretorius, C., Chambers, D., & Coyle, D. (2019). Young people's online help-seeking and mental health difficulties: Systematic narrative review. *Journal of Medical Internet Research, 21*(11), e13873.

Rosen, S., Ham, B., & Mogil, J. S. (2017). Sex differences in neuroimmunity and pain. *Journal of Neuroscience Research, 95*(1–2), 500–508.

Rosser, B. A., Fisher, E., Janjua, S., Eccleston, C., Keogh, E., & Duggan, G. (2023). Psychological therapies delivered remotely for the management of chronic pain (excluding headache) in adults. *Cochrane Database of Systematic Reviews, 8*.

Robinson, A., Flom, M., Forman-Hoffman, V. L., Histon, T., Levy, M., Darcy, A., ... & Montgomery, R. M. (2024). Equity in digital mental health interventions in the united States: where to next?. *Journal of Medical Internet Research, 26*, e59939.

Siddals, S., Torous, J., & Coxon, A. (2024). "It happened to be the perfect thing": experiences of generative AI chatbots for mental health. *npj Mental Health Research, 3*(1), 48.

Stiles-Shields, C., Cummings, C., Montague, E., Plevinsky, J. M., Psihogios, A. M., & Williams, K. D. (2022). A call to action: using and extending human-centered design methodologies to improve mental and behavioral health equity. *Frontiers in Digital Health, 4*, 848052.

Stinson, J. N., Lalloo, C., Harris, L., Isaac, L., Campbell, F., Brown, S., ... & Karim, A. (2014). iCanCope with Pain™: user-centred design of a web-and mobile-based self-management program for youth with chronic pain based on identified health care needs. *Pain Research and Management, 19*(5), 257–265.

Sullivan, M. J., Tripp, D. A., & Santor, D. (2000). Gender differences in pain and pain behavior: The role of catastrophizing. *Cognitive Therapy and Research, 24*, 121–134.

Sundararaman, L. V., Edwards, R. R., Ross, E. L., & Jamison, R. N. (2017). Integration of mobile health technology in the treatment of chronic pain: A critical review. *Regional Anesthesia & Pain Medicine, 42*(4), 488–498.

Tao, T. J., Lim, T. K., Yeung, E. T. F., Liu, H., Shris, P. B., Ma, L. K. Y., Hou, W. K., et al. (2023). Internet-based and mobile-based cognitive behavioral therapy for chronic diseases: A systematic review and meta-analysis. *npj Digital Medicine, 6*(1), 80.

Thomson, C. J., Pahl, H., & Giles, L. V. (2024). Randomized controlled trial investigating the effectiveness of a multimodal mobile application for the treatment of chronic pain. *Canadian Journal of Pain, 8*(1), 2352399.

Twiddy, H., Hanna, J., & Haynes, L. (2017). Growing pains: Understanding the needs of emerging adults with chronic pain. *British Journal of Pain, 11*(3), 108–118.

Urteaga, I., McKillop, M., & Elhadad, N. (2020). Learning endometriosis phenotypes from patient-generated data. *NPJ Digital Medicine, 3*(1), 88.

Wong, C. A., Madanay, F., Ozer, E. M., Harris, S. K., Moore, M., Master, S. O., Weitzman, E. R., et al. (2020). Digital health technology to enhance adolescent and young adult clinical preventive services: Affordances and challenges. *Journal of Adolescent Health, 67*(2), S24–S33.

Wilson, M., Roll, J. M., Corbett, C., & Barbosa-Leiker, C. (2015). Empowering patients with persistent pain using an internet-based self-management program. *Pain Management Nursing, 16*(4), 503–514.

Chapter 11
Cognitive Behavioral Treatment of Pain in Women and Girls with Juvenile Fibromyalgia

Cecelia I. Nelson and Susmita Kashikar-Zuck

Cognitive Behavioral Treatment of Pain in Women and Girls with Juvenile Fibromyalgia

Juvenile Fibromyalgia (JFM) is a poorly understood chronic pain condition characterized by widespread musculoskeletal pain, fatigue, sleep disruption, and frequently accompanied by other somatic symptoms such as headache, dysautonomia, and gastrointestinal distress (Coles et al., 2021; Vincenzo et al., 2019; Weiss & Kashikar-Zuck, 2021; Lynch-Jordan et al., 2023). The majority of adolescent girls with JFM continue to experience symptoms of pain, fatigue, and other symptoms into adulthood, and more than half meet criteria for adult fibromyalgia (FM) in early adulthood (Kashikar-Zuck et al., 2019). Those who experienced the highest levels of pain-related disability in adulthood had a worsening trajectory of mood symptoms from adolescence through adulthood. Retrospectively, adult women who were diagnosed with JFM recounted about their experience with their diagnosis in youth: "It definitely was a trial-and-error period of seeing what actually did help outside of medication," "As a teen, I thought my life was over," and "I got to a point where I got too exhausted to really have friends" (Daffin et al., 2021). From these quotes, it is evident that JFM is life-changing for the youth who experience it. Early multimodal intervention (medicine, exercise, coping skills/behavioral) is therefore critical to mitigate the impact of symptoms on quality of life. Indeed, young women

C. I. Nelson (✉)
Cincinnati Children's Hospital Medical Center, Cincinnati, OH, USA
e-mail: cecelia.nelson@cchmc.org

S. Kashikar-Zuck
Cincinnati Children's Hospital Medical Center, Cincinnati, OH, USA

University of Cincinnati College of Medicine, Cincinnati, OH, USA

L. A. Payne (ed.), *Psychosocial Interventions for Chronic Pain in Women and Girls*, CBT: Science Into Practice, https://doi.org/10.1007/978-3-031-98876-9_11

who received pain education and holistic treatment of their JFM reported the following, "It was that explanation [of the pain gate, pain-stress cycles], that kind of helped things click for me," "The therapist really helped me realize that it doesn't matter if I resent my body. It's still my body, and I'm going to have to make it work," and "Now I'm better at getting that sweet spot of moderate exercise that helps with all the stiffness, and stuff that doesn't make me flare up because I overdid it" (Daffin et al., 2021).

Role of Sex and Gender in JFM

JFM affects young girls at a much higher rate than their male peers (Coles et al., 2021) (>85% are assigned female at birth) and can be highly disabling and disruptive to physical, academic, and psychosocial functioning (Weiss & Kashikar-Zuck, 2021). Additionally, individuals assigned female at birth with FM experience more frequent fatigue, gastrointestinal symptoms, sleep difficulties, and a higher number of tender points than their male counterparts (Yunus, 2001). FM tends to cluster in families, with adolescents with JFM being more likely to have female relatives who also live with FM (Buskila et al., 2007; Yunus, 2001). Given that JFM symptoms overlap with many other conditions [chronic fatigue syndrome, Ehlers-Danlos syndrome, postural orthostatic tachycardia syndrome (POTS)] and that JFM can be comorbid with other conditions (secondary to many rheumatic and autoimmune diseases), the diagnostic journey is often long and difficult for teens (Häuser & Fitzcharles, 2018; Rahman et al., 2014). This process may be especially taxing on young women and girls, who are more likely to experience invalidation and dismissal of pain and fatigue in the medical system (Daffin et al., 2021; Igler et al., 2017) as well as disease-related stigma (Boileau et al., 2023) and are seen by their peers as being more isolated (Kashikar-Zuck et al., 2007). This healthcare journey could lead to mistrust in medical professionals and worsen social isolation, making treatment uniquely challenging.

Cognitive Behavioral Treatment for Pain and Disability in JFM

Given that JFM is a chronic condition lasting into young adulthood that is associated with multiple unpleasant symptoms, significant interference with work and life, social isolation, and high rates of psychiatric comorbidities (Burckhardt et al., 2005; Kashikar-Zuck et al., 2007; Weiss & Kashikar-Zuck, 2021), early identification and treatment for patients, with attention to the social context, is imperative. Cognitive behavioral therapy (CBT) for pain is an effective and rigorously proven approach that is adaptive and available through many different methods of delivery

(Fussner & Lynch-Jordan, 2019; Kashikar-Zuck et al., 2012, 2013). Treatment includes several components, including psychoeducation about the pain experience, relaxation training, behavioral activation, activity pacing, correcting cognitive errors and generating coping statements, and problem-solving skills. Parent and caregiver involvement is critical in younger people with JFM, given the likelihood of family members also living with chronic pain and the impact of the condition on the family system. Youth are encouraged to take greater control and independence in the management of their symptoms. Patients are encouraged to focus on the reduction of disability or engagement in functional behavior throughout treatment.

Methods of Delivery

CBT can be delivered individually (Palermo, 2012) or in a group-based format (Kashikar-Zuck et al., 2012; Simons, 2021). When group-based delivery is possible, many patients prefer it. Following the conclusion of group-based treatment (Kashikar-Zuck et al., 2012), participants indicated that they greatly benefited from the support of other group members and thoroughly enjoyed this aspect of treatment. The involvement of parents or caregivers is critical to long-term treatment success, given that they will likely share some of the responsibility for encouraging teens to utilize and practice their skills. Thus, caregivers should attend sessions that have the potential to impact their behavior with their children (e.g., pain neuroscience education, parent guidelines session, health behavior management, maintenance planning). In the past few years, and especially following the COVID-19 pandemic (Pierce et al., 2021), virtual and hybrid methods of treatment delivery have emerged as options and have been found to be effective (Adamse et al., 2018). With the increase in such telemedicine services, it is important to take certain considerations into account when conducting virtual treatment groups. For example, it is already important to ensure privacy and confidentiality in a face-to-face group setting, but even more so in a remote setting. Patients may find themselves sitting in common areas of their homes or schools, which means that other family members or peers could potentially hear the private health information of other individuals in the group during treatment. Therefore, it is recommended that therapists ensure that their patients (and their caregivers) are in a private space during sessions. When conducting group sessions generally, it is recommended that therapists implement guidelines for contact between group members outside of sessions to facilitate a focus on treatment during sessions (e.g., no exchanging of phone numbers or social media until group conclusion).

Assessment of JFM and Symptoms

JFM is diagnosed by a physician utilizing a set of criteria set forth by Yunus and Masi (1985). The assessment of treatment progress and/or symptom severity in JFM is challenging given the diversity of symptom presentations. Relevant to the completion of CBT for pain and the symptoms that are targeted by treatment, measures of pain, functional disability, and pain catastrophizing could be particularly beneficial. The gold standard for measuring pain is through self-report, often using a numeric (0–10) or Visual Analog Scale (Begum & Hossain, 2019; Williamson & Hoggart, 2005). Functional disability can be assessed through self-report as well, utilizing the Functional Disability Inventory (Walker & Greene, 1991). The Pain Catastrophizing Scale is a useful self-report tool to see how patients think about their pain (Sullivan et al., 1995). Frequent assessment is critical to examine the effectiveness of treatment. Additionally, sharing this data with patients can help acknowledge their successes.

Key Components of Cognitive Behavioral Therapy

Pain Neuroscience Education

Often, teens with JFM have prior experiences with providers where they are advised to engage in relaxation techniques and other coping skills, but they may not be informed about *how* pain works in the brain and *why* these skills are helpful for pain management. A basic education, in lay language and using visuals as necessary, can be provided involving the chemical communication between the brain and body, and the role of the central nervous system in pain processing. Understanding these concepts provides a foundation and rationale for the use of coping skills that facilitate self-management of pain and related symptoms.

- Gate control theory.
  - Many years ago, Melzack and Wall (1965) proposed the “gate control theory” of pain to elucidate the role of the brain in the perception of pain. There have been many advances in pain neuroscience in recent years; however, a basic explanation of the gate control theory still works very well to explain pain processing to younger patients. So, a developmentally appropriate explanation of this theory for an adolescent or young adult may be: “To feel pain, your brain sends signals to your body, and your body sends signals to your brain all through your spinal cord. Your spinal cord has something called a ‘gating mechanism’, which we will call ‘the pain gate’. If the pain gate is open, all of those pain signals can get through, and pain can be very ‘loud’, but we can do things to close the pain gate! If the pain gate is closed, we can turn the volume down on pain and make those signals weaker.”

  - Anchoring the instruction of coping skills in gate control theory can help patients understand why they are learning what they are and why it might be helpful. For example, using a coping skill is one way that we can "close the pain gate." We can also work with patients to identify behaviors that "open the pain gate" and reduce the frequency of those behaviors. It can be beneficial to leverage visual aids in the instruction of this concept, especially for younger patients.

- Autonomic nervous system arousal

  - The autonomic nervous system is responsible for physiological arousal within the body (e.g., the "fight or flight" system and "rest or digest" system). When the body perceives actual or potential tissue damage, psychological stress, or other stressors, the fight or flight system activates. This arousal can cause changes in vision, breathing, heart rate, and digestion with the purpose of preparing the body to respond to a threat.
  - Pain is perceived as a threat to the body, thus activating the fight or flight branch of the autonomic nervous system. Often, behaviors that serve to close the pain gate also activate the rest and digest system, as this relaxation activation is incompatible with fight or flight arousal.

Parent/Caregiver Guidelines

For teens or young adult patients, it is critical to involve parents or caregivers in interventions, as caregivers can also engage in behaviors that open or close the pain gate. Additionally, caregivers can reinforce positive functional behaviors and help patients adhere to treatment recommendations.

Therapists may introduce these concepts as such: "Here are some guidelines for you to follow. It is very important for your teen to have the family support and encouragement while they are learning these new skills. These should be very helpful to you. Try to also get other family members to do the same" (Kashikar-Zuck & Williams, 2023).

1. Encourage your teen to manage their pain and other symptoms independently.
2. Praise your teen when they use the skills they will be learning.
3. Encourage normal activity during pain/fatigue episodes (school and play).
4. Eliminate status checks. Do not ask about pain and how much it hurts or how tired they feel.
5. If medication is requested, follow the doctor's guidelines.
6. Treat pain/fatigue requiring a reduction in activity as you would an illness. Allow them to go to bed and rest for a time. No watching TV, playing games, or special treatment.

These six recommendations are anchored in the theory discussed in the previous section. Many parents struggle to eliminate status checks, as this goes against their instinct as parents to check on and care for their child. Thus, it can be helpful to provide a concrete example of how status checks can open the pain gate. One such example may be asking caregivers, "How does it feel to swallow right now?" Therapists can point out the way that attention to physiological sensations, pain or otherwise, can increase their salience to the brain. This is true for pain as well—patients may be attempting to distract themselves (close the pain gate) when they are again reminded of their pain (opening the pain gate).

Relaxation Training

Patients should anchor their learning and practice of relaxation strategies in what they have learned about gate control theory and their autonomic nervous systems. Relaxation practice is one tool that can be used to close the pain gate. Relaxation techniques such as deep breathing and muscle relaxation are also incompatible with a "fight or flight" state, thus providing a cue to the nervous system to engage in "rest and digest." Patients should practice multiple forms of relaxation to identify which of the strategies works best for them, as this will differ from person to person. Additionally, it is important that relaxation techniques be rehearsed in moments of calm, so that patients are competent in their use when they are experiencing higher levels of pain or stress. These strategies may also be beneficial for use prior to falling asleep.

- Progressive muscle relaxation (active or passive)
  - Active progressive muscle relaxation: Therapists can instruct patients in the tensing and releasing of each muscle group in the body. This may include feet, calves, thighs, stomach, hands, arms, shoulders, and face. Patients should be instructed to engage in deep or diaphragmatic breathing throughout this exercise.
  - Passive progressive muscle relaxation: Therapists should instruct patients to simply relax and release each muscle group in the body. This may include the groups listed above. Some patients benefit from the use of imagery to assist in the progression of relaxation (i.e., "Imagine that a golden light is shining on your body, as it shines on each part of your body, I want you to imagine the tension leaving that part").
  - When introducing muscle relaxation, the therapist and the patient should work together to decide whether active or passive muscle relaxation is most appropriate. Youth who experience muscle pain in particular may be hesitant to tighten muscles due to the possibility of increased pain, making passive relaxation more tolerable.
- Pleasant imagery

  - Many CBT protocols include the introduction of guided or pleasant imagery in which the therapist describes a location that is safe and relaxing for the patient.
  - Therapists should elicit sensory details about a specific relaxing location for the patient. Common examples could be a childhood home, beach, forest, mountains, or anywhere the patient finds calming. It is beneficial to involve all five senses in the imagination process. Therapists should elicit details about what the location looks like, feels like, sounds like, and smells like. Once the patient has adequately described the scene, the therapist can then walk them through it.

- Mini-relaxation
  - Mini-relaxation is a brief relaxation technique that can be done in 30–60 s in a variety of environments (e.g., car, school, work, etc.). Therapists can instruct patients to take a few deep breaths, adding, "as you breathe out, you are going to exhale and say the word 'RELAX'." The goal is to use mini-relaxation throughout the day to remind the nervous system that "you are 'safe and okay' to promote 'rest and digest' in the body, especially when you are busy and maybe do not have time to engage in a full body relaxation."
  - Stickers or other cues (e.g., finishing a meal, standing in line) are a great way for patients to remind themselves to engage in mini-relaxation throughout the day. Therapists may recommend placing stickers on phones, water bottles, or frequently accessed areas (e.g., locker, closet, mirror, fridge) to remind patients to engage in regular practice throughout the day.

Behavioral Activation

Many times, youth with pain avoid engaging in their typical activities, including those that are enjoyable. Over time, this lack of engagement can lead to decreased functioning, increased feelings of depression, lack of motivation, increased fear of engaging in typical activities, and increased pain (Wideman et al., 2013). Thus, youth must find ways to incorporate enjoyable activities into their daily lives to improve these symptoms (Hopko et al., 2003; McCauley et al., 2016).

- Pleasant activity identification.
  - Individuals with JFM are more likely to experience depression, which can lead to a lack of motivation to engage in pleasant activities as well as a feeling of anhedonia associated with typically enjoyable tasks. It can be difficult for patients to identify pleasant activities when they have experienced functional disability or a reduction in typical activity levels. Therapists can assist patients in generating ideas for activities through open-ended questioning, such as:

"What are some activities that you used to enjoy that you have stopped doing?"
"What are some ways that you enjoy being physically active?"
"Tell me about your creative hobbies."

- Activity scheduling
  - Adolescents and young adults are more likely to engage in their identified pleasant activities if they are scheduled ahead of time. Once patients and therapists have identified 3–5 preferred pleasant activities, therapists should work with patients to identify when they are most likely to do them (i.e., after work or school, when first waking up). Sometimes, it is helpful to schedule pleasant activities for patients prior to less preferred or more aversive tasks. For example, some patients may have difficulty finding the energy or motivation to do their physical therapy home exercises or other homework. Thus, it may be helpful to schedule 15–30 min of pleasant activity first, to help the individual get moving. For some patients, this momentum can help them engage in an aversive task. For other patients, they may prefer to schedule pleasant activities following a non-preferred activity to motivate themselves to complete it.

Activity Pacing

Individuals with chronic pain often get into a cycle of over-doing activity (resulting in a flare of pain or other symptoms), taking a rest period, and under-doing activity, and then subsequently over-doing activity again when they feel better. This leads to a vicious cycle where youth are unable to maintain a consistent level of engagement in their daily activities over time and become increasingly sedentary and deconditioned, which can subsequently worsen pain.

To break this cycle (see Fig. 11.1), individuals must work to increase their rest and breaks during periods of over-activity and work to increase their activity level by doing brief or pleasant activities during times of rest. Pacing can be used in a variety of ways depending on the patient's schedule and needs, as some patients with JFM are more impacted by this cycle than others. Some patients may require pacing for a singular activity or specific situation (e.g., a summer camp, grocery

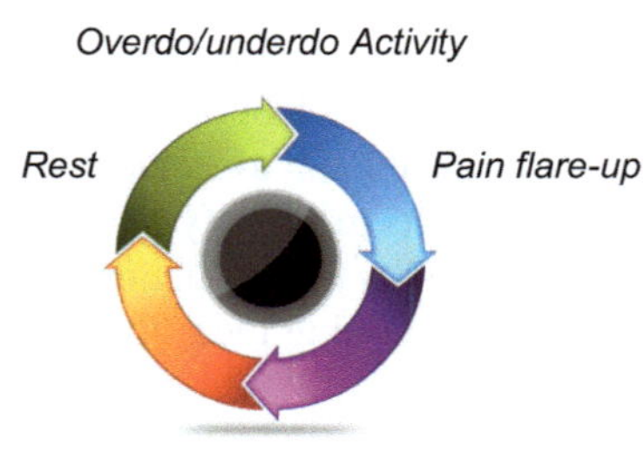

Fig. 11.1 Cycle of pain and under-/over-activity (Kashikar-Zuck & Williams, 2023)

store trips, sports practice) while other patients may require a more general pacing plan for their daily schedule (e.g., school or class schedule, workday). See below for examples of implementing pacing across different situations:

1. Patient with low activity level: Abigail is a 19-year-old with JFM who struggles with fatigue and pain. She has trouble getting out of bed to do the things that she needs to do, like go to class and get groceries. She ends up missing a lot of class time. For someone like Abigail, pacing may look like implementing small trips to stores as opposed to one large grocery trip or planning one outing per day, then increasing to two after a period of endurance building. If Abigail's class schedule is rigorous, a therapist may suggest finding a quiet place to take a break between classes to re-energize.
2. Patient who overdoes activity when feeling good: Joanna is a 14-year-old with JFM who participates in many extracurricular activities (e.g., student council, theater, volunteering). When she is feeling good, she attends school and multiple activities each day, but often crashes and stays home the following day or two. This has caused her to have inconsistencies in her attendance. For Joanna, pacing may look like implementing breaks throughout her school day (i.e., 20 min in the nurse's office twice per day) and taking a break after school before activities begin. In this case, the therapist may also help Joanna establish a pacing plan for her specific activities. As theater practices can be quite long, perhaps Joanna and the therapist could work to establish scheduled breaks throughout the practice.

Cognitive Restructuring

Young girls and women with JFM are more likely than their male counterparts to develop negative or catastrophic cognitive appraisals surrounding pain (i.e., the level of threat that pain poses, or the level of impact pain will have on daily life). Psychoeducation on the impact of thoughts, beliefs, and feelings on pain and fatigue is imperative to developing a patient's self-efficacy and perceived control of pain (Sil & Kashikar-Zuck, 2013). Therapists can anchor this in education about the pain gate ("we know that attention, thoughts, and feelings can all serve as things that open or close the pain gate"). See example below:

- Dr. Jones is doing therapy with Anna, a 16-year-old female with JFM. Anna says the following to Dr. Jones, "I just don't think I'm ever going to get better. If I can't manage in high school, I'll never go to college or get a job." Anna is able to identify that the presence of these thoughts opens the pain gate, but she struggles to find a way to respond to them. The therapist may assist in connecting these thoughts to feelings and behaviors, challenging these thoughts, and working to generate a *coping statement*.
- Identifying the connection between thoughts, feelings, and actions: When prompted, Anna reports that having these thoughts makes her feel anxious and sad (feelings which also open the pain gate). The therapist can then ask if these

thoughts and feelings change the way that Anna acts, to which she responds, "I don't want to look at colleges or work on my applications because I just feel hopeless."

- Challenging thoughts: Dr. Jones could help Anna to identify evidence for and against her thoughts to help her figure out if they are true. "Anna, do you have any evidence that you wouldn't go to college in the future? Do you have any evidence that you would *never* be able to go to college or have a job?"

NOTE: Sometimes, patients have unhelpful thoughts that ARE TRUE (i.e., "I'm going to be managing this for the rest of my life"). In this case, challenging these thoughts may not be helpful, rather, therapists can assist patients in understanding the connection between these thoughts, feelings, and behaviors, and work to generate a calming statement.

- Generate a coping/calming statement: Coping statements are simple messages or responses that patients can develop to respond to their unhelpful thoughts. To assist patients in their generation, a therapist may ask, "What would you tell a friend who said 'insert thought'?" Some examples of coping statements for Anna may be: "I can work on my health" or "I will focus on what I can do now, and think about my options for college when the time comes."

Some patients, especially younger ones, may benefit from the use of vignettes of other pain patients with unhelpful thoughts to facilitate understanding of the connection between thoughts, feelings, and behaviors. A thought diary is a useful tool for helping patients to practice this technique on their own outside of session (Fig. 11.2).

Common Thinking Errors: It can be challenging for patients to identify which of their thoughts may be unhelpful or untrue. Given this, it is helpful to provide patients with an overview of some of the most common thinking errors associated with pain. See below for four of these common errors and a description that can be given to patients (Kashikar-Zuck & Williams, 2023).

1. *Dark or negative glasses*
   - "If you have a good time, or if nice things happen, the dark glasses will still find the things that went wrong or weren't quite good enough. It is the negative things you notice and remember the most, and anything positive is dismissed as unimportant or discredited. Pain is often the dark glasses where it puts a negative spin on everything that happens during the day."
2. *All-or-none thinking*
   - "Do I think about things in only extreme or opposite ways (e.g., good or bad, all or none, black or white)? It is either hot or freezing cold, and there doesn't seem to be anything in between! This might be especially relevant for activities (e.g., school, social activities, sports)."

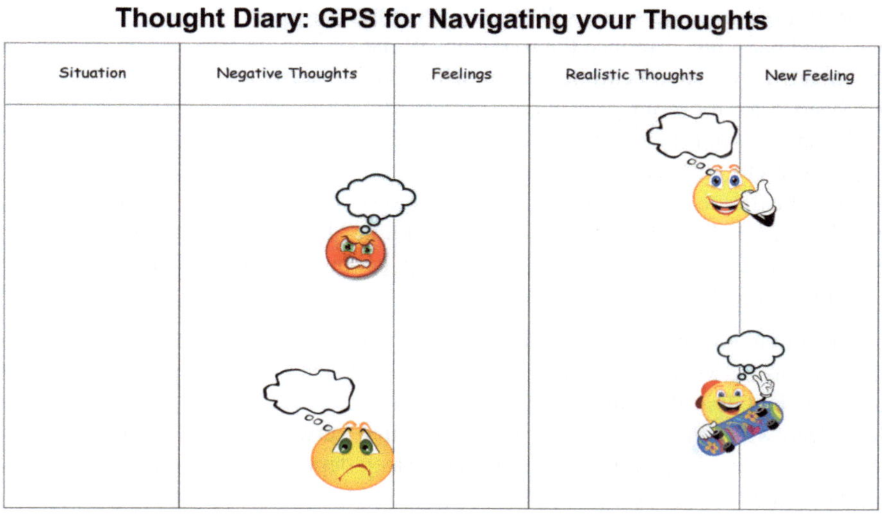

Fig. 11.2 Thought diary example (Kashikar-Zuck & Williams, 2023)

3. *Labeling*
   - "You attach a label to yourself and think of everything you do in these terms. Do I put simple, unfair, or negative labels on myself, people, or things that are more complicated than the label? For example, feeling like the odd person out."
4. *Blaming myself or others*
   - "Sometimes our standards and expectations are too high, and we never seem to achieve them. We tend to set ourselves up to fail. Do I insist or demand that things 'should' or 'must' be done in a certain way? Or we blame our doctors for not finding out what is wrong. These thoughts often start with words such as: should, must, shouldn't, can't."

Health Behaviors

Sleep, hydration, and nutrition are behaviors that all teens struggle with; however, these are critical behaviors for the management of chronic pain in JFM. Therapists can help patients leverage the use of behavior plans (rewards and consequences) to increase hydration and proper nutrition.

The majority of young people with chronic pain struggle with falling and/or staying asleep. Cognitive behavioral sleep medicine strategies can be beneficial for chronic pain patients, whether or not their sleep disturbance is secondary to pain (Cheatle et al., 2016; Husak & Bair, 2020). Therapists can then work with patients and families to assess the best strategies for implementation in their own homes. The following recommendations are common:

- Refrain from using screens 30 min to 1 h before bed
- Avoid napping, or reduce the frequency of naps
- Create a consistent bedtime routine with relaxing activities
- Sleep in a dark room, or use a red light if you need light
- Create a "wind-down" routine for 30–45 min before your bedtime (e.g., reading, shower, etc.) to ready your body for sleep
- Avoid caffeine 5–6 h before bed, avoid vigorous exercise 1–2 h before bed
- Use your bed for sleep only (do not spend time "hanging out" in your bed)
- If it takes longer than 20 min to fall asleep, get out of bed and do a quiet activity until you feel sleepy, then try again

The broad goal of these strategies is to help patients create a strong connection in their brains between their beds, environment, and sleep by minimizing time spent awake in bed. It is also important to emphasize to patients that it is alright if they get less sleep while they are training this connection between the brain and body and getting up more frequently, as this strategic sleep deprivation sometimes facilitates an increased sleep drive (or need for sleep) in the following nights.

Problem Solving

After the introduction and rehearsal of coping skills, it is imperative that therapists work with patients to develop problem-solving skills to facilitate their self-efficacy in the application and implementation of these coping skills in their day-to-day life. Leveraging an example, a basic four-step problem-solving method is proposed (Kashikar-Zuck & Williams, 2023):

- Example: Ellie is a 20-year-old young woman with FM. She attends classes at her local community college in the mornings and then works as a server for a restaurant in the evenings. Sometimes, when Ellie works in the evenings, she is very tired and sore in her classes the following morning. She reported thinking to herself, "Everyone must be thinking that I'm so fidgety and grumpy at school. I should be able to sit still like everyone else." Ellie has started skipping some of her classes the morning after a hard work shift because she fears what people will think of her frequent movement to relieve her pain and stay awake. Problem solving with Ellie may look like:

  – *Step 1: Identify the problem(s)*

    Ellie is very active during some of her work shifts and does not take breaks. She experiences symptom flares the following day.

  – *Step 2: Describe their thoughts, feelings, and behavior*

    Because Ellie is experiencing symptom flares, she engages in more movement during her classes.

Ellie reports having the thought that her classmates are judging her for her pain behaviors.
Thus, Ellie misses class, which makes her feel sad and frustrated.

- *Step 3: Pick strategies from the list of coping skills*

  Given that Ellie is having symptom flares after work, she may benefit from practicing activity pacing around her work shifts to implement more breaks or shorter shifts if possible.
  Ellie and the therapist would benefit from evaluating her unhelpful thinking patterns and generating an alternative thought.

- *Step 4: Apply the coping skills*

  The therapist and Ellie work together to use activity pacing and generation of coping statements/alternative thoughts! They can then evaluate how this worked.

When practicing the implementation of this problem-solving method with patients, it can be helpful to work through a couple of example situations that are common to the patient's life. If patients have difficulty applying the skills to their own lives, describing a vignette of another individual facing a similar challenge can increase understanding and application.

Maintenance Planning

The final sessions of CBT for pain should include a combination of problem-solving and planning for maintenance of skills following the termination of therapy. Having multiple sessions to practice the use of multiple coping skills in different situations is beneficial toward building a patient's confidence in being able to apply the skills on their own, empowering them to manage their pain more independently over time. In the final session, therapists may brainstorm with patients about how to know when a return to treatment (or booster session) is needed.

Considerations for Group-based Delivery

As stated earlier, given the social isolation and challenges associated with JFM, a group-based treatment setting can be particularly beneficial for patients and their families. When conducting treatment with a group, therapists can leverage patient experiences to help with skill application for the entire group (e.g., have patients coach one another). For example, cognitive restructuring can sometimes be better understood when patients can practice with one another's thoughts. Upon teaching the connection between thoughts, feelings, and actions, and developing coping statements, therapists can solicit examples of unhelpful thoughts from the group.

Group members can work together to identify potential coping statements for one member's thought (i.e., "What would you tell Amelia if she shared that thought with you?") instead of generating them for themselves.

Overcoming Obstacles in Treatment

When patients with JFM or other chronic pain conditions begin treatment, they typically express a primary goal related to pain reduction. While pain reduction can occur through improved functioning, this goal can be counterintuitive to successfully learning coping skills, as the goal of treatment for therapists is to teach patients a set of skills to help them function with/through pain. Patients will likely continue to experience pain following treatment completion or have additional symptom flares in the future. It is critical that patients feel empowered to function and live their lives utilizing coping skills, as opposed to utilizing coping skills to reduce pain. Clarifying these goals and the purpose of coping skills from the beginning of treatment and reinforcing them throughout can help create appropriate expectations following termination of treatment. Patients may feel less motivated to engage in coping skills training, knowing that it may not reduce their pain level right away, so for these patients, it may be beneficial to spend time building rapport or spending extra time on education to increase buy-in before skill-building.

Inclusive Treatment Recommendations

Given the invalidation, dismissal, and stigma for girls and women with chronic pain (Boileau et al., 2023; Daffin et al., 2021; Igler et al., 2017), which is often worse for individuals of color (Morais et al., 2022) and gender diverse individuals (Boerner et al., 2025), it is imperative that providers validate the patient experience with empathic listening throughout the therapy process. Providers can build trust with patients by naming patient experiences as invalidating or unjust when warranted (Herbst et al., 2023). Different cultures have different views surrounding pain perception and expression. Given this, it is important that providers approach each patient as a unique individual and practice from a culturally humble framework (i.e., do not assume that all treatments or aspects of treatment apply equally to all cultures).

Therapists should also bear in mind that treatment adaptations may be necessary for neurodivergent patients, such as those with attention-deficit/hyperactivity disorder or autism spectrum disorder. The use of visual learning materials can be particularly helpful for individuals who may struggle with auditory processing or learning. Additionally, patients who struggle with attention concerns may benefit from the inclusion of reminders to utilize coping skills or complete therapy homework. A set of adaptation recommendations for the treatment of pain in autistic youth can be obtained from an article by Han et al. (2024).

The goal of CBT for pain is to build self-efficacy, feelings of control, and empowerment in young people with pain, so that they feel that they have a set of skills to draw upon to manage their symptoms. A strong therapeutic relationship, collaborative spirit, and the therapist's treatment of the patient as a unique individual are critical factors to patient buy-in, which ultimately helps to facilitate change for a very challenging presenting concern.

Conclusions

JFM is a chronic pain condition disproportionately impacting girls and young women, which is comprised of many unpleasant symptoms and a lengthy diagnostic journey that can be challenging to cope with. Evidence-based treatment for JFM is multi-modal and includes CBT for pain, movement-based or physical therapy approaches, and other holistic and integrative treatments. CBT can be done with patients in an individual or group setting, though group settings may be uniquely beneficial due to the isolation that patients with JFM experience. Treatment can also be remote or virtual, or in-person, allowing for patient/provider flexibility and increased access to treatment. CBT for pain involves a variety of evidence-based components, including pain neuroscience, relaxation and distraction skills, activity pacing, pleasant activities, caregiver involvement, cognitive strategies, and problem solving. Providers should prioritize validating patient experiences, building patient self-efficacy and control, and a strong therapeutic relationship to facilitate positive change.

Resources for Patients and Families

Web Resources

- The website for the US Pain Foundation (https://uspainfoundation.org/) contains many resources for patients and families, including connections to support groups.
- Pain psychologist, Dr. Rachel Zoffness, PhD, has an informational website (https://zoffness.com/resources) with resources, podcasts, applications, and other information for patients and caregivers.
- Creative Healing for Youth with Chronic Pain is a non-profit organization with a website (https://mychyp.org) that contains many resources, webinars, and activities for patients, providers, and caregivers.

Print Resources

- "Pain in Children and Young Adults: The Journey Back to Normal: Two Pediatricians' Mind-Body Guide for Parents" by Lonnie Zeltzer, MD & Paul Zeltzer, MD.
- "When Your Child Hurts: Effective Strategies to Increase Comfort, Reduce Stress, and Break the Cycle of Chronic Pain" by Rachel Coakley, PhD.
- "Conquering Your Child's Chronic Pain" by Lonnie Zeltzer, MD.
- "The Chronic Pain and Illness Workbook for Teens: CBT and Mindfulness-Based Practices to Turn the Volume Down on Pain" by Rachel Zoffness, New Harbinger Publications.

Mobile Applications

- "WebMAP Mobile" is freely available for Android and iPhone. The app instructs individuals in several pain coping skills based upon a brief cognitive-behavioral program for teens. This application is based upon an intervention for pain that has been tested in multiple clinical trials through Seattle Children's Hospital (Palermo et al., 2020).

References

Adamse, C., Dekker-Van Weering, M. G., van Etten-Jamaludin, F. S., & Stuiver, M. M. (2018). The effectiveness of exercise-based telemedicine on pain, physical activity and quality of life in the treatment of chronic pain: A systematic review. *Journal of Telemedicine and Telecare, 24*(8), 511–526.

Begum, M. R., & Hossain, M. A. (2019). Validity and reliability of visual analogue scale (VAS) for pain measurement. *Journal of Medical Case Reports and Reviews, 2*(11).

Boerner, K. E., Fox, D. A., Du, L., Metzger, D. L., Marshall, S., Moore, E. M., Oberlander, T. F., et al. (2025). Experiences of gender-diverse youth living with chronic pain. *Pediatrics, e2024067035*.

Boileau, N. R., Thompson-Phillips, K. A., Goodin, B. R., Lynch-Milder, M. K., Evans, C. T., Adetayo, T., Wakefield, E. O., et al. (2023). Pain-related stigma and its associations with clinical and experimental pain severity in youth with chronic musculoskeletal pain conditions. *Journal of Pediatric Psychology, 48*(10), 842–851.

Burckhardt, C. S., Liedberg, G. M., Henriksson, C. M., & Kendall, S. (2005). The impact of fibromyalgia on employment status of newly-diagnosed young women: A pilot study. *Journal of Musculoskeletal Pain, 13*(2), 31–41.

Buskila, D., Sarzi-Puttini, P., & Ablin, J. N. (2007). The genetics of fibromyalgia syndrome. *Pharmacogenomics, 8*(1), 67–74.

Cheatle, M. D., Foster, S., Pinkett, A., Lesneski, M., Qu, D., & Dhingra, L. (2016). Assessing and managing sleep disturbance in patients with chronic pain. *Anesthesiology Clinics, 34*(2), 379–393.

Coles, Weissmann, & Uziel. (2021). Juvenile primary fibromyalgia syndrome: Epidemiology, etiology, pathogenesis, clinical manifestations, and diagnosis. *Pediatric Rheumatology, 19*(22). https://doi.org/10.1186/s12969-021-00493-6

Daffin, M., Lynch-Milder, M. K., Gibler, R. C., Murray, C., Green, C. M., & Kashikar-Zuck, S. (2021). A qualitative study of risk and resilience in young adult women with a history of juvenile-onset fibromyalgia. *Pediatric Rheumatology, 19*, 1–9.

Fussner, L. M., & Lynch-Jordan, A. M. (2019). Cognitive behavioral therapy in pediatric patients with chronic widespread musculoskeletal pain. *Handbook of Cognitive Behavioral Therapy for Pediatric Medical Conditions*, 185–199.

Han, G. T., Heavner, H. S., Rains, T. R., Hoang, A. H., & Stone, A. L. (2024). Chronic pain in autistic youth: Clinical prevalence and reflections on tailoring evidence-based interventions from an interdisciplinary treatment team. *Children, 11*(3), 312.

Häuser, W., & Fitzcharles, M. A. (2018). Facts and myths pertaining to fibromyalgia. *Dialogues in Clinical Neuroscience, 20*(1), 53–62.

Herbst, R., Corley, A. M., & McTate, E. (2023). Clinical framework for dismantling antiblack racism in the clinic room. *Clinical Pediatrics, 62*(10), 1129–1136.

Hopko, D. R., Lejuez, C. W., Ruggiero, K. J., & Eifert, G. H. (2003). Contemporary behavioral activation treatments for depression: Procedures, principles, and progress. *Clinical Psychology Review, 23*(5), 699–717.

Husak, A. J., & Bair, M. J. (2020). Chronic pain and sleep disturbances: A pragmatic review of their relationships, comorbidities, and treatments. *Pain Medicine, 21*(6), 1142–1152.

Igler, E. C., Defenderfer, E. K., Lang, A. C., Bauer, K., Uihlein, J., & Davies, W. H. (2017). Gender differences in the experience of pain dismissal in adolescence. *Journal of Child Health Care, 21*(4), 381–391.

Kashikar-Zuck, S., & Williams, S. (2023). *Fitness integrative training manual for teens (FIT Teens): Virtual/Hybrid FIT Teens Group Protocol.* Cincinnati Children's Hospital and Medical Center.

Kashikar-Zuck, S., Lynch, A. M., Graham, T. B., Swain, N. F., Mullen, S. M., & Noll, R. B. (2007). Social functioning and peer relationships of adolescents with juvenile fibromyalgia syndrome. *Arthritis Care & Research, 57*(3), 474–480.

Kashikar-Zuck, S., Ting, T. V., Arnold, L. M., Bean, J., Powers, S. W., Graham, T. B., Lovell, D. J., et al. (2012). Cognitive behavioral therapy for the treatment of juvenile fibromyalgia: A multisite, single-blind, randomized, controlled clinical trial. *Arthritis & Rheumatism, 64*(1), 297–305.

Kashikar-Zuck, S., Sil, S., Lynch-Jordan, A. M., Ting, T. V., Peugh, J., Schikler, K. N., Lovell, D. J., et al. (2013). Changes in pain coping, catastrophizing, and coping efficacy after cognitive-behavioral therapy in children and adolescents with juvenile fibromyalgia. *The Journal of Pain, 14*(5), 492–501.

Kashikar-Zuck, S., Black, W. R., Pfeiffer, M., Peugh, J., Williams, S. E., Ting, T. V., ... & Myer, G. D. (2018). Pilot randomized trial of integrated cognitive-behavioral therapy and neuromuscular training for juvenile fibromyalgia: The FIT Teens Program. *The Journal of Pain, 19*(9), 1049–1062.

Kashikar-Zuck, S., Cunningham, N., Peugh, J., Black, W. R., Nelson, S., Lynch-Jordan, A. M., Lovell, D. J., et al. (2019). Long-term outcomes of adolescents with juvenile-onset fibromyalgia into adulthood and impact of depressive symptoms on functioning over time. *Pain, 160*(2), 433–441.

Lynch-Jordan, A. M., Connelly, M., Guite, J. W., King, C., Goldstein-Leever, A., Logan, D. E., ... & Fibromyalgia Integrative Training for Teens Clinical Trial Study Group and the Childhood Arthritis and Rheumatology Research Alliance Pain Workgroup Investigators. (2023). Clinical characterization of juvenile fibromyalgia in a multicenter cohort of adolescents enrolled in a randomized clinical trial. *Arthritis Care & Research, 75*(8), 1795–1803.

McCauley, E., Gudmundsen, G., Schloredt, K., Martell, C., Rhew, I., Hubley, S., & Dimidjian, S. (2016). The adolescent behavioral activation program: Adapting behavioral activation as a treatment for depression in adolescence. *Journal of Clinical Child & Adolescent Psychology, 45*(3), 291–304.

Melzack, R., & Wall, P. D. (1965). Pain mechanisms: A new theory. *Science, 150*, 971–979.

Morais, C. A., Aroke, E. N., Letzen, J. E., Campbell, C. M., Hood, A. M., Janevic, M. R., Campbell, L. C., et al. (2022). Confronting racism in pain research: A call to action. *The Journal of Pain, 23*(6), 878–892.

Palermo, T. M. (2012). *CBT for chronic pain in children and adolescents*. Oxford University Press. https://books.google.com/books?id=Ey4d_oR7zqcC

Palermo, T. M., de la Vega, R., Murray, C., Law, E., & Zhou, C. (2020). A digital health psychological intervention (WebMAP Mobile) for children and adolescents with chronic pain: Results of a hybrid effectiveness-implementation stepped-wedge cluster randomized trial. *Pain, 161*(12), 2763–2774.

Pierce, B. S., Perrin, P. B., Tyler, C. M., McKee, G. B., & Watson, J. D. (2021). The COVID-19 telepsychology revolution: A national study of pandemic-based changes in US mental health care delivery. *American Psychologist, 76*(1), 14.

Rahman, A., Underwood, M., & Carnes, D. (2014). Fibromyalgia. *BMJ, 348*. https://doi.org/10.1136/bmj.g1224

Sil, S., & Kashikar-Zuck, S. (2013). Understanding why cognitive–behavioral therapy is an effective treatment for adolescents with juvenile fibromyalgia. *International Journal of Clinical Rheumatology, 8*(2), 213. https://doi.org/10.2217/IJR.13.3

Simons, L. (2021). *GET living: Graded exposure treatment for children and adolescents with chronic musculoskeletal pain*.

Sullivan, M. J., Bishop, S. R., & Pivik, J. (1995). The pain catastrophizing scale: Development and validation. *Psychological Assessment, 7*(4), 524.

Vincenzo, A., Ashraf, T. S., Nada, S., Bernadette, F., & Christos, K. (2019). The juvenile fibromyalgia syndrome (JFMS): A poorly defined disorder. *Acta Bio Medica: Atenei Parmensis, 90*(1), 134.

Wakefield, E. O., Zempsky, W. T., Puhl, R. M., & Litt, M. D. (2018). Conceptualizing pain-related stigma in adolescent chronic pain: A literature review and preliminary focus group findings. *Pain Reports, 3*, e679.

Walker, L. S., & Greene, J. W. (1991). The functional disability inventory: Measuring a neglected dimension of child health status. *Journal of Pediatric Psychology, 16*(1), 39–58.

Weiss, J. E., & Kashikar-Zuck, S. (2021). Juvenile Fibromyalgia. In J. N. Ablin & Y. Shoenfeld (Eds.), *Fibromyalgia syndrome*. Springer. https://doi.org/10.1007/978-3-030-78638-0_14

Wideman, T. H., Asmundson, G. G., Smeets, R. J., Zautra, A. J., Simmonds, M. J., Sullivan, M. J., Edwards, R. R., et al. (2013). Rethinking the fear avoidance model: Toward a multidimensional framework of pain-related disability. *PAIN®, 154*(11), 2262–2265.

Williamson, A., & Hoggart, B. (2005). Pain: A review of three commonly used pain rating scales. *Journal of Clinical Nursing, 14*(7), 798–804.

Yunus, M. B. (2001). The role of gender in fibromyalgia syndrome. *Current Rheumatology Reports, 3*(2), 128–134.

Yunus, M. B., & Masi, A. T. (1985). Juvenile primary fibromyalgia syndrome. A clinical study of thirty-three patients and matched normal controls. *Arthritis & Rheumatism: Official Journal of the American College of Rheumatology, 28*(2), 138–145.

Index

L. A. Payne (ed.), *Psychosocial Interventions for Chronic Pain in Women and Girls*, CBT: Science Into Practice, https://doi.org/10.1007/978-3-031-98876-9

MIX
Papier aus verantwortungsvollen Quellen
Paper from responsible sources
FSC® C105338

If you have any concerns about our products,
you can contact us on
ProductSafety@springernature.com

In case Publisher is established outside the EU,
the EU authorized representative is:
Springer Nature Customer Service Center GmbH
Europaplatz 3, 69115 Heidelberg, Germany

Printed by Libri Plureos GmbH
in Hamburg, Germany